ABOUT THE AUTHOR

Prudencio Damboriena was born in Spain in 1913. He took his M.A. in philosophy at the Collège Ecclesiastique, Marneffe, Belgium, his S.T.L. at the Bellarmine School of Theology, Shanghai, China, and his doctorate in Church history at the Pontifical Gregorian University, Rome, where he later became dean of the department of missions.

He was a missionary in India, China, and the Philippines from 1936 to 1954, and in Colombia from 1963 to 1966. He is associate professor of historical theology at the School of Theology, St. Louis University, and pastoral theology editor for the *Catholic Theological Encyclopedia*. Among his books are *Fe Católica e Iglesias y Sectas de la Reforma,* and *El Protestantismo en la América Latina.*

Tongues As of Fire

PENTECOSTALISM IN CONTEMPORARY CHRISTIANITY

Tongues As of Fire

PENTECOSTALISM IN CONTEMPORARY CHRISTIANITY

by Prudencio Damboriena, S.J.

CORPUS BOOKS: Washington & Cleveland

CORPUS PUBLICATIONS

EDITORIAL OFFICES: *1330 Massachusetts Ave., N.W. Washington, D.C. 20005*

SALES & DISTRIBUTION: *2231 West 110th Street, Cleveland, Ohio 44102*

Library of Congress Catalog Card Number: 70-79228

FIRST PRINTING 1969

Printed in the United States of America

CONTENTS

INTRODUCTION

The number of books and articles on Pentecostalism is already enormous. Perhaps a short account of my contacts with its members and the new aspects I have discovered in the movement will explain the reasons for the addition of another volume to the existing literature.

I first became acquainted with Pentecostals in the China of the pre-Mao days. They constituted a small but aggressive group, not much loved by the rest of the missionary community, and their activities and temper gave me a glimpse of the Asiatic Pentecostalism I would subsequently encounter in India, the Philippines, and Indonesia. Later, while doing research at Union Theological Seminary, New York, I made regular trips to Harlem, lower Manhattan, and Brooklyn to watch in the store-front churches the work of the American Pentecostals among the newly arrived Puerto Ricans and the more settled groups of Negro congregations. A few years after, while teaching at the Gregorian University, Rome, I asked the Dean of the Theology Department if I might offer a course on Pentecostalism. He was taken by surprise: the theme did not fall within the ambit of his own theological interests, and seemed rather "way out" to be offered as a course at a Pontifical University. But he agreed for the sake of the seminarians from the North American College and a few candidates for the missions who might be interested in it.

My former students still remind me of our difficulty in handling the subject in Latin, then obligatory in lectures. But, on the whole, we did not waste our time. I realized that there was an embryonic Pentecostal theology worth exploring, and my students realized that, in view of the pastoral ministry for which they were being prepared, Pentecostalism was a far more lively subject than some of the courses included in their theological program.

My Roman lectures, however, would have remained in my files had it not been for further and richer experiences with the Pentecostal phenomenon. During the last decade it has been my privilege to visit the Latin American continent five times, from northern Mexico to Temuco in Chile, and from Recife to Santa Catarina in Brazil. One of my purposes was to study more closely the advances of Pentecostalism in different republics, to talk to its leaders, and to try to understand the Christian motivations of the movement. This new experience, added to contacts with friendly correspondents in both Americas and in mission lands, has convinced me of the necessity of preparing a book that would contain for ministers, priests, and lay people essential information about the beliefs and practices of our Pentecostal brethren. If I am not mistaken, ignorance of Pentecostalism and prejudices against it are shared equally by the Catholic and Protestant communions.

The book is developed on three levels: historical, theological, and missionary-ecumenical. Pentecostalism has a rich past and is the modern version of a well-defined trend in Christianity that reaches from some of the Pauline churches to contemporary neo-Pentecostals. The historian is impelled to delve more deeply into this rather neglected facet of Pentecostalism. The character of my research does not permit me to go into further details, but I have at least pointed out the highlights of this historical development. In the past the theological doctrines and religious practices of Pentecostals have more often been caricatured than objectively described, and only now do we begin to realize that Pentecostalism involves much more than the "manifestations of the Spirit" by which it has been commonly known. I therefore devote a rather long chapter to those doctrines that Pentecostals share with the rest of Christianity, without thereby neglecting the importance of their "peculiarities." Authorities such as John Mackay and Henry P. Van Dusen have often referred to the missionary spirit of Pentecostalism, but no effort has been made to evaluate the depth and extent of its penetration or to analyze the reasons for its aggressive zeal, which amazes and sometimes antagonizes the other churches. I have attempted to fill this gap, and thus show that, when speaking of Pentecostals, we are not now dealing with an obscure "sect," born almost seventy years ago in a small Midwest town, but with a world-embracing movement, in fact with the fastest-growing of American-born religions.

Until recent times, the relationship of the traditional Christian churches with Pentecostalism has been anything but cordial. We have inclined more to shun their "interference" with the work of our churches than to extend a friendly hand to those who also have been baptized in the same Christ. The ecumenical movement may bring about changes. On our part, the first step in the right direction will be an effort to know from authoritative sources what Pentecostals believe, how they worship, and how they conceive their work in the world. Such knowledge, if leavened by even a minimum of Christian love, might convince us that, viewing the whole spectrum of Christian denominations, Pentecostals are not the most widely sundered of our "separated brethren."

It would be difficult to acknowledge the debt I owe to Pentecostals of four continents. Even when they realized that I did not agree with them on a number of points, they were wholly cooperative in providing the necessary information. The officials in charge of the Pentecostal Archives at the Oral Roberts University, Tulsa, Oklahoma, were especially helpful.

PRUDENCIO DAMBORIENA, S. J.

SCHOOL OF DIVINITY
ST. LOUIS UNIVERSITY

CHAPTER ONE

BACKGROUND OF THE HOLINESS AND PENTECOSTAL MOVEMENT

Pentecostalism generally is thought to be a product of the American religious ethos, but in its own self-estimation it traces its origins to the primitive Church. Pentecostals point out that in the first Christian communities of Rome, Thessalonica, and Corinth there were groups of believers who led lives segregated from the world, aimed at perfection, and who were endowed with charismatic gifts, the best manifestation of which was "speaking in tongues" as the Apostles and disciples of Jesus did on the day of Pentecost. Such gifts also played an important role in the Pauline churches. The charismatics appeared at worship meetings and, by their prophetic utterances and stirring prayers of thanksgiving, kept alive the enthusiasm of the new faith. Some of them, however, overestimated the value of their gifts and were called to task by Paul.

This speaking in tongues (glossolalia) was, in the opinion of an Episcopalian admirer of Pentecostalism,

> an integral part of the apostolic religious life. If one reads the New Testament objectively, he finds that it tells us stories of men who received not only new ethics, but a new life which was given far beyond the ordinary capacities. When this divine power was given to man, his character improved, his love and patience increased, and he was given greater vision and perception of spiritual things. *Receiving this divine power was known as being filled with the Holy Spirit.*[1]

Charismatic gifts were also in evidence in subapostolic times, and very often the laity was specially favored with them. In the *Didache* the favored ones were known as "prophets" and enjoyed special rank in the life of the Christian community: they taught, led in giving thanks, and helped the clergy in the service of the poor. Their charismatic gifts appeared generally during religious services, although some of them were evident precisely in the help the prophets rendered to their brethren. The Church did not grant hierarchical authority to them; they were under the jurisdiction of the elders and bishops, and their relationship with the authorities was generally smooth, for the Church was glad to accept their help and saw their gifts as normal blessings from the Holy Spirit.[2]

Pentecostals find in Montanism, an enthusiastic movement of the second century, something like their parent church. Montanus, the founder, who prior to his conversion was a priest of the ecstatic cult of Cybeles, claimed to have received a fuller revelation of the Spirit than that possessed by the Church. " 'Behold,' said the Spirit through Montanus, 'that man is a lyre, and I sweep over it as a plectrum. Man sleeps; I wake. Behold, it is the Lord who puts the hearts of men out of themselves and gives a heart to them.' "[3] Associated with two "prophetesses," Prisca and Maximilla, Montanus proclaimed that the Spirit had revealed to him secret things, among others, the beginning of a new era (the era of the Paraclete), the impending return of Christ, and the founding of a new Jerusalem placed between Tymion and Pepuza, in Phrygia. In the words of W. H. C. Frend:

> It was a revival of the wilderness theory of the Coming, and it was heard gladly. People summoned by the prophets to attend the inauguration of the Millenium abandoned homes and families and work to stream into the countryside. Wars and rumors of war were freely prophesied, and death by martyrdom, prepared for by continence and fasting enjoined as the command of the Holy Spirit.[4]

According to historian Eusebius, Montanus at times "became beside himself, and being suddenly in a sort of frenzy and ecstasy, he raved and began to babble and utter strange things, prophesying in a manner contrary to the custom of the Church handed down by tradition from the beginning."[5] Montanism acquired a new status when Tertullian, one of the pillars of the Church, joined its ranks and became its first theologian. His entrance into the sect also marked the beginning of friction between the hierarchical Church and the defenders of charismatic tendencies among some of the faithful. Professor Baus explains the rise of the tension:

> The New Prophecy, as the movement was called, took up again the form of religious enthusiasm so much esteemed in the primitive Church, which regarded certain individual believers as specially favored messengers of the Spirit and as prophets who placed

their gifts at the service of the community. False prophets, illusionaries and swindlers among them, here and there, brought discredit on prophecy and created mistrust of any "bearers of the Spirit" that might arise. There had also been tension between those favored by the Spirit and those who wielded ecclesiastical authority. . . . This time, however, it came to a clash between prophecy and authority, which led to the exclusion of adherents of the movement from the community of the Church.[6]

Tertullian, with his gifts and theological acumen, soon made Montanism a controversial issue. There was much to be said in favor of the movement. It offered a staunch and badly needed opposition to Gnosticism. Its followers led an ascetical life and won the name of "soldiers of Christ." Among the requirements of those *koinonoi,* or participants in the sufferings of Christ, were the rejection of the secular world and the proclamation of the name of Christ to their fellowmen. But Church leaders noticed also that all too often Montanists vastly distorted the genuine Christian claims, and falsified Christian tradition. The time had come to intervene: "The Church," says a Lutheran theologian,

rejected Montanism because she recognized these reformatory efforts as out of harmony with the principles of the Gospel, her judgment here being entirely correct. She freed herself from responsibility for the charisms claimed by the few, asserted more clearly the authority of biblical revelation, and prepared the way for the forms of a compact organization. The conflict had, therefore, a most important influence upon the development of the Church.[7]

By the beginning of the fourth century the charismatic gifts fade from the scene. Even earlier, Iraeneus, who had praised their role in the primitive community, observed that the possession of charisms was reserved to a very few. Such had also been the view of Origen around the middle of the third century: "The Holy Spirit gave signs of his presence at the beginning of Christ's ministry, and after his ascension he gave still more; but since that time signs have diminished, although there are still traces of his presence in the few who have had their souls purified by the Gospel, and their actions regulated by its influence."[8]

The decline occurred, according to Catholic historians, because those gifts had been given to the early Church in order to arrest the minds and sustain the faith of the Christian communities, especially during the time of persecution. In the words of Duchesne, "If visions, prophecies, and miraculous cures did not go out of sight entirely from the Church, very soon they became incompatible with the regular order of liturgical services, until they completely disappeared from the Christian life."[9] St. John Chrysostom attested to their almost total absence from the Church.[10] And St. Augustine, in one of his sermons, asked his listeners:

> Who in our days expects that those on whom hands are laid so that they may receive the Holy Spirit [in Confirmation] should forthwith speak with tongues? . . . These were signs adapted to the times. For there behooved to be that betokening of the Spirit in all tongues to show that the Gospel of God was to run through all the tongues over the earth. But that thing was done for the betokening, and it has passed away.[11]

Modern Pentecostals, while acknowledging most of these facts, do not endorse this interpretation. They assert rather that the decline of charismatic gifts was a sure sign that the Church had abandoned its original fervor and had succumbed to pagan influences in theology and liturgy. As contributing causes they adduce the Church's increasing hierarchization, the fight against heretical factions, and a kind of obsession for logical definition of truth. The result was an overly institutionalized Christianity, a theology based exclusively on theoretical and non-experimental principles, a rationalist understanding of Christian life, the elimination of the freedom of the spirit and of the spontaneous understanding and practice of Christ's message: "Early in the history of the Church began a process of centralizing and organizing, and of formulating hard and fast creeds. While this was necessary as a defense against false cults, it tended to check the free moving of the Spirit, and to make Christianity a matter of orthodoxy rather than of spiritual vitality."[12]

In the Middle Ages

The Middle Ages were not the most propitious time for enthusiastic movements. Christian Europe (at least in its western portion) formed a close-knit religious and cultural block. Doctrinal and ecclesiastical authority became centralized in the hands of the bishops and the papacy, creating a monolithic Christianity. After the conversion of the Arians in Lombardy and Spain in the middle of the seventh century, religious dissent practically disappeared from the Church. Only in the eleventh and twelvth centuries did it reappear in Europe. Its centers were in southern France, northern Italy, and Bavaria. Ronald Knox states:

> It was still the Languedoc, cut off even by a barrier of speech from the France of Paris and of the court; its Mediterranean trade exposed to Eastern influence; the remote fastness of its hill-country which offered a ready asylum to the persecuted.... Those were also the days of the troubadors, when Languedoc was distinguished by a free and easy society, rich, cultured, independent, impatient of authority, tolerant of foreign affairs and even friendly to the despised and persecuted Jews.[13]

It seems wrong to include among the enthusiasts the Fratricelli, the Poor of Christ, the Flagellantes, and other extreme factions within the Mendicant Orders. Such groups, despite their eccentric attitudes, never abandoned the Church or refused to accept its fundamental doctrines. They were rigorists who intended to return to the "unmitigated rule" of their founders and proclaimed the need to recapture the "spirit of primitive Christianity." Even when they criticized certain aspects of the Church's life or warned its authorities by apocalyptic prophecies, they stayed in the Church or returned to its fold after admonition. Among such charismatics we find Abbot Joachim of Fiore of Calabria, whose theories about the history of salvation seem to have inspired some of our modern Pentecostals. In his *Commentary on the Apocalypse,* Joachim divided history into three ages: (1) The Age of the Father covered the period of the Old Testament dispensation, when men lived under the Law and in the characteristically married state of the patriarchs: (2) The Age of the Son, or the time of New Testament grace, was characterized by a hierarchical Church and the discipline of clerical life: (3) The Age of the Holy Spirit would usher in a *spiritual* Church, dominated by mysticism and hence requiring no organized ministry. Joachim allowed forty-two generations for each period, and therefore expected the age of the Spirit to begin around the year 1260.[14]

The case was different with other individuals and groups: Peter de Brys, Tnacheln, Eckart of Shonam, Lambert de Begue, Arnold of Brescia, Hugo de Speroni, the Waldensians, and the Cathars, or Albigenses. The latter have attracted the attention of historians because of their affinities with some of our contemporary religious enthusiastic movements.[15] Cathari in Greek means "the pure." In France they were called Albigenses, from the town of Albi, where their influence was strongest. In Bavaria their heterodox leanings won for them the nickname of *ketzer*, the heretics. The new faith seems to have been brought from the East by traders, pilgrims, and perhaps even by missionaries during the Second Crusade. The movement had taken deep root in the country of Toulouse, whose archbishop could write in 1473 to the King of France: "The Catholic faith is receiving tremendous attacks in our diocese and the bark of Peter is undergoing such a buffeting from these heretics that it is almost at the point of sinking."[16]

> Dressed in black, austere, of an undoubted purity of morals, for they practised absolute continence, sober to the point of abstaining from all food produced by carnal intercourse, such as milk products and eggs and meat, poor indeed, but having at their common disposal very large financial resources, the clergy of the Catharists and the *Perfect* found among all classes of the population an audience which the Catholics were in the process of losing in a large number of places.[17]

Catharist theology was typically dualistic. In the beginning, they said, there were two principles: that of good and that of evil. From the principle of light (good) derives whatever is light and spirit; from the principle of evil comes all that is matter and darkness. Thus, the phenomenal world and the God of the Old Testament who created it are evil. Hence also, at the end, the whole material world will be destroyed by fire from heaven. Man's purpose in life consists in liberating his soul from the flesh that surrounds it. Those who fail to achieve this are doomed to consecutive reincarnations. In consequence of the evil nature of matter, Cathars denied that Christ could have assumed a truly human body, but only a glorious one. Mary never gave birth to the Son of God. Christ was created in heaven and passed through Mary only as through a channel.[18] Cathars emptied the sacraments of their salvific value and reduced them to the level of symbols. The Eucharists lost its traditional meaning, and for the Mass was substituted the eating of the "consecrated bread" taken before meals. Others made the hearing of the Scriptures an equivalent to communion. The Catharists distinguished two types of churches: one that is righteous, made up of those who received the imposition of hands and did penance; the other that of the wicked, in which they included the Catholic Church, comparing it to the harlot of the Apocalypse, with the pope as the anti-Christ.[19]

As substitutes for the traditional doctrines, the Cathars proposed their own way of salvation centered around a spiritual baptism administered by the imposition of hands and called *consolamentum*. It was a rite indispensable for salvation, and any person dying without it was doomed to damnation or to return (through metempsychosis) to the world in the form of an animal. Before submitting to the ceremony, married men needed the consent of their wives to loose the nuptial bonds and consign their husbands to God. The *consolamentum* was preceded by a period of initiation in which the candidates had to be tried and submitted to the regime of the *perfects.* If the results were not satisfactory, the tests could be repeated one year later. The initiation ended with the handing of the Gospels *(traditio libri)* to the candidate.[20]

Cathars rejected baptism by water as being the devil's invention, for water, they maintained, remained simply water and was incapable of playing any part in forgiveness of sin or salvation. The rite of *consolamentum* was at times called baptism of the spirit or spiritual baptism. While receiving it, the candidate made a confession of his sins and placed his hope in the Holy Spirit, who was about to come upon him.[21] The requirements imposed by the new baptism were so rigorous that many had to consider very carefully whether they could assume the burden. On principle they were promised impeccability, but few believed in this because they found it at odds with personal experience; and since a "second penance" was excluded, many preferred to postpone the reception of the "blessing" until their deathbed.

For those who never took the *consolamentum,* or had fallen from it, Catharism invented a kind of sacred euthanasia called *endura.* This could be administered to sick person and even to children in order to "liberate" them from the burden of their bodies. Philip Schaff comments:

> The *endura* has been called the most cruel practice the history of asceticism has to show. It was a voluntary starvation unto death by those who had not received the *consolamentum.* Sometimes these religionists waited for thirteen days for the end to come.... Parents are said to have left their children without food and mothers to have withdrawn their breast from nursing infants in executing the rite.[22]

Those who remained faithful to the pledges of their spiritual baptism led very apostolic lives. All the *perfect,* being in some sense ordained, were required to preach. The sect had a profound zeal for evangelism and often prepared its own translations of the New Testament in the vernacular. The purity of life of its members made a deep impression upon contemporaries, and even St. Bernard once remarked that there were no people more Christian than the Cathars.[23]

From this excursus, which is relevant also to the doctrinal section of the book, it is evident that, despite a number of external affinities, the Cathars were essentially different from any enthusiastic movement of modern Christianity. Catharism was the negation of, and not merely a deviation from, traditional Christianity, and it has no place in any religious system whose immutable foundation is Jesus Christ, God and Savior of mankind.[24]

The Churches of the Reformation

The great leaders of the Reformation, Luther, Calvin, Zwingli, Bullinger, and Melanchthon, did not show, either in their writings or in their practice, much love for enthusiastic perfectionism, and those who followed that trend were soon listed as "deserters" of the new faith. This hostility was scorned by the enthusiasts, who insisted that the Reformers had not gone far enough in their efforts to renew Christendom but had all too quickly compromised their principles in order to curry favor with secular authorities, even against the "clear words of the Gospel." The mutual opposition sprang from many causes. The basic tenet of the primitive Reformation, a fixed text of the word of God, present in the pages of the Bible as the unique norm for human conduct, left little room for the pervasive inspiration of the Holy Spirit advocated by the perfectionists. The concepts of "fallen nature" and of "fiducial faith" likewise ran counter to some of the most cherished ideals of the enthusiasts, who were activists at heart and firmly believed in the possibilities of perfection and of human progress.

The concrete event that revealed the irreconcilability of the two sides was perhaps the Peasants' War (1524), in which Luther abandoned his communities to the hands and whims of the secular princes:

> The principal victors in that civil war were the princes who centralized, regardless of religious confession, their control in civil jurisdiction and religion, and with the slogan *cuius regio, eius religio,* established either a Catholic or a Protestant Christianity in the spirit and with the precedent of Constantine, no longer, however, on the ecumenical basis of an empire, but on the particularist basis of princely absolutism.[25]

The historian may wonder whether the leading Reformers made an effort to grasp the nature of the message or the particular emphasis presented by the enthusiasts. Bullinger was persuaded that the birth of Anabaptism was due "to the malice of its leaders and to diabolical suggestion against the purity of our doctrine and ministry."[26] Luther wasted much time attacking his enemies, and in 1525 wrote his violent treatise *Against the Robbing and Murdering Hordes of Peasants,* which contained accusations frequently unjustified. In 1534 he answered the objections of Caspar Schwenkfeld to his eucharistic doctrines, calling him "the mad fool, possessed of the devil, [who] does not understand anything and does not know what he is babbling"; wishing that "the Lord punish Satan in you and in your spirit"; and hoping that "all who have part in you, Sacramentarians and Eutychians, together with your blasphemies, be your destruction."[27]

The enmity outlasted the first Reformers. In the words of G. H. Williams:

> The major Protestant Reformers and their associates were the bitterest foes and persecutors of the Anabaptists. [Later on] Protestant scholars and polemicists drew a composite portrait of them as fanatics and revolutionaries. Except for Mennonite circles, the consequence was that, up until the nineteenth century, Anabaptist was synonymous with Munsterite or Muntzerite, i.e., seditious, polygamous, licentious, tyrannical.[28]

These unsavory incidents (which remind us of the cold reception given to the Holiness movements by the historical churches) explain the reaction of Pentecostal historians and theologians to the Reformation of the sixteenth century:

> In the sixteenth and seventeenth centuries, when the noble and illustrious Reformers were throwing off and breaking from under the galling yoke of Romanism, and launched what is commonly called Protestantism, they: (1) failed to reform the Creeds; (2) adopted the law of [fiducial] faith when they should have adopted the law of love; and (3) failed to reserve a right place for the leadership of the Holy Ghost and conscience.[29]

The groups of the left-wing Reformation, Anabaptists and Quakers, to whom we must add for a later period the French Camisards, present a number of facets of significance in the study of the Pentecostal movement. All of them had begun by rejecting the theology of a visible and state-directed Church. Anabaptists, for instance, "ascribed to the state no Christian character, but regarded it as belonging, with the whole unbelieving world, to the kingdom of darkness; true Christian magistrates were unnecessary . . . since the two kingdoms were already in opposition, and there could be no doubt which would conquer."[30] In matters of faith, Quakers, Anabaptists, and Camisards sought guidance, not in any "dead book," but in the living word of the Spirit. God, Anabaptists maintained, had throughout the ages raised up prophets and chosen messengers to transmit his message to redeem mankind:

> Muntzer saw Wittemberg becoming the center of an idolization of Scripture, which came dangerously close to making a paper pope out of the Bible. . . . True salvation consisted *in the eternal word of God;* every preacher must have revelations because otherwise he could not announce the good tidings. . . . The central issue with Muntzer was the living conception of God who directly addressed men while Luther reasoned that Scripture had been given to men because they could not endure God's speech. "They [the Anabaptists] talk directly to God," exclaimed Luther with a shudder upon hearing of Muntzer's claim.[31]

Quakers were still more radical and derived their guidance entirely from the "Inner Light." That Light was not "an impersonal abstraction, a substitute for God or Christ; it was Christ, manifesting himself in the hearts of men; it was he whom the heathen, obedient to the Light, were obeying, even though they had not heard of his earthly existence."[32] George Fox suspected all external forms of religion and was persuaded that the simplest might wait upon the Spirit. His message (which can also be found in Denck, Bohme, Schwenkfeld, and certain Anabaptists) was the belief in the need (and sufficiency) of an immediate contact of the soul with God. "There is," he said, "a mystical but divine light which, if followed honestly and steadily, infallibly leads to God; and that without the Bible or any ordinance."[33]

All these movements advocated likewise a "return to simplicity" in liturgy. The Anabaptists restricted their religious services to the preaching of the word, excluding ornaments, sacred music, or any other ceremonies; the Quakers introduced a silent liturgy which, down to our times, has remained the symbol of a liturgy-less community within the Reformation.[34] In ecclesiology Anabaptists and Quakers tended to promote a Church composed exclusively of "pure and sinless members" completely independent of state control. Anabaptists accepted one sacrament, baptism, administered only to adults; Quakers preferred to give it up completely:

> The only thing that is important is that which comes "out of the heart of man" (Mk 7:21). Here is a religion of the highest order, but it is by no means surprising that the recognition of its significance appeared only by slow and painful degrees. In the untutored yet clear mind of George Fox there came the recognition that this revolution was to be taken seriously. Since the new creation is everything, all else is secondary; therefore no particular acts, not even the historically honored ones like baptism and the bread and wine, can be requirements. This was his fundamental insight. Whatever else it was, it was not trivial.[35]

Historians have discovered among Quakers and Anabaptists clear manifestations of enthusiastic outbursts, similar in kind, if not in frequency, to those of the modern Pentecostals. Among Anabaptists,

> some simulated little children in preparation of the kingdom, the imminent advent of which was discussed and calculated with enthusiasm. Group confessions led to disclosures which alarmed spouses; children of seven or eight lay in coma; and there were other attempts at simulating death with Christ to the world. Glossolalia broke out. There was lewdness and unchastity, and the extraordinary disclosure of a woman who said she was predestined to give birth to the anti-Christ.[36]

The Quakers, too, loved "going naked in the streets for a sign." On certain occasions, "men, women, and children were strangely brought . . . to fall, foam at the mouth, roar, and swell in their bodies."[37] Their annals refer to Friends who would "fall into violent trembling and sometimes vomiting in their meetings, and pretending to be violently acted upon by the Spirit."[38] Apparently Fox accepted without complaint practices that contributed so much to the spread of his message. Similar eccentricities occurred in Boston, Cambridge, and Salem when Quakers, dressed in sacks, with their heads covered with ashes, or even *in puris naturalibus,* as "signs of wonder" (Isaiah 20:2-3), invaded the chapels of other denominations.[39] Even Roger Williams, the advocate of religious freedom, repudiated such conduct which, in the long run, could not contribute to the good name of Christendom.

The French Camisards were also given to that type of manifestation. After the revocation of the Edict of Nantes (1685), French Protestantism had been declared illegal in the realm of the *rex christianissimus,* and its followers forced to wander in search of a refuge for themselves and for their children. It is not known whether, before these political restrictions, they were already given to enthusiastic religion. The fact is that, deprived as they were of their own preachers and chapels, they began to find inspiration and consolation in thoughts of the world to come. Emile Léonard defends the spiritual and physical health of the Camisards, while acknowledging in their "trances" and glossolalia clear precedents for the practices of modern Pentecostalism.[40] Some of the visionaries were girls trained in the art of prophecy by a certain Monsieur Ferré: they "talked in languages they could not have known; made prophecies or told of things which were happening at a distance and were proved to be right by the event."[41]

During that period of persecution many Camisards fled from France, some finding shelter in Germany with the Pietists of Zinzendorf, others in England among the dissenters. Here they seem to have converted Anne Lee, the foundress of the Shakers[42] in America. In John Wesley's *Journal* we find an entry regarding his meeting with a Camisard who "seemed to have strong workings in her breasts, with deep sighing; her head and hands and by turn every part of her body seemed also to be in a state of convulsion. . . . She spoke much, all in the name of God . . . of fulfilling prophecies, of the coming of Christ, and the spreading of the Gospel all over the world."[43]

Methodist Contribution

With Methodism we come a step closer to the immediate origins of Pentecostalism. Theologically, Pentecostals are children of Wesley. Similar doctrines were professed by Methodists on both sides of the Atlantic. They agreed on Christianity as a "religion of experience," assurance of salvation, justification as something "inferior" and different from the "new birth," the role of the Holy Spirit in the life of the individual, ecclesiological and sacramental doctrines based on Pietistic insights, and, most of all, holiness and sanctification as the goal attainable by every true Christian. A moot point is how much the present-day emotionalism of the Holiness bodies owes its origin to Wesley and his followers. Historically there is no doubt that Wesley made large use of intensive, at times hysterical, emotions in his evangelistic campaigns. In the words of one of his biographers:

> Wesley, by recounting over and over again the marvelous happenings which had accompanied him, expected to arouse a similar

> experience in his listeners. The very peak of his success took place when ten, fifteen, twenty persons of the audience fell in a heap, yelling, groaning, weeping, screaming under the impulses of violent, epileptic spasms. These, in the mind of the Methodists, were evident signs of the approaching birth of the new man, the true Christian, the regenerate. When these extraordinary manifestations took place, Wesley himself, under the impulse of mob psychology, would break off his sermon. It was useless to continue since God himself had intervened. With awe and respect, he would draw near those convulsive, jerking forms, and invite the listeners (in a voice which trembled with emotion) to associate themselves with him in praying to God that the soul of that man or woman might break loose from the accursed fetters of its sinful life and might straightforward find its way to the true life of the children of God.[44]

Wesley's own attitude to such "personal manifestations of the Spirit" remains ambivalent. According to Ronald Knox, the founder of Methodism fostered them. Such phenomena constituted the proof of God's blessings he was looking for to confirm the supernatural origin of his work. Writing to his brother Samuel who had objected to such eccentricities, John replied:

> The matter which divides us is a question of facts. You deny that God can produce such effects. I affirm it because I have heard them with my ears and seen with my eyes. . . . I have seen many persons who had been changed in a moment pass [through those trances] from one spirit of fear, horror, and despair, to another of love, happiness, and peace. . . . These are my living arguments.[45]

"To suggest," concludes Knox, "that, at any period of his life, Wesley regretted or discouraged them, is plain contradiction of the evidence."[46] Others, however, also familiar with Wesleyan sources, are less apodictic in their conclusions. First, they claim that Wesley denounced in his writings the excesses that had taken place during those manifestations; and second, he never considered them as prerequisites for the admission of new members into his societies. "Wesley," writes L. M. Starley, "states that the Methodists do not lay claim to them, but expect only the ordinary gifts and operations which every Christian is privileged to seek and reject."[47] "Reject" does not mean that Wesley repudiated charismatic gifts in the life of the Church. He was convinced that such gifts were always a blessing and had by no means disappeared with the passing of primitive Christianity. If his contemporaries did not usually enjoy them, it was because the Spirit "could not work such gifts in men whose love had waxed cold and for whom Christianity remained a dead form."[48]

Methodism, born in England, was destined to see its most glorious days in America. By 1765 two Methodist preachers, R. Strawbridge and P. Embury, had arrived as immigrants. Other groups followed and began itinerant work either by themselves or in the company of the ministers of other denominations. They also founded new societies and linked them to those of the original Wesleyan Connexion. The latter task was done mainly by Francis Coke and Francis Asbury, the true founders of Methodism in America. After the War of Independence which, because of the loyalty to England of many preachers and church members, decimated the ranks of the nascent Methodist societies, the followers of Wesley began their work of reorganization. The consecration by Wesley himself of Thomas Coke as the first Methodist bishop, and his appointment, together with Asbury, to head the movement in America, was a definite step in that direction. Wesley's idea of Church had always been hazy. In England his societies could be compared to the *ecclesiolae* within the Church of England.[49] In America, on the contrary, their relation could be stated in terms of the whole Catholic Church. He desired Methodism "to have an organized life of its own, fulfilling the need for group fellowship and discipline and concentrating on the mission of the Church, while remaining within the framework of the Church, united with her by common doctrine, ministry, sacraments, and worship."[50] By 1784 that dream had become a reality and taken the name of the American Methodist Episcopal Church, an autonomous body which ordained its clergymen, administered the sacraments, had legal titles to churches and properties, and possessed a fully empowered legislative organism with a Superintendent elected by a General Conference: "The test of the new organization would be its ability to meet the challenges of a rapidly expanding western frontier, a national population in which 90 per cent were members of no church, and the competition of rival denominations in a society based on religious liberty."[51]

For almost a hundred years the basic doctrines and techniques of expansion for Methodism in America did not greatly differ from those in use in England. Once again, emphasis was laid on the need of the new birth; preaching and literature were keyed to "holiness unto the Lord," and the camp-meeting "schools of holiness" were geared to the "precipitation" of the experience of "perfect love." From the beginning itinerant preachers formed the task force of Methodism. Their aim was to convert sinners through a powerful experience of the forgiveness of Christ, accompanied by physical manifestations of that conversion which Jessie Lee, one of the first American converts, described: "I have been at meetings where the whole congregation would be bathed in tears and sometimes their cries would be so loud that the preacher's voice could not be heard. Some would be seized with trembling and in a few moments drop to the floor as if they were dead, while others were embracing each other with streaming eyes and all were lost in wonder, love, and praise."[52]

The American Religious Awakenings

Pentecostals claim a direct lineage from the religious revivals. We must therefore sketch some of their characteristics insofar as they have influenced our contemporary Holiness and Pentecostal movements. Beginning from the eighteenth century, writes L. Jamison, "revivalism has been endemic in American Protestantism. That impulse has been expressed in various degrees of intensity and ubiquity, yet it has never been entirely absent from the American scene, and it has left its mark on the structures and ideas of every Protestant body."[53]

There have been four main waves of revivalism: from 1725 to 1750; from 1795 to 1835; from 1875 to the end of the century; and the fourth, during and after the two World Wars, is still vigorous. All of them, besides becoming to a great extent national in scope and outreach, were characterized by the following aspects: 1) An emphasis on direct inspiration and religious emotionalism: "The aim of the revivalist preacher was always to stimulate a direct confrontation of the sinner with God."[54] 2) Personal sanctification as a possible, or even necessary state for the converted individual. (This had been a "pervasive element in the religion of John Wesley, and the theme was elaborated with variations in most revivals." 3) Universalism, or an anti-Calvinistic emphasis which, rejecting the *decretum horribile* of predestination, stressed the possibility and probability of salvation for all. 4) The millenarian expectation of the second coming of Christ, not only as the Parousia of the kingdom of God, but also as a hope that thereby all problems and the evil of the world will find a definite solution.[55]

Of all revival movements the two which fall within the period under our study are the second and, partly, the third. The first (the

Great Awakening) under the leadership of Jonathan Edwards and George Whitefield, took place before the establishment of Methodism on American soil. The fourth, obviously, is developing with the preaching campaigns of the Holiness and Pentecostal denominations.

The Second Awakening (1795–1835) centered around Kentucky, the Appalachians, and Tennessee, but it spread also into other areas, mostly New York, New England, and Pennsylvania. By that time the effects of the Great Awakening had largely ceased. The American Revolution, disrupting the usual patterns of church life, had contributed to the spread of rationalism in the form of a militant deism. Perry Miller has referred to the "urbane rationalism" of men like Jefferson, Washington, and other statesmen of American independence. Thomas Jefferson had gone so far as to prepare an expurgated version of the New Testament from which he had removed those supernatural and miraculous elements which he deemed "unacceptable" to the enlightened men of his time. The person of Jesus was reduced to the level of a moral teacher of the highest ideals, but deprived of any divine attributes.[56] Hence "something of an extraordinary nature seemed necessary to arrest the attention of a giddy people who were ready to conclude that Christianity was a fable and futurity a dream."[57]

This necessity the revival tried to achieve in different ways. The casual preachers of former times were replaced by professional evangelists, thus inaugurating the era of "modern revivalism." Their main instruments were the camp meetings and an intense emotionalism which "confounded infidelity, awed vice into silence, and brought numbers beyond calculations under serious impressions." The camp meetings at the Red River and at Cane Ridge (with as many as 20,000 listeners coming from distances of fifty and even one hundred miles) became landmarks in the history of American revivalism:

> Preachers were encouraged to exhort the throng simultaneously from preaching stands and suitable distances. People would drift from one stand to another. They would gather in smaller groups to hear recent converts relate their experiences, and then burst into hymns of praise. And the conversions that were effected released tidal waves of feeling. With the traditionally slow cycle of "guilt, despair, hope, and assurance" being compressed into a few days and even a few hours, the emotional stress was agonizingly intensified and cut deep into normal restraint. Not only were there outbursts of weeping and shouts of joy, but frequently in the frenzied excitement of the moment, men and women were suddenly

swept into physical "exercises" (falling, jumping, running, jerking) which were attributed to the smiting power of the Spirit.[58]

At the end of the period, the man who would set revivalism on a new road began his work, Charles Grandison Finney (1792–1875). In 1821 he had left a law office to devote his life to saving souls.

> [He] not only developed techniques for promoting conversions and a new style for pulpit oratory, but he transformed also the whole philosophy and process of evangelism. . . . The difference between [Edwards and Finney] was essentially the difference between the medieval mind and the modern temper. One saw God as the center of the universe, the other saw man. One believed that revivals were "prayed down," and the other that they were "worked out."[59]

Emotionalism was at the root of Finney's preaching, although he generally endeavored to keep the audience within the bounds of a restrained fervor. He was six feet, two inches, slim, blond, blue-eyed, and handsome, and has remained the symbol of the best that revivalism can offer. When he spoke from the pulpit, guilt-ridden listeners quailed and fainted under his gaze. "For a decade, he was the most sought-after preacher of the United States, and thereafter until his death, he was considered the national dean of evangelists. There was also a mystical element in his make-up, which explained to those who knew him many of his eccentricities."[60]

Finney became famous as well through the "new measures" he developed. He held services at "unseasonable hours" or protracted them for days until his audience would "break down." His sermons included emotion-loaded prayers for the conversion of sinners. Women were invited to pray aloud for the return of their husbands to God, while he pointed out specific individuals whose conversion he was seeking by means of prayer-circles and other devices. Finney was accused of "indulging in harsh, colloquial, and even irreverent language," but he did not pay much attention and sometimes challenged his critics to watch him working at the "anxious bench." But many remained unconviced. "The spirit of the anxious bench," said J. W. Nevin, "is at war with the spirit of the catechism. . . . The bench is against catechism, and the catechism is against the bench."[61]

This Second Awakening is usually held in small esteem by the historical churches. It failed, they say, to build up a "theocratic nation under God" and in its pursuit of a "religious democracy" it engendered the denominational forms of American Protestantism which still endure.[62] "Democracy," states R. H. Niebuhr, "has not only permitted the continuance of old divisions of Protestantism; it has allowed, if not encouraged, the growth of new groups. Large as the number of naturalized denominations is, it is exceeded by the native-born. Most of them trace their origins to some extensive or localized revival in America such as the Second Awakening."[63] But the revival was also the starting-point for a large number of educational, social, and benevolent societies such as the American Educational Society (1816), the American Bible Society (1816), the American Colonization Society (1816), the Sunday School Union (1817), the American Tract Society (1826), and the American Home Missionary Society (1826). Another, and perhaps the most precious, of its by-products was the marvelous Protestant missionary outreach to Asiatic countries which began at that period with the foundation of the American Board of Commissioners for Foreign Missions (1810), and the American Baptist Missionary Society (1810). Historians have also seen in these and similar societies the beginning of ecumenical ventures in those parts of the world: "For the first time in American history, members of more than two denominations cooperated in an outward, visible organization, in what we should now class as movements in the field of Life and Work. . . . These societies were national, with a nation-wide conception of their missionary work. This helped to give some of the more provincial denominations . . . a broader outlook."[64]

The Third Awakening followed at the end of Civil War. Hostilities had served, among other things, to wipe out a good deal of the political nativism of the 1850's, along with its anti-Catholic overtones. Protestant churches went through a period of pietism and produced a number of great revivalists: Dwight L. Moody, Samuel P. Jones, R. A. Torrey, J. W. Chapman, and the most famous of all, Billy Sunday. The scenery of the revival had also moved from the farmland to the great industrial cities. "Water," said Moody, "runs down the hill, and the highest hills are the great cities. If we can stir them, we can stir the whole country." The first part of the revival (and the only one connected with our subject) evolved around the personality of D. L. Moody and his associates. After a much publicized tour in England, they came back to America resolved to apply here the methods of "fighting sin." Executive committees of ministers and laymen took charge of the preparatory work, while prominent businessmen assured financial backing for the campaigns. Moody and Sankey, his accompanying singer, stormed the cities and spoke to audiences of more than 10,000 people in halls, tabernacles, theaters, and open-air spaces. They relied heavily on "prayer meetings" at which audiences (often made up of drunkards, gamblers, and hard-core sinners) submitted themselves to being prayed over until they were "converted." Moody made full use of his "weeping-power" and easily moved his listeners to tears. The people would shout hallelujahs, amens, or make any kind of hysterical noise, but only to a certain point, because Moody's personality was strong enough to stop the emotionalism and get back to more serious business.[65]

In the long run, the revivals tended to create in American Protestantism a state of nausea and fatigue. There was too much theatrical organization and business-like procedure in the whole enterprise. Before the end of the nineteenth century, enthusiasm for the Awakening had dwindled, and even Methodism shared the growing indifference. At the same time, however, there were others who, attributing this negligence of the "only method of saving souls" to the snares of the devil, would take it as evidence that God had forsaken the historical churches, and that a revolution was needed to bring them back to primitive Christianity. These people became the pioneers of the Holiness and Pentecostal churches.

In conclusion, we notice throughout the centuries a trend in Christianity that points to the existence of a more mystical and less legalistic interpretation of Christ's message. That trend is seen in the early Church and can be detected (though it was largely an underground movement) during the Middle Ages. It reappears, with renewed vigor, in some of the branches of the radical Reformation, and takes more definite shape with Methodism. But the trend, in order to mature and take final form, required a specially prepared ground. This was found in the Awakenings and in the democratic forms of American religion during its moves to the Western frontiers. By the middle of the nineteenth century the "dissolution" and "worldliness" of the historical churches had paved the way for the change. The newcomers exalted the "old religion" and proclaimed that holiness was available to, and should be sought by, man in the present life. That moment signaled the birth of the Holiness and Pentecostal movements.

CHAPTER TWO

HOLINESS CHURCHES IN AMERICA

Pentecostalism made its world appearance in two steps: as a revivalist movement devoted to restoring the doctrine and practice of Holiness among the people of God; and as a dissident religious body that, unsatisfied with internal sanctification, wanted to manifest it with charismatic signs. With the Holiness movement (which embodies the first aspect) we already have the essence of a new development in Christianity; Pentecostalism (promoter of the second) will serve to bring it to completion. One cannot be disengaged from the other.[1]

In the history of the Church most dissenting movements have searched for a scapegoat for their dissatisfaction. The Holiness movement adherents singled out Methodism, accusing it of sinful negligence in matters pertaining to the very nature of its vocation. Then a number of collateral reasons were added to justify their withdrawal from the parent church and for starting a new denomination. In this case, however, Methodist sources reveal that the basic accusation, that Wesley's church in America had forgotten many of the ideals of Holiness that had animated its first days, was largely justified. The injunction given to the original preachers had been: "to save any souls you can; to bring as many sinners as possible to Repentance; and with all your power to build them into that holiness without which they cannot see the Lord." "All our preachers," said the *Plain Account of Christian Perfection,* "should make a point of preaching perfection to believers constantly, strongly and explicitly; and all believers should mind this one thing, and continually agonize for it."[2] Methodism's aim in the New World had been, therefore, to spread Christian holiness over these lands. Its ministers, before their formal reception, were expected to preach that man can be perfect in love in this life.

Decline of Methodism

And yet, by the end of the Second Awakening, observers were detecting that American Methodism was drifting away from these original ideals. The deistic bent of the nation's intellectuals was flatly opposed to "exaggerations" in the practice of religion. The camp meetings were being abandoned because, as they came more under the direction of "reasonable preachers," they could not "precipitate" in audiences the true conversions that come through the experience of true love. According to M. E. Gaddis, the slackening was caused as well by the increasing autocratic character of the episcopacy; the decline of class meetings; the passing of the frontier itinerancy; and the general environmental circumstances.[3] Pentecostals saw other alarming symptoms in the life of the mother church:

> Local congregations neglected spiritual matters to pander to social wants of the people. In the seminaries, to be sure, earnest men grappled with the new learning and the ethical issues which urban poverty and industrial strife had raised. The new faith of Modernism which they brought forth was deadly serious about righting social wrongs. But it rejected the ancient doctrines and the old-fashioned revivals which hitherto had made war on sin so effective. The masses of church-goers either misunderstood or suspected it. To most laymen the Social Gospel seemed nothing more than a sanction for church festivals and Sunday school dances. The shallow faith prevailed that education, democracy, and Christianity were soon to usher in the earth's most glorious age.[4]

Another embarrassing problem entered into the picture with the issue of slavery. The Methodist churches had among their church members no less than half a million slaves, and the law issued by the General Conference of 1784 prohibiting "buying or selling the bodies and souls of men, women and children, with an intent to enslave them," had become a dead letter. Many of the pastors and theologians of the Midwest and South defended slavery as "a political question with which the Church must not meddle." The attitude became provocative. In 1816 the Negro members of the Methodist societies in Philadelphia, aggrieved at such un-Christian conduct, founded their own African Methodist Church. Four years later their New York brethren gathered into another African Methodist Episcopal Zion Church.[5] It was a warning to Methodism that issues might arrive that could force certain groups to start their own denominations.

Certain sections in Methodism were making efforts to recover the ancient heritage of holiness. In 1839 Thomas Merritt launched in Boston a periodical, *Guide to Christian Perfection,* destined to be very influential for the Holiness cause. In New York, Mrs. Phoebe Palmer and her husband held, in the parlor of their home, "Tuesday Meetings for the Promotion of Holiness" and inspired hundreds of preachers "to seek and find what they believed was perfect love." During their preaching tours in the states on the eastern seaboard, "great numbers of listeners professed the second blessing and pledged to uphold the banner of holiness in their home communities." Even Charles Finney endorsed the campaign, while admitting that his own revivals "would become more and more superficial and finally cease to exist unless something effectual was done to elevate the standard of holiness in the Church."[6] Books dealing with perfectionism, such as *The Higher Christian Life* (1859), by W. E. Boardman, and *Guide to Holiness* (1860), by Mrs. Palmer, sold hundreds of thousands of copies at home and abroad and became best sellers in religious literature. After the Civil War some leaders saw in perfectionism the only remedy to the ills caused by the hostilities. "If we keep to this doctrine of perfection," said John C. McClintock, who later became president of Drew Seminary, "then the century is ours. Our work is a moral work, that is to say, the work of making men holy."[7]

The reaction of official Methodism to the demands of these "budding rebels" was never well articulated. The dissenters accused the Church of "loss of simplicity in worship" and decried the "abominable use" of sitting during prayer and the needless employment of pews, choirs, and organs, which they felt tended to convert the chapels into "heathen churches." In 1840 a number of Methodist bishops called attention to the fact that Holiness was "a leading feature of early Methodism" and promised to take the steps needed to return to the "primitive way."[8] But, in the opinion of the historians of Holiness, little was done to change the trend:

> For several years before 1867 . . . there was [in Methodism] a growing opposition to the subject of entire sanctification as a distinctive experience. This opposition came from the pulpit and pew, and was often met with at the local camp-meetings. The opposition became at times so violent that in many places the professors of this experience found little or no sympathy or encouragement at these annual meetings.[9]

Disenchanted by the coolness of the official reception, the promoters of Holiness decided to go their own way. By 1758—the *annus mirabilis* of the Holiness movement—they had launched revival campaigns that some have rated "as intense and as deep as those of Whitefield in 1740." In 1867, during a series of revivals at Vineland, New Jersey, directed by W. Osborn, A. Cockman, and J. Inskip, those present at the meetings established a National Camp Meeting Association for the Promotion of Holiness, which later became the National Holiness Association and extended its action to various parts of the country. The machinery, comments Synan, was already in operation and could have easily been transformed into a particular denomination of more than one million members. The delegates to some of their conventions asked for such a step, but "leaders steadfastly counseled against *come-outism* and directed the delegates to remain loyal to their denominations. However, this insistence on loyalty caused the movement to fragment, as groups in different annual conferences left the churches piecemeal in disputes over local conditions."[10]

As a next step, American Holiness leaders moved to Great Britain. While the Palmers were preaching at Leeds, Sheffield, Manchester, and Birmingham, James Caughey conducted campaigns with conversions and professions of Holiness in other parts of the British Isles. Meanwhile, Dwight Moody and William Boardman helped Canon Batterly to start what later would become the Keswick Revivals. In England, "the shirt-sleeve exuberance of the American camp-meeting gave way to a more thoughtful atmosphere, and individual experience turned towards social needs despite the encouragement which Anglican participants gave to the mystical elements in Holiness teaching."[11] Meanwhile, in the United States attention was distracted by the rise of a radical form of Holiness revival, more intent on Puritan standards of dress or behavior than on perfect love. This departure from orthodoxy hurt the Holiness groups, but it did not stop them. The event marked rather the beginning of a frontal attack against official Methodism. Typical was J. P. Brooks's book, *The Divine Church,* a refutation of ecclesiastical organization, soon to become the manual of "come-outism." The effects of that verbal and written offensive were soon evident. By 1860 B. T. Roberts had founded the Free Methodist Church of America, and twenty years later Daniel S. Werner was quitting Methodism to start his own Church of God, Anderson, Indiana. The defections were accompanied by lengthy controversies between the opposing parties. From 1885 to 1895 the Holiness awakening reached its peak of acceptance, when Inskip preached Holiness to the Mormons at Salt Lake City, and Quakers and Cumberland Presbyterians joined in the praises of the new revival.

Separate Denominations

The idea of forming separate denominations was gaining ground. Four main factors seemed to push it: (1) the persistent opposition of ecclesiastical officials to independent Holiness associations and publishing agencies; (2) the recurrent outbursts of fanaticism among persons connected with, but not members of, the Holiness associations; (3) the outbreak of strenuous attacks upon the doctrine of sanctification; and (4) the increasing activity of urban Holiness preachers in city missions and social work.[12]

The response of Methodism to these flare-ups of rebellion was, once again, equivocal. Some if its branches, for instance the Methodist Protestant Church in 1877 and the Wesleyan Connection ten years later, adopted an official stand favoring the second blessing, and several of their bishops shared the same view. The position of the Southern Methodist bishops was still more firm. In 1870 they declared the need for a "general and powerful revival of Scriptural holiness" and criticized their preachers for their insufficient stress on Christian perfection: "The infrequency of its proclamation from the pulpit and the irregularity of its experimental power in the Church has proved a serious detriment . . . to our mission. . . . Let us more than ever reassert this grand doctrine."[13] A few years later came the warnings: "No self-constituted and irresponsible 'association,' with its many objectionable features, must be allowed to stand forth before the world as the only, or even as the chief, exponent of holiness. The honor and the very existence of the Church is involved here. . . . The Church must assert her prerogatives and be true to her character. . . . She must vindicate the claim that her highest aim is to spread Scriptural holiness over the land. In order to do this every Methodist pulpit must continue to ring out clear and strong on the doctrine of the higher Christian life, and every preacher must exemplify the doctrine he preaches."[14]

The objections raised against the attempts made by the Holiness associations to lead in the pursuit of the same objectives were the following: 1) "Holiness" was "a novelty," and a departure from original Wesleyan theology. "The holiness associations, the holiness prayer meeting, the holiness preacher, are all modern novelties. They are not Wesleyan. Wesley would have never admitted them into the Methodist system."[15] 2) The new world trends, marked by fast-moving scientific and industrial developments, counseled against the acceptance of any "old-fashioned methods" of enthusiastic religion. 3) Perfectionists were "disparaging the doctrine of the New Birth at all stages of spiritual growth" as taught clearly in Methodism. 4) Methodist leaders called into question the Holiness tendency of limiting the name "saint" and "sanctified person" to the few people who had reached the state of perfection, while denying it to the larger body of believers. 5) Methodism could not approve certain charismatic gifts (mainly divine healing) which their adversaries claimed to have belonged to the original Wesleyan message. 6) Two other factors had to be kept in mind: first, sanctification could never become universal in the Church if left in the hands of independent organizations and unrecognized agencies; and second, the whole problem ought to be discussed and solved "in connection with the established usages of the Church." The document ended with this stern warning:

> We do not question the sincerity and zeal of these brethren. We desire the Church to profit by their earnest preaching and godly example. But we deplore their teaching and method insofar as they claim a monopoly of the experience, practice, and advocacy of holiness, and the fact that they separate themselves from the body of [our] ministers and discipline.[16]

End of Dialogue

These words signaled the end of any semblance of dialogue among parties holding such antagonistic views of Christianity. The Holiness movement was already a fact, and no adverse criticism, opposition, or disdain on the part of the parent church would stop it. The movement had the blessing of the best revivalists of the time who so often have directed the destinies of American religion. Holiness had also caught the imagination of many citizens who found in the new doctrines more solid spiritual food and religious experience than the older churches offered. What they did not realize was the new and deep wound of division the movement was opening in the mystical body of Christ. The men "who issued the call for the first gathering of the National Holiness Association in 1867 little knew they were inadvertently laying the groundwork for the formation of dozens of new denominations."[17] One wonders if the unawareness was due to the fact that some well-known theologians of the preceding century, while repudiating the idea of a *sect* as contrary to the essence of the Gospel, had accepted that of *denomination* as something useful to the Church. "All societies," wrote Gilbert Tennent, "who profess the foundational principles thereof, notwithstanding their different *denominations* and diversity of sentiments in small things, are in reality but one Church of Christ, but several branches [more or less pure in minute things] of one visible kingdom of the Messiah."[18] The results of this principle would become disastrous to the Holiness and Pentecostal cause.

The decades from 1880 to the end of the century were vital for the building up of a "Holiness mentality" and the beginning of Holiness denominations. The disintegration process followed the old patterns. Well-known preachers of Holiness toured the country, denouncing the "easy, indulgent, accommodating and mammonized" beliefs and practices of the official Church, gathering around them followers with similar aspirations, and organizing "bands under Spirit guidance" or more commonly "Holiness Associations." In order to keep the initial enthusiasm high, the organizers set up conferences and camp meetings in various parts of the country. The Holiness press, technically backward, but apt to keep alive the high-pitched fervor of its readers, helped in the fight against their more powerful adversaries. Before the end of the century, hundreds of Holiness preachers were devoting full time to the work. The success was more rapid in the West and South than in the East.[19] To those disturbed by the disruptive nature of the new movement, the Holiness leaders retorted that they constituted a truly "invigorating element" in the Church. But disruption and chaos existed certainly in their ranks. This precisely led them to ask if the time had not come to start "separate denominations" as distinct from the rather loose type of associations. The majority opted for this solution. To this was added the fact that some of their "missions" and Bible Schools were already producing "a class of converts who could not feel at home in stylish downtown congregations, but rather nurtured a sense of freedom and fellowship among the sponsors who offered a welcome respite from bitter and fruitless controversy. The result was the organization by 1900 of scores of independent Holiness congregations in cities large and small."[20] The outlook, as viewed by the mother church, was not encouraging. In the words of one of its historians:

> Through twenty years following 1880, Methodist leaders in both the North and the South witnessed a growing disruption of fellowship in their communions which they seemed powerless to halt. The bishops were generally sane and conservative and deeply

religious men. They were anxious to keep Methodism evangelical and thoroughly Wesleyan. On the other hand, however, wealthy city congregations and their cultivated pastors had rebelled against the class-meetings, the revivals, and the old standards which the early generation thought to be evidence of holiness. Recently this part of the Church had seemed an easy prey of the young university men who were rapidly forsaking traditional Methodist theology.[21]

It has been said that Methodism was not the only tradition which provided supporters and members to the Holiness and Pentecostal movements. There is a grain of truth in the affirmation. Individuals and small groupings from other denominations, mainly Baptists and Presbyterians, embraced the doctrines of sanctification and joined the ranks of the Holiness churches. Their presence might have contributed to the adoption of church policies borrowed from the Baptist tradition. Nevertheless, the National Holiness Movement, the parent body of most American perfectionist denominations, "was almost exclusively a Methodist phenomenon, led by Methodists, and appealing mainly to Methodists." In Clark's view this was only "natural in view of the practical monopoly held by Methodism at that time on the perfectionist tradition, including the revival, the class-meeting, and testimony technique which has been always the strongest support of holiness."[22]

Regarding the question of which elements in American Protestantism prepared the way for the extraordinary development of the enthusiastic denominations, theologians, sociologists, and historians have proposed these tentative answers:

1. American religious pluralism has often tended to the multiplication of denominations. Freedom of belief has led to countless varieties in the theological and liturgical fields. "Freedom in worship," writes R. H. Niebuhr, "seems to give way to undisciplined inventiveness and formlessness. While the sermon remains the central feature in most Protestant meetings, the term *preaching* now includes not only the proclamation of the Gospel ... but lecturing on political, humanitarian, and literary themes, ritualistic rhapsodizing and rote repetition of holy phrases. Not only the sacraments of baptism and the Lord's Supper, but feet-washing, holy-rolling, and ecstatic dancing, speaking in tongues, and the handling of snakes can be found by the curious student of religious customs as he visits the meeting of groups in America that call themselves Protestant."[23]

2. The historical churches had often adapted their policies to the

economic status of their membership. Richer denominations placed a premium on worldly success and adopted a paternalistic attitude towards the unsuccessful and underprivileged. "Small wonder, then, that the latter were frequently prompted to withdraw from religious associations which verbalized fellowship instead of practicing it, and would not minister adequately to the acute needs of the less fortunate."[24] Students of political science also have asked if there was more than political coincidence between the Holiness movement and the agrarian revolt of the late 1890's which culminated in populism and the presidential candidacy of William Jennings Bryan in 1896. Both had an agrarian background; and both took place in the Midwest and Southern States. The aim of populism was to debunk the "monopoly powers" of the Eastern Establishment; while the Holiness leaders were fighting against the "autocracy" and the ecclesiastical power of the Methodist hierarchy.[25]

3. A number of experts rate the "economic degradation" of the prospective members among the main factors in the rise of Holiness denominations. The theory, applied earlier to European churches by M. Weber and E. Troeltsch, has been revived for the American Holiness movement by E. T. Clark:

> These sects originated among the religiously neglected who find the conventional religion of their day unsuited to their social and psychological needs. As a result, finding themselves ill at ease in the presence of the effete and prosperous *bourgeoise,* their emotional natures unsatisfied by a middle-class complacency, their economic problems disregarded by those who have no such problems to meet, and their naive faith and simple interpretation smiled upon . . . the poor and the ignorant revolt and draw apart into groups that are congenial.[26]

4. Others, headed by Joachim Walch, see in the estrangement of these Holiness bodies an attempt to establish, through a religious experience, a direct contact with God, the sacred and the nouminous. Since the traditional ways (liturgical and sacramental) of the historical churches failed or became inadequate, the man in the street turns to those preachers who offer him a short-cut to God. The leaders of these movements know it and "strive for and claim to attain an immediacy of revelation with the *noumenous* objects, whether through a fresh revelation, emotional conversation and exaltation, mystical union with the divine. . . . The sectarian ideal involves also a return to the fancied

immediacy of some normative movement, such as the Apostolic Age of Christianity."[27]

These combined reasons explain some of the basic historicosociological aspects of the Holiness movement. Such elements were present more than elsewhere in nineteenth-century American society in which "religious experience" (understood as that "wrestling with God which all men must go through on their way to salvation"), and emotionalism constituted the most evident manifestation of popular Christianity. Reservations are in order, however, about the motif of material poverty among the rank and file in Holiness denominations. Most of its members came, it is true, from the more humble strata of society. But to state that they joined the new communion "to look for an escape from their hard lot into a heaven of bliss and comfort which was foreign to their everyday existence," or to fancy that "they usually picture a coming time when the judgment of society shall be reversed and they shall change places with the prosperous and comfortable, who shall be cast down, while the poor are exalted,"[28] is grossly to misinterpret their motivation. Holiness and Pentecostal people do not now—and probably never did before—join the new church for socialistic or even humanitarian motives. The Pentecostals I have known in four continents would not be willing to exchange their peace of soul, their closeness to God, and the ineffable experience of the second blessing for any of the material comforts of an affluent society. Not enough attention has been paid by the experts to the reasons advanced by the Holiness and Pentecostal groups for their separation. And yet they must be taken into account if we want to have a close look at the whole picture. Here are the most important reasons:

1. *Departure from the true faith* on the part of the historical churches. Darwin's evolutionism, Kant's rationalism, Schleiermacher's religion of experience, Bushnell's theories on Christian Nurture, and Rauschenbusch's Social Gospel had robbed American Christianity of its genuine spirit. "A confusion of theologians, philosophers, and poets came to exert more influence on many a fashionable pulpit than did the word of God. The Bible was largely forgotten."[29]

2. The *dead formalism* of their theologies and liturgies. The sad state of the latter could be seen in the elaborately dressed choirs whose members in many cases made no profession of religion, but were sneering skeptics, thus transforming the religious services into "operatic performances" and allowing spirituality to be "frozen to death."[30]

3. The *worldliness* to which the historical churches had succumbed. "Separation from the world," the watchword of the early Church, had become a dead issue in Methodism, and traditional prohibitions (from card-playing to abstentionism) were rescinded by the official Church.[31]

4. The *substitution of experimental religion* by a mere knowledge and external profession of faith. All the new theories were "so foreign to the Bible and to the experience of the founders and the early propagators of the various Protestant denominations that their spiritual children sighed for a return of the old-fashioned proclamation that 'whosoever will' may have a personal knowledge of God."[32]

5. *Resistance,* on the part of the historical churches, *to the endorsement of these urgently needed reforms,* or even to receive into their membership those who professed such views. As a consequence:

> Since reformation and holiness were resisted in the Church, then there must be a separation if there was to be genuine spiritual identity. A Christian union should be formed that would reassert the intrinsic doctrines of the Bible and the vital matters of Christian service, whose ultimate objective would be "to restore primitive Christianity and bring about the union of all denominations."[33]

It is not easy to assign exact dates for the foundation of the various Holiness bodies. The very smallness of some of them and the anonymity of their founders add to the difficulty. The denominations began to mushroom all over the United States and Canada during the second half of the nineteenth century and the first part of the twentieth century. Some were short-lived. Others survived, either independently or by joining forces with groups of similar ideals. The "erupting process" began around 1880 and came to a halt before the beginning of World War II. In mission territories, however, the splintering process continues and has reached its greatest acceleration in sub-Saharan Africa.

The list of the ecclesial communities of the Holiness movement has never been completed. For the United States and Canada such sources as the *Yearbook of American Churches,* Frank Mead's *Handbook of Denominations,* or E. T. Clark's *Small Sects in America* contain ample information. Chéry, Seguy, and Colinon have compiled a useful list for France; Block-Hoell is almost exhaustive for the Scandinavian countries; Sundkler and D. Barrett have done good introductory work for

Africa; Mullert, Algermissen, and Hutten have covered the German-speaking lands; and Crivelli and the present author have attempted a similar effort for Latin America. J. Gründler's *Lexikon der Christlichen Kirchen und Sekten,* 1961, contains new entries of importance. But all previous efforts at classification have been amply surpassed by W. J. Hollenweger's magnificent ten volume manuscript, *Handbuch der Pfingstbewegung,* (Geneva, 1965–67), now available at a few libraries in America. And yet, it is more than doubtful that our research for new names has been exhausted. Anyone familiar with a concrete region of the world where Holiness and Pentecostals are at work is aware of the existence of new groups never mentioned by any of the sources.[34]

Here I shall limit myself to the most important American Holiness groups. They are, to a great extent, responsible for many off-shoots in mission lands, and are characterized by their insistence on perfectionism, theological fundamentalism, and hopes of the imminent second coming of Christ. Those groups, however, which embrace among their basic doctrines the "gifts," and mostly that of speaking with tongues, must be transferred into the category of Pentecostal denominations. This distinction is necessary for any clear ideas on the subject. Excluded also from this list are certain small Methodist churches, some German "perfectionist" groups still attached to their parent churches, the Mennonites, the Quakers, and the United Brethren. Certain writers mention here the Church of the Nazarene. This certainly started as a Holiness or even Pentecostal group. But in 1924 it dropped the name Pentecostal and, as can be discovered from conversations with its officials, now shuns the title of Holiness, not because there are no perfectionist elements in its theology, but perhaps in order to differentiate itself from the cheaper type of religious enthusiasm used (and abused) by some Holiness denominations. For different reasons I have decided to omit from this section the movement called Moral Rearmament. It embraced Holiness ideas when Frank Buchman founded it (1921), and even in the early days when it was known as the Oxford Group Movement. But lately it has become a syncretistic organization where non-Christian religions are given almost the same prominent place as Christianity. I have also decided to shift Father Divine's Peace Mission from the Pentecostal camp where Clark places it to that of Holiness where, in spite of all its eccentricities, it belongs of its own right. The Holiness groups born outside the United States will be mentioned in the chapter on missions.

Important American Holiness Groups

Church of God, Anderson, Indiana. The place name distinguishes it from many other "churches of God" (Mead speaks of at least 200 independent religious bodies in North America which bear that title) within and without the Holiness fold. As mentioned above, the church began to function in 1880 under the leadership of D. S. Werner. Theologically the denomination is strictly fundamentalist; it insists on the second coming of Christ, and refuses to distinguish between the visible and invisible Church, thus recognizing the Lord's people in all communions. The church practices foot-washing and baptism by immersion, but leaves optional the reception of the Eucharist. It is said to have one of the best Sunday-school systems in the country. The ministerial work is voluntary. The denomination claims 250,000 followers in its total community. The members are very zealous, and the group is known for "its liberal attitude to co-operative movements, religious education, and general church procedure."[35]

The Pilgrim Holiness Church. Its purpose is to preach the "whole Gospel," namely, salvation from actual sin through justification, and from original sin through sanctification. It believes in the textual inspiration of the Bible, in the Trinitarian and christological dogmas, in the pre-millenial coming of Christ, in divine healing, and in the evangelization of the whole world.[36] In its actual organization the church is a merger of several bodies: the International Apostolic Church Union, started by Knaff in Cincinnati; the Holiness Christian Church, born from Holiness revivals in Pennsylvania at the beginning of the century; a Pentecostal Rescue Mission from New York; some California groups discontented with the policies of the Nazarenes; the Pentecostal Brethren of God in Christ, from Ohio; and the People's Mission, of Colorado Springs. The mergers have taken place in a span of forty years. Even with all these additions, the Pilgrim Holiness Church seems to have stopped growing. At present it has 50,000 members scattered in a good number of States and in Canada. Its missionaries work also in foreign lands: in Mexico and in several South American countries; in the Philippines and in the West Indies. Both men and women are ordained to the ministry. In polity the Church follows the Methodist pattern with local units, district organization, and a General Conference meeting every four years.[37]

Pillar of Fire. The symbol of fire has been dear to Holiness bodies, several of which have adopted it as a title for their organization. Like a few other American contemporary religious movements the Pillar of Fire owes its beginnings to the ardent activities of a lady, Mrs. Alma White, foundress, first "bishop," and theologian of the organization (1862–1946). Unsatisfied with the lukewarmness of the Methodist Church, of which she was a member in her home state of Kentucky, she moved to Denver, Colorado, where she took over the pulpit, organized camp meetings on her own authority, and began to recruit people who sympathized with her Holiness ideas. These activities brought her into conflict with the Methodist church authorities. The frictions encouraged her to found her own denomination under the title of Pentecostal Union, which in 1917 was changed to Pillar of Fire. The first headquarters were at Denver, but later they moved to Brooklyn, New York. The theology of the denomination is Methodist in inspiration, but fundamentalist in interpretation. Only the fact that its constitutions have an enthusiastic flavor and insist strongly on "second baptism" puts it in the category of the Holiness bodies. The Pillar of Fire for a long time has seemed to be a family property: Mrs. White was succeeded in her "episcopal" job by her two sons. The denomination, with only 5,000 members, can afford it.[38]

Other Holiness Bodies. Of all the other individual Holiness bodies, there is hardly any that deserves more than a passing mention. There are, for instance: a Church of the Gospel, founded in 1911 in Massachusetts, and claiming to adhere to early Methodist principles, with sanctification as one of its fundamental beliefs; a Christian Nation Church, which, in spite of its early beginnings in 1892, numbers only a few hundred followers, rejects any contact with other religious societies, and is opposed to "adornment in attire, clubs and lodges, remarriage after divorce, marriage between the saved and the unsaved, church festivals and entertainments, slang and jesting, tobacco and snuff";[39] and a Christian Congregation, organized at Kokomo, Indiana, in 1887, prevalent in a few rural sectors, with seven congregations and 1,250 members. The same can be said of the long list compiled by Gründler under the heading of Der Perfektionierte Glaubensstand. Their influence is either local (as in the case of many of the South African denominations) or so small that they fail to appear in the official lists of the Yearbooks.[40] The case is somehow different with certain of the major mergers or with some of their missionary associations. A sample of each one of the groupings will suffice for our purpose.

Churches of God in North America (General Eldership). A few German emigrant churches in America joined with other denominations in the revivals of the nineteenth century. One of their pastors, John Winebrenner, from Harrisburg, Pennsylvania, aroused the criticism of his co-religionists for such participation and for the perfectionist ideas he was embracing. By 1823 he had severed relation with his church, and two years later formed a new congregation under the title of the Church of God. By 1830 the founder and six preachers who had joined him had changed its name to the General Eldership of the Church of God. The words "in North America" were added in 1845, and "Church" became "Churches" in 1903. Thus, with the "nominal" question solved, the new church began to expand, though even at present we cannot speak of any great development since it has only 401 congregations and a total membership of less than 40,000. Doctrinally, the denomination is fundamentalist: the Bible considered as the only rule of faith and practice; baptism by immersion only, the Lord's Supper and feet-washing are the only and always obligatory ordinances; insistence on the work of the Holy Spirit; localism stressed as the only personification of the Church ("each local church is a Church of God and should be so called"); and a strict code of morality for all the members of the denomination. The church is organized into seventeen elderships or conferences, some of them in mission territories. The highest authority is vested in the General Eldership, composed of an equal number of ministers and lay people. Its headquarters are at Harrisburg, Pennsylvania.[41]

The Christian and Missionary Alliance. This is probably the strongest and best-organized denomination within the Holiness movement. It does not call itself a church, although it functions as such for all practical purposes. It originated in 1881 under the leadership of A.B. Simpson, a Presbyterian minister who left his church to work among the abandoned masses of New York City. "Strongly evangelical and fundamentalist, the Alliance stands for the literal interpretation of the Bible, the atonement wrought by Christ, the reality of supernatural experience, separation from the world, the premillennial return of Christ, Spirit baptism and practical holiness."[42] Simpson's theology expressed itself in a fourfold Gospel: Christ the Savior, the Sanctifier, the Healer, and the Coming Christ. The denomination is ruled by a General Council which meets annually. The local churches are self-maintaining and self-supporting.

Its members rank among the most missionary-minded groups in the Holiness communion. They work in Africa, the Near East, India, Vietnam, Thailand, Japan, New Guinea, among overseas Chinese, and in Indonesia. In Latin America they carry on an active and often proselytizing work among Catholics. They have over a thousand missionaries, a mighty number for a denomination whose domestic membership is around 70,000. This explains the fact that its overseas membership doubles that at home. At the beginning of the century, the Alliance went through a serious crisis which revolved around the doctrine and practice of "charismatic gifts." Divine healing was accepted as part of the ministry of the Church, but the case was different with "speaking with tongues." Some promoted it; others squarely opposed it. The church remained neutral for a while, until in 1907, during the services held at the campus of the Alliance-operated Missionary Training School at Nyack, New York, some of its members began to be "blessed" with glossolalia and to promote it as an essential tenet in the life of the Church. The matter was brought to the authorities, and A. B. Simpson took his stand on it: speaking with tongues was not a basic part of the Church's message, and the Alliance discarded it from its creed. The decision proved to be costly: the Alliance lost many congregations and much property at home and in the mission lands. But the decision saved the Church from losing "its primitive spirit."[43]

Peace Mission. Father Divine's Peace Mission can be placed in many categories or in none. F. Mayer classifies it among the "Egocentric Cults." Algermissen ranks it among the "Redeemer Sects," because it "venerates the founder as a real redeemer, the perfecter of Christ's work." F. Mead does not find a niche for it in his long list of American denominations. Understandably, there was much of a "cultic reverence" toward the man who received from his followers the titles "King of the Universe," "Source of Imagination," and "Holy Magnetic Body." His eccentricities also gave the impression that all the attention was directed to his person. However, the practices of the movement resemble much more those of the Holiness groups than those of Pentecostalism. Perfectionism and divine healing were among the chief features of the Peace Mission. The "contagious joy," a consequence of "divine experiences" of his disciples, resembled that of many perfectionists after the reception of the second blessing. In one point only, but an essential one, the two movements differ: Holiness is fundamentally Christian, while in Father Divine's preaching there was not even a minimum of authentic Christian belief and doctrine. Clark has accused its founder of not possessing "intelligible doctrines," and for the "chaotic surge of unthinking and superstitious people around him." Father Divine died in 1965. His incoherent thoughts were a strange blending of Theosophy, New Thought, and dualistic Gnosticism under the cloak of a Christian vocabulary detached from its original meaning.[44]

For the remaining Holiness bodies in the West the lists compiled by Clark, Mead, Gründler, and Hollenweger are very extensive. To those already mentioned we may add the following: the Church of God as Organized by Christ; the Church of Christ in Christian Union; Herald of His Coming; the Church of Daniel; Kodesh Church of Emmanuel; Metropolitan Church Association; the Church of the Living; the Catholic Church in Zion; the Church of the Full Gospel; the House of the Lord; Swedish Holiness Mission; the Missionary Bands of the World; Igreja Evangelica Holiness of Brazil; the Hephzibah Faith Mission Association; Faith Holiness Mission; Peniel Mission; United Christian Mission; Church Brotherhood; the Church of God (Apostolic); the Church of Daniel's Band. These denominations, while working in mission lands and in Latin America, have produced off-shoots of the same kind, thus enlarging immensely—and not always in a manner that helps Christian unity—the family of Holiness churches.

CHAPTER THREE

PENTECOSTAL DENOMINATIONS

The Holiness groups prepared the way for the Pentecostal movement. C. W. Conn even states that, "in reality, the Pentecostal emphasis is simply an extension of the earlier Holiness concepts."[1] For Kendrick, the contribution of Holiness to Pentecostalism was twofold: to popularize "the need for the experience of sanctification or second blessing"; and to produce "another wave of motor-phenomena which includes tongues."[2] The new denominations, therefore, would be made up of persons who, accepting, but not satisfied with mere sanctification, required also that such a condition be manifested externally by charismatic gifts of various kinds, and this as the normal way offered by the Spirit to every Christian. A French writer has compared the Holiness experience to the tasting of the gifts of the Spirit, leaving to Pentecostalism the full enjoyment of them.

American Pentecostals were not the first "glossolalists" and faith healers of modern times. They had been preceded in the Old World by the British Irvingites, a group which, haunted by the thought of the imminent second coming of Christ, claimed to have been endowed with such gifts. Even on this side of the Atlantic and before the rise of Pentecostalism, there were a few outstanding preachers in the nineteenth century known as the "Gift-People," such as R. B. Swan in Rhode Island, W. J. Wathall in Arkansas, D. Avery in Ohio, the members of the Swedish Mission in Minnesota, and others. The gifts would appear either in the ministers or among the members of their congregations. In Mooreland, Minn., "the power of God would fall, people dropping to the floor and speaking in other tongues. Prophecy and visions were also listed among the demonstrations."[3] The manifestation of gifts was also a part of the revivals of another famous preacher of the time, R. G. Spurling:

> His services were generally of an emotional nature.... The emotion that made the worshipers weep, laugh, and shout was not some indefinable psychological delirium, but vented the exaltation they received from the presence of God. As the congregation dispersed

> from the meetinghouse in their wagons and ox-carts or on foot, they departed with praises of God. From over the fields and hills would come the sound of rejoicing from some happy person or family. . . . Spectators and worshipers came from distant regions . . . to attend the new outbreak of revival, for a new thing was seen under the sun. Spiritual awakening had become a blessed reality.[4]

At the beginning, this bestowing of charismatic gifts was known as the Latter Rain Movement, a name borrowed from the words of the prophet Joel (2:23), about a former and latter rain. In Pentecostal exegesis, the former rain pointed to the first great spiritual outpouring of the Holy Spirit on the day of Pentecost, while the latter rain indicated a gift which would be given only when the last days of the world were at hand. For some unknown reason, Pentecostals had been entrusted to carry this message to the unbelieving world.[5] Thus Pentecostalism marked the beginning of the last age in the history of mankind and the approach of the second coming of Christ.

> This resurgence of Pentecostalism is conceived as a dispensational outpouring of the Spirit of God, likened to the rains that are essential to the ripening of the harvest, and linked definitely to the immediate return of Christ in power and glory. . . . Wherever the Pentecostal baptism is experienced, the imminence of the return to earth of the Lord Jesus is believed and taught.[6]

The cause of Pentecostalism received a definite impulse from the publication, in 1895, of R. A. Torrey's book, *Baptism with the Holy Spirit.* Torrey's stand was clear: every Christian is entitled to receive the gifts of the Spirit, and there is no substantial difference between the primitive Church and that of our day: the gift "is for every believer, in every age of the Church's history." The book achieved its purpose. Within the short span of thirty years, America witnessed the birth of dozens of clearly Pentecostal bodies and denominations. In other words, for many contemporaries, the experience of the gifts of the Spirit had become a distinctive feature of the full Gospel.[7]

In order to see the initial and, as it were, tangible demonstration of the Pentecostal phenomenon, the reader is invited to consider a small Midwest town, Topeka, Kansas, on January 1, 1901. C. P. Parham, a former Methodist minister who had by this time embraced Holiness and chiliastic doctrines, had opened there a modest Bethel College for the training of evangelists. The students had heard from him the need of spiritual gifts: "Though I honor the Holy Ghost in anointing power both in conversion and sanctification, yet I believe there is a greater revelation of his power. The gifts are in the Holy Spirit and with the baptism of the Holy Spirit the gifts, as well as the graces, should be manifested."[8] They had also "deduced" from the reading of the Bible that "in apostolic times, speaking in tongues was considered to be the initial, physical evidence of a person having received the baptism of the Holy Spirit." Consequently, they had asked for themselves, in their night vigils, that ineffable experience. One night the Spirit came upon one of them. Her name was Agnes Oznam:

> When I learned that the Holy Spirit was yet to be poured out in greater fullness, my heart became hungry for the promised Comforter, and I began to cry out for an enduement of power from on high.... It was nearly eleven o'clock in the evening when it came into my heart to ask that hands be laid upon me that I might receive the Holy Ghost. As hands were laid upon me, the Holy Ghost fell upon me, and I began to speak in tongues, glorifying God.... It was though rivers of living waters were proceeding from my innermost being.[9]

From that day on, says one of their historians, Pentecostal believers teach that "baptism in the Holy Spirit is to be sought and may be received with the evidence of tongues."[10] The experience of Miss Oznam marks the beginning of the Pentecostal Movement. Soon the marvels of Topeka spread to all parts of the country, but nowhere more amazingly than at the Azuza Chapel in Los Angeles, California. The chapel had been a shabby stable where a few Negroes used to attend Sunday services under pastor W. S. Seymour, a former friend of Parham. Brother Seymour was, according to a reporter from the Los Angeles *Times*, a "meek and plain-spoken man," and a rather poor orator who spoke the language of the uneducated people and had nothing of the "arm-waving thunderers" of his class.[11] However, the meetings that had begun with a few people ended in overflowing congregations of seekers of the second blessing. Pentecostals believe that "among the thousands of cathedrals and parish churches with which the world was filled, there was not at that time another which God chose for the glorious preaching of eternal life." "People," one eye-witness stated, "came from all over the world to that Pentecostal mecca during the three years that the services continued day and night." The fruits of the preaching were summed up in the weekly publication *The Apostolic Faith* of December 18, 1906:

> Hundreds of souls have received salvation and healing. The Lord is in Los Angeles in different missions and churches in mighty power. . . . The waves of Pentecostal salvation are still rolling in Azuza Street mission. From morning till late evening, meetings continue with about three services a day. . . . The revival has spread . . . through the States . . . and across the ocean. The blood of Jesus Christ prevails against every force and power of the enemy.[12]

The Pentecostal movement was on foot, and even the historical churches had to take note of its presence. The reasons behind the success were partly those already mentioned for the Holiness denominations. There was also the appeal of the Pentecostal message to the poorer sections of the population. In the words of Brumback:

> The world awakened slowly to the fact that the presence of the poor in the Movement was an evidence that Christ himself was present among them. . . . While Pentecostalism was spurned at the beginning because its calling was not replete with the very wise after the flesh, the mighty and the noble, this very feature afterwards became one of its strongest attractions to a world in which the underprivileged are the majority.[13]

Pentecostals emphasized religious experience instead of orthodox doctrine; the second grace and deliverance from sin, instead of the hellfire motives of many revivalists. But, most of all, they asked their listeners to imitate the spiritual and contagious joy of the men and women who had received the Spirit, their power to speak in tongues and even that of performing miracles upon sick bodies, "just like at the time of the apostles."[14]

In the following years Pentecostalism moved into all the States of the Union and crossed the border into Canada. Everywhere revivals were followed by the foundation of ecclesial communities. Revivals held at Galena, Kansas, achieved special fame in the annals of the movement because, during the evening services, "people who had not walked for years without the aid of crutches had risen from the altar with their limbs so straightened that they were enabled to lay aside the crutches, to the astonishment of the audience."[15] Meanwhile, G. B. Caswell, C. G. Mason, and J. Tomlinson conducted revivals in North Carolina, Georgia, Florida, and Tennessee.

> In the mountains of Tennessee and North Carolina the Holy Ghost had been poured upon man in a continuous effusion, from which would go spreading waves of influence to all the world . . . The Church [of God] had been born and nurtured, then had gathered

> strength through his graces that it might assist in taking this faith everywhere.[16]

In turn, Parham and his associates took the message to Texas, where "many scores were converted, sanctified, and baptized with the Holy Spirit; many were healed in answer to the prayer of faith, and others possessed with evil spirits were delivered."[17] Chicago and its area were covered in 1905 by J. C. Sinclair, F. A. Sandgren, W. H. Pieper, and W. H. Durham. Their efforts were directed mainly to the large communities of emigrants, chiefly Italians, then pouring into the city and often left without assistance by the clergy of their own church. It was also in Chicago that Aimée Semple McPherson, the foundress of the International Church of the Foursquare Gospel, "received a new touch of God and experienced a miraculous healing."[18] Miss Marie Burgess, a convert from Chicago, moved into New York and preached in missions and cottages until 1907 when she opened a Glad Tidings Hall on the west side of Forty-second Street. Pentecostals commissioned from Chicago and New York took Pentecostalism to Canada.[19]

The whole movement received a considerable boost from the fundamentalist crisis then shaking the historical churches of America. "By and large," writes Jamison, "it was the partisans of the fundamentalist-conservative wing who succeeded in forming new sects."[20] By 1910 the term Pentecostal movement was applied "to all groups who taught the need for the experience of the baptism in the Holy Spirit evidenced by the speaking with tongues." But its followers lived in scattered, small congregations, often under the direction of poorly trained leaders. Pentecostals from various states and with diverse tendencies convened in 1914 at Hot Springs, Arkansas, in order to recognize a General Council which, in time, became the powerful Assemblies of God. The conferees seemed satisfied with the new situation. "God," they said, "has brought us out of old, dead ecclesiasticism and denominationalism. He has made us a free people, and we are not going back to 'Babylon' any more."[21] The meeting had been convened with several aims in mind. The movement needed a broader basis than the local assemblies, if possible a central organization. Doctrinal issues had to be settled and cooperative efforts devised in the fields of communication and in ministerial training. All this, they thought, was also required because the Spirit had been

> so aggressive that almost every city and community in civilization had heard of the Latter Rain outpouring of the Holy Ghost, with

> many signs following . . . while hundreds of missionaries had gone forth until almost every country on the globe had heard the message and also the prophecy which has been predominant in all this great outpouring, which is: "Jesus is coming soon" to this old world in the same manner as he left it to set up his millennial kingdom and to reign over the earth in righteousness and peace for a thousand years.[22]

The convention fulfilled some of these expectations, and "the most blessed spirit of fellowship had prevailed through the gathered host; hearts were blended together and a most blessed spirit of love, unity, and peace was manifested."[23] Many of the participants, and the small congregations they represented, became absorbed into the Assemblies of God. The statement issued by the new body was couched in words which, at first sight, gave the impression that little or nothing had been changed of the "primitive freedom of the Spirit." Time and leadership would suffice to close ranks and make of the Assemblies one of the most tightly knit denominations of our days. A new convention in 1916 named a General and Executive Presbytery, elected officers, created departments, and even determined the fiscal policies that were to regulate the lives of individuals and congregations.[24]

It was obvious, however, that the founding of the Assemblies of God could not bring about the end of particularisms. Numerous groups doubted the intentions of the mergers. "It seemed to be difficult for them to grasp the fact that independent, autonomous churches could be associated in a cooperative fellowship without losing their spiritual liberty. This feeling of uncertainty was intensified by the disruptive preaching of radical, independent men who had opposed from the first any form of church organization."[25] As we shall see, many Pentecostal groups preferred to go their own way. Once again in the history of the Church since the Reformation, a denomination was born internally splintered and gave no immediate hope of cooperation with the other branches of Christendom.

The Era of Persecutions

It is helpful to add here a few words on what Pentecostal writers call the "era of persecution" in the growth of the movement. Chronologically, this period seems to extend from the time of "foundations," all through the twenties, and almost to the eve of World War II. It is difficult for the outsider to assess the seriousness of the situation. The insistence on "persecution" becomes rather monotonous. There was no bloodshed and there were no martyrs, but expulsions and excommunications of Pentecostals by the mother-churches occurred. Chapels were closed to some preachers; ridicule was poured upon leaders and faithful because of the "manifestations of the Spirit"; and challenges came from pulpit and press against the supposedly charismatic blessings Pentecostals claimed. These "persecutions" were often followed by stern prohibitions against any contacts with the new demoniations. The warning of one of the historical churches read:

> The session declares most emphatically that our Confession of Faith gives no room for holding, teaching, or expressing sympathy for, participating in, or attending the so-called "Pentecostal" or tongues meetings. . . . From this time onward, no man or woman will be allowed to hold membership in this church who is sympathetic with, has part in, or attempts to bring this teaching among our people, or attempts to send members or attendants of this church to places where this so-called Pentecostal movement holds sway.[26]

The "culprits" who fomented the persecution covered the whole spectrum of the historical churches. Methodists and Baptists, more directly affected by loss of members to Pentecostalism, tried to stem the flow with stern measures. The Christian and Missionary Alliance and the Church of the Nazarene were simply fighting for survival when they opposed Pentecostal claims in the matter of glossolalia. There had been a time when, owing to similar doctrinal positions in a number of issues, Pentecostalism had hoped to draw many members from fundamentalist denominations. Hence its disappointment when the Fundamentalist Convention of Chicago in 1928 passed the following resolution:

> Whereas, the present wave of modern Pentecostalism, often referred to as the "tongues movement," and the present wave of fanatical and unscriptural healing which is sweeping the country today has become a menace in many churches and a real injury to the sane testimony of Fundamental Christians, Be it Resolved, That this convention go on record as unreservedly opposed to modern Pentecostalism, including the speaking with unknown tongues, and the fanatical healing known as the general healing of Jesus and his apostles, wherein they claim the only reason the Church cannot perform these miracles is because of unbelief.[27]

The Pentecostal attitude in face of such opposition was and is a blend of self-defense, explanatory remarks about the inevitability of the situation, and a certain humility to acknowledge that, in spite of the sublime holiness they are supposed to possess, Pentecostals remain, after all, "children of the dust." Few today will be willing to accept without qualifications the list of causes for opposition once adduced by D. Gee: "tradition, doctrinal disagreement, unbelief, fear, jealousy, and conviction." One would have rather to begin by pointing out what should be considered the main reasons for discord: the strange behavior of many Pentecostals in the practice of their faith, and their excessive charismatic claims vis-à-vis the other Christian denominations. To answer that " the emotional excesses were a reaction against the stiffness and formality of the churches from which they came," or that "there were few leaders in those days with enough experience in orgiastic behavior to be able to distinguish it" from the true presence of the Spirit,[28] may relieve Pentecostals from responsibility, but it is not enough to accuse the historical churches of misinterpreting the true situation. There is also here a danger of seeing in the resistance of the churches a mere opposition to glossolalia as such, when the fact is that, very often, the objections were aimed simply at the excesses (moral and otherwise) which very often accompanied that phenomenon. If "immoral behavior" in some of the early leaders was enough to "embarrass" Pentecostals, it became something bewildering to those who did not belong to the fold. The same consideration applies to the "holier than thou" attitude taken by many early Pentecostals. Contemporaries could not see in that "spiritual pomposity" a sign that Pentecostalism was a God-sent movement. One does not know whether the divisiveness which Pentecostalism spread in the Church at the precise moment when Protestant Christianity was taking (for instance, in Edinburgh, 1910) its first step on the road to ecumenism, had anything to do with their opposition to the movement.[29]

The above considerations do not exonerate the historic churches which indulged too much and too often in attacking the underprivileged groups of believers, who became "trouble-makers," "holy jumpers," or "holy rollers," with all the derogatory connotations attached by the masses to those names. The last epithet in particular was extremely offensive and for the Church of God, Cleveland, became almost a *casus belli.* "At what time," says its historian, "this sacrilegious taunt was first used against the Pentecostal people cannot be positively determined, but it seems to have been used almost from the beginning of the Movement. . . . The indignity of the epithet was too disgusting to the Church of God which refused to acquiesce to it." "Be it known," read a resolution passed in 1915, "to all men everywhere and to all nations that we, the Church of God . . . do hereby and hereafter disclaim and repudiate the title of Holy Rollers. In consequence of this decision, we herewith give general notice to the public that all references . . . to this name by the public press or otherwise will be considered and treated as a slanderous and malignant offense."[30] Whether the incident was worth the trouble, is another point. It was, in any case, a symptom of the tense relations between the older and the newly-arrived churches. The former not only forgot that they themselves had been an object of name-calling at one or another period in their history,[31] but also that their actions sowed the seeds of future misunderstandings. Our present-day mutual alienation can be traced, to a great extent, to those unfortunate beginnings.

European Expansion

Parallel to the Pentecostal drive within the United States and Canada came the expansion of the movement into foreign lands. For methodological reasons, we shall divide the outreach into two sections: the Pentecostal penetration into European countries, and its development in mission territories and in Latin America. Because of its many similarities with the original movement, European Pentecostalism deserves to be treated together with that in the United States. The branches of Asiatic, African, and Latin American Pentecostalism, with all the peculiarities attached to their development, will find their place in the chapter devoted to Pentecostal Missions.

The first Pentecostal thrust into the Old World took place in Norway through the activities of a British-born Methodist pastor, T. C. Barratt, who was then working at the City Mission in Oslo. When Barratt came to the United States in 1905 to collect funds for his Norwegian project, he was informed of the events taking place at the Azuza Street Chapel in Los Angeles. There he went and, "at a hectic meeting, he received the gift of speaking with tongues."[32] Back in Norway with a band of followers, Barratt held his first Pentecostal religious services which included "trembling, dancing, glossolalia . . . 'holy laughter' and even the loss of consciousness."[33] Then came the foundation of a Norwegian Pentecostal Movement, the issuing of Principles of Faith, and the foundation in 1916 of an independent Pentecostal congregation. Norway has at present 70,000 Pentecostals, of which

40,000 are considered full members. They support more than 160 missionaries in foreign lands, while at home they already surpass the other two non-Lutheran bodies, namely the Baptists and Methodists. Norwegian Pentecostalism is in a phase of evolution "from uncontrolled ecstasy to controlled emotionalism, from spontaneity to organized evangelistic training and regular parish work, from enthusiastic interdenominationalism to Pentecostal doctrinalization."

Bloch-Hoell sees evidences of this transforming process in the birth of "new and radical Pentecostal assemblies reviving all the enthusiasm of original Pentecostalism and emphasizing ecstasy and miraculous experiences even more than the early Movement."[34] Barratt and his disciples took the Pentecostal message into the other Scandinavian countries. He entered Sweden in 1907 and won over to his side a Baptist minister, Levi Pethrus, who soon became the head of the Swedish Pentecostal Church with two main centers at Stockholm and Uppsala. With the years, the movement has become a strong spiritual force in an officially Lutheran country where religious influence is one of the lowest on the Continent. The Pentecostal churches of Sweden have a membership of 120,000; take an active part in witnessing and street-preaching; direct a Bible Institute at the Kaggenholn Castle; and (before Moroccan independence) used to broadcast from Tangiers their message to the neighboring African countries. There are more than 500 Swedish Pentecostals working in mission lands.[35] Barratt paid a number of visits to Denmark.

At the beginning certain much-publicized conversions, as those of actress Anna Larsen and others, seemed to promise days of glory and expansion for the movement. But time has not borne out such hopes, and the community there has remained a small one of 5,000 members.[36] Finnish Pentecostalism seemed stagnant for a number of years. Only the sufferings of the post-war period and the Russian occupation led the Finns to join the ranks of the movement. With new material prosperity, the advance has come again to a standstill and the total community remains at 40,000. Pentecostals have sent missionaries to Japan and several African countries. A certain unnecessary antagonism to the Lutheran church has strained their mutual relations.[37]

Several Pentecostal groups, some of Scandinavian origin, others of a more autochthonous type, were at work in Germany before World War I. Among its pioneers mention must be made of Jonathan Paul (who had stayed in 1907 with Barratt in Norway), Heinrich Dallmeyer, and Emil Humburg. The latter founded at Mulheim in the Ruhr a Christian Alliance which developed certain visionary and prophetic trends that were not always welcomed by the other Christian communities. In 1945 it changed its name into Christlicher Gemeinschaftsverband (Union of Christian Assemblies), possibly the largest present Pentecostal denomination in Germany. There is also a Christen-Gemeinde Elim, founded in 1907. Of a more bellicose spirit was the Deutsche Volksmission Entschieneder Christen (The Mission of Resolute Christians of the German People), founded in 1934 and established in certain sectors of southern Germany. It has introduced the dedication of children to Christ in place of infant baptism; it shuns communion with "sinful Christians," and makes appeal to the charisms of the Spirit.

After 1945 Germany became the cradle of a few national Pentecostal denominations. An industrialist by the name of Hermann Zaiss founded a Gemeinde der Christen-Ecclesia (Community of Christians Church) which rose to popularity between 1951 and 1957. It borrowed doctrines and practices from various American organizations, and spread its influence into Swizerland and Holland. The "commemorative meal" (the Lord's Supper) must be preceded by personal conversion for which there is available a "penitent's bench" similar to that of the Salvation Army. The specialty of Zaiss before his death in 1958 was healing, a gift which "every sanctified Christian can and ought to possess." Hundreds of thousands of patients from all walks of life attended his healing sessions. Of late, the activities and strength of the denomination seem to be declining.[38] A missionary of Swiss origin, Christian Rockle, started in 1946 in the state of Wurttemberg a Philadelphia-Verein (Philadelphian Community) which, at least to a certain extent, may be classed among the Pentecostal bodies. Its members are convinced that they possess an "unction" still superior to the gifts of the second baptism, "a kind of hypostatic union with the Holy Spirit" (Algermissen). At present they are sanctified and, in the millennial kingdom, they will act as the "high priests of Christ." They believe in glossolalia, visions, prophecies, revelations, and bodily healings. In 1957 they started a "school of prophets" in imitation to the Old Testament institution begun by Samuel.[39]

As was to be expected, after 1945 Western Germany suffered a systematic "invasion" of American Pentecostal denominations. The Assemblies of God, the International Foursquare Gospel, several branches of the Churches of God and of Christ, the Apostolic Faith Mission, and others began to work among the refugees from the East and extended their activities to other populations. People raised in Pietistic circles have become the easiest converts to the movement. More than once authorities in both state and church have warned the faithful to resist practices and beliefs that violate the basic tenets of the Reformation. Algermissen, while acknowledging the dangers of an overzealous and overpromising Pentecostalism, has invited the historical churches to self-examination in view of the spiritual yearnings of so many baptized Christians within their own ranks.[40]

The information we possess regarding the status and progress of Pentecostalism in the rest of Continental Europe is deficient. In Switzerland a European Missionary Crusade for a Better Christian Life has its headquarters at the Hotel Rosat in Chateau d'Oex. It was founded by a Canadian, John T. Owens, and is devoted to circulating Pentecostal literature in various languages and to conducting correspondence in a number of European countries. Other small communities, of Scandinavian and British origin, are established among the French and German-speaking inhabitants of the country. There is likewise a Swiss Pentecostal Mission whose membership is put at 3,000, with a few missionaries in Africa.[41] From all appearances, the Pentecostal presence passes almost unnoticed in countries like Austria and Belgium. The latter, however, did send some missionaries to its former Congolese colony. Holland has some 10,000 Pentecostals.

In Italy, however, its penetration became for a moment a matter of worry. The time was well chosen: the chaotic years after the Italian military defeat in World War II with its aftermath of hunger, misery, and resentment against the old order, either political or ecclesiastical. Pentecostalism hurried to send in teams of Italo-American preachers who met with extraordinary success in the poorer sections of the great cities, Rome and Naples in particular, as well as in the rural populations of Calabria and Sicily. The leaders often joined hands with the political left in order to attack the Catholic Church. This fact needs to be taken into account in order to understand (not, indeed, to justify) the "persecutions" they were subjected to by the civil, usually local, authorities. Italian Pentecostalism is of a special brand. Its main purpose seems to be to attack the Establishment. Glossolalia is practically absent from its religious services and the doctrine of the second baptism occupies a rather marginal rank. Insistence is on divine healing, with many "miraculous" cases attributed to the preachers. These, and the many charitable institutions, financed by their American branches, that promoted a spirit of true Christian love, constitute the secret of their success. After a field study of the situation, I am ready to accept the estimate that Pentecostals in Italy numbered, for a time, at least 100,000, the largest group in Western Europe. How many of them will persevere in the now prosperous peninsula is harder to ascertain. According to Nichol:

> The Assemblies of God in Italy, the main division of all Pentecostal bodies, maintains close contact with three organizations in the United States: 1) The Christian Churches of North America which contributes liberally toward the support of national workers; 2) The Italian branch of the Assemblies of God (USA), which underwrites the cost of translating and printing Gospel literature, as well as improving the work of Sunday schools; and 3) The Assemblies of God (USA), which has been responsible for building the six-story Rome Bible Institute that can accommodate 100 students.[42]

This total dependence on foreign help and support may be one of the weaknesses of Italian Pentecostalism and may, in the long run, prove detrimental to its indigenous growth.

In Portugal, Pentecostalism has only 5,000 members. Its influence, however, extends to the African "provinces" of Mozambique and Angola with a total community of 12,500 in the first and 1,500 in the second.

In Spain, Pentecostalism has been officially forbidden for the last decade, and it is doubtful that it will be included in the new Law of Associations being promulgated for non-Catholic denominations. This will depend on whether it is welcomed by the Confederation of Evangelical Churches of the nation.[43] According to Père Chéry, the main Pentecostal denominations (native or imported) in France are: the Assemblies of God; the Catholic Apostolic Church; the Church of the Latter Rain ("extremist and of an impatient eschatology"); the First Pentecost Church; the Bethesda Hall; Pentecostal Baptists; the Revival Mission; the Free Pentecostals; the Pentecostals of the Living Water; and the Pentecostal Evangelists. The chief centers of expansion are on the Normandy Coast, in the Maritime Alps, in the regions close to Paris and at the Bouches-de-Rhone, where some denominations have set up their headquarters.

French Pentecostalism offers these peculiarities. Its adherents are recruited largely from the millions of immigrant workers who have flocked in from other European countries and from overseas. Uprooted from their homelands and without ministrations of their own, they have found in Pentecostalism a "first spiritual aid" which has led them to the full acceptance of the Pentecostal message. One of their preachers, Clement de Cossec, has also begun to work among the gypsy groups of the land. In matters of belief and practice, one finds a wide range of differences: from the uneducated who hardly know the rudiments of Pentecostalism, to the initiated who teach holiness, practice glossolalia, and divine healing without any of the inhibitions of certain other European groups. The total Pentecostal community stands at 30,000, "although the number of those who attend the religious services or are in favor of the Movement might be far higher." They also have some missionaries working in the former French colonies of Africa.[44]

For the countries behind the Iron Curtain, I rely solely on two sources: the American J. T. Nichol, and the usually well-informed German Kurt Hutten. One ought to begin by stating that our reports about these territories are a blend of historical facts regarding the beginnings of Pentecostal work, considerations regarding the injustices, restrictions, and prison terms to which Pentecostals have been subjected, and a few vague notions about their present numerical strength and activities, as for example: "There is something romantic and revolutionary about the Pentecostal Movement in the Soviet Union. . . . The movement is banned. . . . Its meetings take place in circumstances which appeal to young people . . . in mountains . . . forests . . . half-dark rooms. All meetings are secret and conspiratorial." Hence also the unreliability of our figures. Those of Russia vary from the 250,000 accepted by Nichol, to the 100,000 adduced by Hutten; from 10,000 to 3,700 in Poland; while the 80,000 quoted by Hutten for Rumania are not even mentioned by Nichol in his survey of European Communist lands.[45] On the other hand, it is evident that those Pentecostals who keep and propagate their faith do so at the cost of heroic sacrifices. The case of Yugoslavia applies a fortiori to other Communist territories:

> The devotion of both clergy and believers is impressive. Many Pentecostals come to worship on foot and on bicycle from distances of up to fifteen miles. Their prayer sessions last until three in the morning. There is no Bible-training institute for educating young pastors; therefore Dragutin Volf (the pastor) translates correspondence-course materials that have been donated by the Assemblies of God (USA), prints them on a duplicating machine, and distributes them to the Yugoslavian pastors.[46]

In Great Britain and Ireland there are at least two indigenous Pentecostal bodies: the Apostolic Church, and the Elim Foursquare Gospel Church, as well as a good sampling of the main American denominations. The Apostolic Church was started in 1916 by W. O. Hutchison, in strict line with the principles of Pentecostalism, while stressing also the role of the "prophets" in the life of the Church. Its numerical strength has never been great (only 7,500 members in 1962), but the movement has expanded into some African territories, mostly to Nigeria, where it is said to have 50,000 members. The Elim Four-square Gospel Church began in Northern Ireland under the leadership of George Jeffreys and his associates. Its historian states:

> It arose in an atmosphere of insecurity concerning political changes, and amid marked religious tensions. It was nourished by the old revivalistic techniques in England and Wales in the period of economic unrest in the twenties and early thirties. . . . Ignoring the dominant traits of Protestantism, it reasserted fundamental beliefs. It accepted, however, an Arminian rather than a Calvinistic theology, for Arminianism blends more easily with revivalism and evangelism which, together with Pentecostalism and Adventism, characterized the Elim movement.[47]

The Elim Church has gone through various crises, owing partly to the diminished role of Great Britain in world affairs, and seems also to have lost much of its initial aggressiveness. Numerically it has never recovered its pre-war levels. The total constituency is made up of some 27,000 followers, to which we may add 7,000 others in mission territories.[48] In theology and worship there is also a clear shift between the rough fundamentalism of the early days to the more liberal presentation of our times. Among the American Pentecostal denominations in Great Britain, the Assemblies of God holds first place. They have some 20,000 followers and are strongest in Wales and in the populated areas of the great industrial cities. Of the other groups, the Church of Christ (12,000 members) is becoming popular, while the Church of God, Prophecy, has so far gathered only a few hundred members. In general, British Pentecostalism is adopting in doctrine and worship many of the bourgeois elements of its European partners. Not all Pentecostal groups feel happy about the shift.[49]

Particular American Pentecostal Denominations

The lists of American Pentecostal bodies are elastic and range from the twenty-two denominations given by C. Kendrick, or the twenty-six by Bloch-Hoell, to the forty classified by E.L. Moore, the "sixty" suggested by Algermissen, or the "three dozen prominent sects," together with the "unclassified numerous independent churches and small groups of the same character," spoken of by E. T. Clark.[50] My selection appears in all the lists so far available. The churches included therein show the following common traits:

> They run true to the uniform type, and, save for some bizarre elements, there are few differences among them. Theologically they are usually pre-millenarian and look for the imminent second coming of Christ to destroy this world order. They are literal biblicists, hold to plenary and verbal inspiration, and ascribe divine authority to their own interpretation of prophecy. Their morality is generally of the puritan type, in opposition to the jewelry, fashionable and expensive clothing, amusements, and general worldliness of their better-placed neighbors. The conventional churches and regular ministry are regarded as having corrupted or departed from the faith of Bible religion. . . . Religious education, in the modern sense, is often discounted or opposed, as is also modern biblical and scientific learning. The preachers are usually uneducated and often unsalaried. The revival technique is exclusively employed in gaining adherents; conversion and salvation are accomplished by the direct agency operating through emotional channels, and the "gift of the Holy Spirit" is the highest boom bestowed upon the faithful. Divine healing is practiced by nearly all of these sects.[51]

This description may be verified in the following instances selected as typical because—judging from their numbers and organizational strength—they seem most adequately to represent American Pentecostalism.

Apostolic Overcoming Holy Church of God, a church founded in 1916 in Mobile, Alabama, by a Negro Methodist preacher, W. T. Phillips. He had joined first the Apostolic Faith Mission, but soon left it with his flock in order to form his own organization. Its original title, "Ethiopian," was changed in 1927 to "Apostolic." Phillips named himself "bishop," and in that capacity, he still runs the church. It is active in fourteen American States and has missions in the West Indies and in some African countries. "Voluntary offerings" and tithes from which not even the bishop is exempt cover the expenses of the denomination and of the ministry. The Apostolic Overcoming Holy Church of God is a typical charismatic body. As we read in its *Manual:* "We believe in the baptism of the Holy Ghost as it was on the day of Pentecost. We believe all those who receive the Holy Ghost will speak with other tongues." Its religious services can be taken as the pattern of what goes under the name of a Negro enthusiastic liturgy. It includes (at least on occasion) foot washing and divine healing, and the whole service is carried out without any semblance of order. There is an uninterrupted dialogue between the preacher and his audience. Hymns have given way to spirituals, and the rhythm is marked by drums, tambourines, shouts of approval, and the clapping of hands and the stamping of feet, and the whole ceremony may end up by speaking with tongues or the ecstatic dances of the participants. Unlike many other Negro Pentecostal bodies, this one forbids "marriage to unsaved men and women, the use of snuff, foolish talking, jesting, and the use of slang."[52] The church in 1962 had almost 80,000 members.

Assemblies of God, General Council, the strongest of all Pentecostal bodies. Inaugurated by the Hot Spring, Arkansas, Declaration of 1914, it has its headquarters at Springfield, Missouri, and claims a home and foreign membership of over one million persons. The denomination is a product of American ingenuity which succeeds in giving to an essentially disrupting movement the unity needed for normal operations.[53]

Apostolic Faith Mission was established by Parham, the true founder of Pentecostalism. But his leadership was soon challenged by many others who saw in the formation of a larger and closely-knit organization the only remedy for the fissiparous tendencies within the movement. The ideas were discussed for some time and the new denominational structures were formalized at the Hot Spring Convention. The appeal had been addressed to "all the churches of God in Christ, to all Pentecostal and Apostolic Assemblies who desire with united purpose to cooperate in love and peace to push the interests of the kingdom of God everywhere."[54] The convention intended: 1) to achieve better understanding "of what God would have us to teach, that we may do away with so many divisions, both in doctrine and in the various names under which our people are working and incorporating"; 2) to conserve, build up and not tear down the work already done at home and in foreign lands; 3) to cooperate in the missionary enterprise; 4) to charter the churches of God on a legal basis; and 5) to consider the possibility of starting a common Bible training school and a literary department.[55] The proposals were accepted. The convention issued a policy regulating the independence (at least relative) of the local churches and their relation to the central governing body. Doctrinally the progress was limited, and participants had to be satisfied with affirming something that, "no matter what their background, all those present could suscribe to," namely the sufficiency of the Holy Scriptures as the rule of faith and practice. The Statement of Fundamental

Truths would be compiled two years later. The name Assemblies of God, General Council was adopted "amid great joy and shouting." Local assemblies were authorized to form district councils; ministerial credentials were denied to all persons who were divorced and remarried, and a periodical, *Christian Evangel,* was recognized as the official organ of the denomination.[56]

The Assemblies of God have flourished. They function in each of the States of the Union, with greatest vigor in the Midwest and South. In 1914 they had 118 churches with an approximate membership of 6,703. Since then, 192 congregations per year have been added with an annual increase of over 10,000 members. The 1963 figures for the 44 home districts were: 8,302 churches, 14,832 ministers, and 514,000 members. The Assemblies engage in extensive missionary activities that in 1963 expanded to 72 countries, with "thirty additional nations with other Pentecostal work, much of it carried on by organizations with which the Assemblies of God have some degree of fellowship or working arrangement." In the same year the community in mission lands had almost reached the one million mark, with 12,437 native ministers and 5,694 churches.[57] The number of missionaries was eight hundred. The Assemblies of God are governed by a presbyterian-congregationalist policy-making organ, the General Council, which meets every two years. The administration is in the hands of the General Presbytery. The District Council is in charge of the religious activities within more restricted territories. As we shall see in a later chapter, the Assemblies of God have been responsible for the minimal doctrinal systematization that exists among Pentecostal bodies. True to their beginnings, the Assemblies endorse the main points of Fundamentalism and add, as peculiar tenets, the baptism of the Spirit attested by the speaking with other tongues, divine healing, and the imminent second coming of Christ. They preach a puritan type of morality, condemn worldliness, extravagance in dress and entertainment, and carry on an all-out battle against alcoholism.

Pentecostal Holiness Church. A merger (1898) of two original Pentecostal bodies: the Fire-Baptized Holiness Church and a similar group from North Carolina that joined together and adopted the present name. A third body, the Tabernacle Pentecostal Church, asked to be admitted in 1915. The headquarters of the church are at Franklin Springs, Georgia. The denomination bears traces of deep Methodist influence more in policy than in doctrine. In keeping with the episcopal organization, the church is divided into conferences: general, annual, missionary, and district. As we gather from the *Discipline* of the church, its doctrines are strictly Pentecostal: the two works of grace, the second baptism, as the first, and divine healing and sanctification as a second—and progressive—work of grace. Candidates to "water baptism" are given a choice between baptism by immersion or aspersion. Parents are also allowed "the option of requesting either dedication or baptism for their children." In matters of divine healing, the Pentecostal Holiness Church allows its followers to consult doctors and follow their prescriptions. Its foreign missions are found in Hong Kong; India; South, West, and Central Africa; Mexico; Cuba, and in a number of other South American republics. The church has shown interest in the appropriate theological training of its ministers, and runs several junior and Bible colleges and a theological seminary at Greenville, South Carolina. The church's growth has been fair: 192 churches and 8,096 members in 1916; 1,331 churches and 60,665 members in 1965.[58] At headquarters its publishing house issues the *Pentecostal Holiness Advocate,* the official organ of the denomination.

The International Church of the Foursquare Gospel. The anecdotic and romantic aspects of Sister Aimée (née Kennedy), the Canadian-born girl who, during a revival at Chicago, was won to the cause of Pentecostalism, her evangelistic campaigns, her brief sojourn as a missionary in China, the death of her husband Robert Semple, her return to the United States, and her second marriage and later love affairs have been told and retold in a number of publications. Here we limit ourselves to her role as foundress of her church. It is said that "she had a rare ability for personalizing every event, and a lively eloquence gave to everything she said embroidery and high coloring."[59] According to E. T. Clark, "Sister" possessed also all the qualities necessary for a messiah of ardent souls:

> Handsome in appearance and fluent in speech, she knew the secrets of crowd psychology. Her preaching services were highly dramatic, and she used publicity, costuming, lighting effects, music, and personal charm to secure the most striking effects. Her message was the most simple orthodoxy; she claimed and exercised the gift of healing and tongues, and professed to be under the direct guidance of God; she abounded in good works to the poor; she turned the opposition of the regular preachers to her own advantage and to the discomfiture of her enemies.[60]

Mrs. McPherson settled down in Los Angeles in 1918. Three years later she had founded the Echo Park Evangelistic Association and began the building of the famous Angelus Temple, destined to be the center of all the activities of her denomination. Its name seems to have been the result of a "prophetic vision" of four faces she saw in 1921; they represented "a perfect gospel; a complete gospel for body, for soul, for spirit, and for eternity; a gospel that faces squarely in every direction." "In my soul," she says, "there was born a harmony that was struck and sustained upon four full, quivering strings, and from it were plucked words that leaped into being: *The Foursquare Gospel.*"[61] Its legal incorporation took place in 1927. A church flag, red, yellow, blue, and purple, with a red cross on a Bible background, and a big *4* over it is displayed on all buildings of the denomination.

To the student of Pentecostal movements there are few puzzles that can compete with Mrs. McPherson's organization. Doctrinally, the Foursquare Gospel does not offer novelties that cannot be found in other Pentecostal bodies. The foundress' theological piece, *The Foursquare Gospel,* makes for rather boring reading and seems deeply inspired by A. B. Simpson's definition to present Christ as the savior of the world, the baptizer with the Holy Ghost, the healer of our sickness, and our coming king. What distinguishes this denomination is, in addition to the dynamic personality of Sister Aimée herself, the great capacity for organization she possessed. She was one of the first to make radio broadcasting a powerful instrument of evangelism. She inspired her followers with a devotion whose sincerity had to be shown in works. For this purpose she started a missionary training institute, the Lighthouse of International Foursquare Evangelism, and sent the graduates (whom she ordained as ministers) to all parts of the nation and abroad. They carried with them a sense of evangelism often bordering on a proselytism uncommon at the time. In polity, the denomination felt the omnipresent hand of the foundress to organize, to rule, to command. She presided over all conventions, boards, and cabinet councils, and kept to herself the power of veto against the board of directors. The latter were composed of five persons appointed by the president at the annual convention.

Thanks to this close-knit organization, Aimée McPherson was able to build up one of the more solid Pentecostal churches in the world. After her death (September 27, 1944) and funeral: "one of the most spectacular ever to be conducted in the Los Angeles area" *(Life),* Sister Aimée's mantle was inherited by her son, Dr. Rolf K. McPherson, who had shown some of the foresight and executive qualities of his mother.

There are at present over 500 churches and chapels of the Foursquare Gospel in the United States. The Angelus Temple continues to be a center of revivals and conversions—in 1949, 26,842 persons "confessed Christ as their Savior." Eight hundred and six foreign mission stations under the responsibility of 961 missionaries constitute its major task force in 22 nations from Latin America to Africa and Asia. The different estimates in membership—79,012 in the *Yearbook of the American Churches* (1960), and 122,907 as reported by Frank Mead (1956)—may be due to the criteria followed in the counting or to the fact that the higher statistics include the members to be found in mission territories. This expansional work is backed by a solid financial fund to which the members of the church contribute in a very substantial way.

> We believe [says the Declaration of Faith] that the method ordained of God to sustain his ministry and the spread of the Gospel after his command is tithing and is generally accepted throughout all Foursquare churches, not only as God's method to take care of the material and financial needs of his church, but to raise the spiritual morale of his people.[62]

The Church of God, Cleveland, Tennessee. Its earliest beginnings go back to the 1890's when Spurling and his associates decided to form a Christian Union with a number of like-minded Pentecostal individuals who had abandoned their Baptist denominations. During 1903 and 1904 they were joined by other leaders, among them a well-known preacher, A. J. Tomlinson, who were planning similar organizations. By 1907 the group had decided upon a joint effort, the Church of God, with Tomlinson at its head. Not all were satisfied with the choice because "he had not been blessed with tongues." But the "blessing" came in the following year, and the man was confirmed in his position. The next crisis occurred in 1923 and centered around the person of the general moderator, who was accused of misuse of funds and (after the U.S. Supreme Court had backed the decision of the General Assembly) stripped of his powers. He was succeeded by F. J. Lee as General Overseer. Many feared the total collapse of the church. But C. W. Conn says:

> All in all the Church suffered no great loss in numbers, although the disillusionment was a great blow. Other ministers had been expelled in times past, but this was by far the severest test to which the Church had been subjected. The Church of God manifested remarkable facility in holding its balance. Despite its losses to Tomlinson, there was a gain in every department of the church.[63]

After his expulsion, Tomlinson started another organization with the same name of Church of God. A subsequent internal defection gave rise to the Third Church of God, World Headquarters, directed at the present writing by his son, Bishop Homer A. Tomlinson, from Queens Village, New York. The new office holder considers himself the true head of the only Church of God; he has traveled through Asia, Africa, and Australia with his banner of "Peace on earth," and claims the supernatural powers of a semi-god in whose hands rests the well-being of mankind.[64] But the departure of the older Tomlinson brought peace and prosperity to the church over which he had once presided. Its new structures were modeled on Methodist patterns: with a General Assembly, state and annual conferences, district quarterly meetings, and a fair amount of independence for the local communities.

Doctrinally, the Church of God, Cleveland, Tenn., offers no surprises. It is Pentecostal to the core, with glossolalia and divine healing keeping their primitive importance. Its leaders, afraid of the inroads of worldliness into their ranks, reaffirmed in 1960 their belief in "holiness, in stated doctrine, in principles of conduct, and as a living reality in our hearts." Ministers must guard "against conformity to the world in appearance, in selfish ambition, in carnal attitudes, and in evil associations."[65] The severity of this group against wearing jewelry, is a common feature with other Pentecostal denominations.

The Church of God carries on an active evangelical program at home and in foreign countries. The annuals count with understandable joy the new lands they have entered since their first missionary was sent (1910) to the Bahamas. They cover no less than 45 countries from Australia and Japan, through the Middle East, Tunisia, and Spain, to Angola in Africa, and most of the Latin-American republics. In 1951 the denomination merged with the Full Gospel Church in South Africa, thus becoming "a world-encircling movement . . . which in programs and methods has kept pace with its time, but in doctrine, in fellowship, and in mission has remained the same Church it was at the turn of the century."[66] According to the latest statistics, the denomination has 3,575 churches, 3,411 ordained ministers, and a total membership of 205,465.

The Pentecostal Church of America, Inc. The Hot Spring Convention of 1914 which led to the formation of the Assemblies of God was not a total success. Certain groups had refused to attend it; others preferred not to join the new organization, perhaps for fear of failure. "This feeling of uncertainty was intensified by the unfavorable preaching of radical, independent men who had opposed from the first any form of church set-up." Further theological discussion encouraged the dissenters to go their own way. This departure was favored by two Chicagoans, J. C. Sinclair and a layman, George Brinkman, editor of the *Pentecostal Herald*. They had an advantage over the Assemblies: a less precise doctrinal statement and more liberal conditions of membership. They did not want to create "unscriptural lines of fellowship and disfellowship, but to affiliate on the basic principles of love, righteousness, and truth," accepting "the Word of God in its entirety, and conducting ourselves in harmony with its divine principles."

The formal organization of the church took place in 1919. There was bickering about the name to be adopted: first it was "Pentecostal Assemblies of the U.S.A.," then, "Pentecostal Church of God," and finally, Pentecostal Church of God in America. Nor were its leaders agreed on the site of its headquarters. These moved from Chicago to Ottumwa, Iowa, and then from Kansas City to Joplin, Missouri.

The highest governing body of the Church is the General Convention, followed by an Executive Board, assistant superintendents, executive secretaries, and so on. Local units enjoy much freedom in conducting their own affairs. The liberality of the early years in doctrinal matters has been changed into Statements of Faith which are not different from those of the other Pentecostal bodies. The denomination has its publishing and youth programs. The rather backward missionary situation of the early days began to improve in 1949 with the establishment of a missions department. At present, it has 300 mission churches in 13 countries abroad. The church is also very active among the American Indians. Its membership is put at 115,000, with 1,150 churches and 1,200 ordained ministers.[67]

Pentecostal Assemblies of the World, Inc. E. T. Clark defines this as "a Latter Rain Sect which follows the somewhat general practice of tracing its history direct to the day of Pentecost by way of Los Angeles and similar revivals."[68] Originally it was an interracial body until in 1924 the white constituency withdrew to form the United Pentecostal Church. The organization of the group was due to the Trinitarian controversy in matters of baptism. There were those who, basing their belief on "Scripture alone," maintained that baptism had to be administered "in the name of Jesus only." The breach with the Assemblies of God became a fact after the latter took a definite Trinitarian position in its Statement of 1916.

To the outside world, this denomination is best known for some of its puritanic features: "secret societies are opposed, as are church festivals and collecting money on the streets; the wearing of jewelry, attractive hosiery, bobbed hair, bright ties, low-neck dresses are forbidden. Divorce is not permitted when both man and wife have the baptism of the Holy Ghost; but when the unbeliever in a marriage contract procures a divorce, the believer may remarry."[69] Its doctrines include foot washing, divine healing, and speaking with tongues. The government is patterned on Methodist lines: a General Assembly presided over by a bishop, secretaries, and district leaders. Departing from the policy of most Negro churches, this one has missions abroad. At home the Pentecostal Assemblies of the World have 600 churches and 50,000 members.

United Pentecostal Church, Inc. This constitutes a strange but apparently strong merger made up of segments of Pentecostal groups which shifted from one church to another until they found their equilibrium. The "parent body," if one may so call it, was the white congregation which in 1924 withdrew from the Pentecostal Assemblies of the World. In 1931 it was joined by other small factions not associated with either of the previous organizations. Thus appeared the Pentecostal Assemblies of Jesus Christ, which in 1945 merged with the Pentecostal Church. In the following years these bodies received a Canadian Pentecostal branch. The cause of the trouble was again the doctrine of "oneness," namely the denial of the mystery of the Trinity and the adoption of a "Jesusology" as the center of their beliefs and sacramental life. It all began in 1914 when Frank J. Ewart received a "revelation" and started to preach that the Jehovah of the Old Testament, the Jesus of the New Testament, and the Holy Spirit were only manifestations of the one true God. Hence baptism had to be administered only in the name of Jesus, and the ceremony had to be repeated for all who had previously received the sacrament with a Trinitarian formula.

> The Godhead is plainly taught in the creation of man who was made in the image and likeness of God. Man is a threefold being —body, soul, and spirit, but only one person; therefore, it is understood and clearly seen that God is a threefold being, Father, Son, and Holy Spirit, but only one person, and that one is the Holy One, Jesus Christ our Lord. He is not the second person, but is the First and the Last, the Alpha and Omega, the Beginning and the End, and there is none beside him.[70]

The theological basis could not be more shallow. However—and the phenomenon has happened before in Church history—the "Jesus-cult" as a "higher form of Christianity" attracted many Pentecostals who submitted themselves to re-baptism. The new denomination fascinated many by its stern puritan regulations which included among "the activities which are not conducive to good Christianity and godly living," the following: "Theatres, dances, mixed bathing, women cutting the hair, make-up, any apparel that immodestly exposes the body, all worldly sports and amusements, and unwholesome radio programs and music." Since all these evils are vividly evident on television screens, the denomination also disapproves "of any of our people having television sets in their homes."[71] The United Pentecostal Church continues to fascinate some people. The activities of its pastors and missionaries are on the increase. According to the latest reports, the United Pentecostal Church has 1,800 churches, the same number of ministers, and 200,000 members.

Alongside these major and more characteristic Pentecostal denominations, there exist others which, in order to lead their own either prosperous or languishing lives, refuse to join hands with any denomination. Here are the names of a few:

CHURCH	MEMBERSHIP
Church of Our Lord Jesus Christ of the Apostolic Faith	50,000
The Church of God, Holiness	23,500
Calvary Pentecostal Church	20,000
United Holy Church of America, Inc.	26,000
Triumph the Church and Kingdom of God in Christ	8,000
National David Spiritual Temple of Christian Church Union	30,000
International Pentecostal Assemblies	5,000
Fire Baptized Holiness Church of America	6,000
The Original Church of God, Inc.	6,000
Congregational Holiness Church	4,087
Apostolic Faith Mission	2,888
The New Apostolic Church	5,000
The Church of God in Christ	35,000
The Free Christian Zion Church of Christ	1,800
The Churches of God, Holiness	8,000
The Emmanuel Holiness Church	1,200
The Pentecostal Free-will Baptist Church	10,000
The Pentecostal Church of Christ	1,234
Elim Missionary Assemblies	4,000
The Christian Church of North America	20,000
Open Bible Standard Churches, Inc.	26,000[72]

Dozens of smaller units whose membership never surpasses a few hundred followers have been omitted from our consideration, as have cultic denominations, which, even if they retain in their doctrines and practices some Holiness and Pentecostal features, generally deny or ignore the original theology of Pentecostalism.

Neo-Pentecostalism. This chapter cannot be concluded without a brief mention of neo-Pentecostalism. The movement made its appearance around 1960, and takes different shapes according to circumstances. It was first promoted by some pastors of suburban churches, such as Dennis Bennett, Episcopalian Rector of St. Mark's Church, Van Nuys, California; Harold Bredesen, pastor of the First Reformed Church of Mount Vernon, New York; Howard Ervin, pastor of Emmanuel Baptist Church, Atlantic Highlands, New Jersey; Larry Christenson, pastor of Holy Trinity Lutheran Church in San Pedro, California; and James Brown, minister of the Upper Octorara United Presbyterian Church, Parkersburg, Pennsylvania. These ministers (some of whom became proficient in glossolalia) have fostered the speaking in tongues among select groups in their congregations, and encouraged organizations for those blessed with the gift.

A number of popular and well-edited periodicals *(Trinity, Abundant Life, Pentecost, The Voice of Healing, Herald, Miracle Magazine, Pentecostal Holiness Advocate)* are actively engaged in promoting the charismatic revival. The leaders have also moved to the campuses of nationally-known universities (Yale, Princeton, Notre Dame, Harvard) or even to denominational seminaries to teach students the motivations and techniques of the new "direct approach to God." The cause of neo-Pentecostalism has been greatly enhanced by the active presence of eminent individuals from the world of arts, finances, politics, and literature who have become advocates of the spiritual experience.

This church-sponsored neo-Pentecostalism had been preceded in America by a parallel lay-organization of religious enthusiasm of the holiness type called The Full Gospel Business Men's Fellowship International (FGBMFI). Founded in 1953 by Demas Shakarian, a wealthy Californian of Armenian extraction, and fully backed by Oral Roberts and its own powerful organization, the FGBMFI represents a new version of Pentecostalism adapted to the lives and tastes of well-to-do Americans. (To the outside observer it offers many similarities with Moral Rearmament, so much in vogue in the fifties, but it is more mystically oriented than the movement started by Frank Buchman.) It already has some branches in foreign countries.

The organization uses its conventions around the country to spread Pentecostal ideas and to show to those attending them how easy it is to be filled with the Spirit and to speak in tongues—as well as the great benefits derived from the method by individuals and society at large. Among the main speakers one often finds the already mentioned clergymen favorable to Pentecostalism, or special guests like David Du Plessis and Oral Roberts whose chief task is to convince their listeners that there is nothing in neo-Pentecostalism that can be opposed by the historical churches to which they belong.

Neo-Pentecostalism feels specially proud of its penetration among certain groups of Roman Catholics in the United States. Apparently the first infiltrations took place at the University of Notre Dame. From there they have extended to a few other campuses and to restricted circles of avant-garde Catholics in various cities. Nuns in good standing in their congregations or for some time already out of their communities often form the most enthusiastic elements of the groupings. At the beginning they constituted an underground organization but, of late, they have come out in the open and have even begun to hold "nationwide" conventions. They have their own chaplains, and—often in the company of Christians of other denominations—get together in the chapels of secluded monasteries, spend long vigils speaking and singing in tongues. One of their accompanying theologians is making efforts to show the compatibility between the Catholic doctrines of Church, sacramental life, and hierarchical authority and the Pentecostal tenets about charismatic gifts and the direct intervention of the Holy Spirit.

These trends are already disturbing the historical churches of the Reformation. Several commissions appointed by authorities to study the phenomena from the scriptural, confessional, and psychological aspects have come out with conclusions which are either totally negative or extremely cautious regarding the place of glossolalia within the framework of Christianity. In American Lutheranism one branch permits its private exercise "for the individual's personal edification," while another thinks it scripturally unfounded and psychologically dangerous. The Episcopal Church has dismissed glossolalia as a "heresy in embryo" and directed its faithful to seek the gifts of the Spirit in the sacramental life of the Church. Likewise the studies and reports from theologians of the historical churches are opposed to the supernatural character of the gift and try to explain it by various psychological approaches.

The reaction of classical Pentecostalism to these imitators of the original phenomena remains a blend of approval and skepticism. Surely they are happy at seeing that their movement, seemingly circumscribed to outcasts of church and society, is moving up and making inroads into respectable sections in Christendom. The acceptance on the part of educated and well-to-do people of the most controversial aspects of their teaching and practice represents for them a victory and a confirmation that they were not misled. And the insistence on the role of the Holy Spirit in the life of the Christian is an asset for their expansion within and without the United States. And yet, the new outburst is viewed with serious reservations.

In many ways neo-Pentecostals do not appear to be legitimate children of Pentecostalism. The main body of their beliefs is in sharp contrast with those of the Holiness denominations except in the particular point of glossolalia. Pentecostalism, as we shall see, professes a stern, conservative theology which must be accepted by all its members, while many neo-Pentecostals hold a Christianity which has been diluted by liberal and radical interpretations of the Gospel. Genuine Pentecostalism has also emptied sacraments of their intrinsic worth in order to give place to the exclusive operation of the Holy Spirit. Why do not neo-Pentecostals do the same, or even quit their churches and join some of the branches of the movement?

As far as practical Christianity is concerned, the contrasts are still sharper. Neo-Pentecostals do not need divine healing except for a few spectacular cases because they have substituted for it a blind faith in the progress of medical science. And there is little in common between the easy-going life of a member of the Full Gospel Business Men's Fellowship International and the faithful Pentecostals who shun worldliness and preach the Gospel message with a heavy accent on the imminent second coming of Christ. Neo-Pentecostalism seems to have picked up one awe-inspiring aspect of the movement, leaving aside others equally important and intrinsically connected with the Pentecostal interpretation of Christianity.[73]

CHAPTER FOUR

PENTECOSTAL THEOLOGY

Historians find it most difficult to characterize theologies in which subjectivism plays a leading role. One is hard put to say with K. Algermissen that "Pentecostal Christianity has no dogmas because each one of its followers considers himself inspired by the Holy Spirit."[1] It does, however, become extremely difficult to pin down the beliefs of persons whose theology is based on unscholarly biblicism or who do not take into account the data of theological research or the consensus of Christian tradition. If in certain European and North American sectors the situation shows a few signs of improvement, the general outlook is far from clear.

Pentecostals claim the possession of "doctrinal purity" or what they call "a theology of the full Gospel." In the words of C. W. Conn: "There is absolutely no evidence that their people consider themselves other than simple, orthodox Christians."[2] Pentecostals, in the opinion of Du Plessis, have preserved what is best in Protestantism:

> They have the Anglicans' creed and sense of God's greatness; the Congregationalists' belief that Christianity is a layman's religion; the Quakers' practice of waiting for the Holy Spirit; the Brethren's emphasis on the word of God; their own unequaled zeal for evangelism; plus the power of the Apostles received at Pentecost.[3]

In line with other Holiness groups, Pentecostals believe they are part of the "great Protestant family," destined to carry on that "perpetual reformation" which belongs to the essence of Protestantism. Luther, they add, was God's instrument in the sixteenth century against the evils of humanism and of the papacy. The Almighty made use of the Great Awakening and Methodism to fight the forces of deism. In our time Pentecostals continue their opposition against the evils of the day symbolized for them in "German rationalism" and other "modernistic errors." "These modern radicals," one of their historians states, "constitute the strongest threat against modernism, and a wholesome competition to stimulate the larger churches to action."[4] From a different angle, Pentecostal theology belongs to the fundamentalist wing in modern Protestantism. "We," concludes Campbell, "are the branch of Christendom which used to be called fundamentalist. We would prefer to be called conservatives, or more correctly, evangelicals."[5]

Pentecostals have not formulated their beliefs in any uniform way. The differences, however, generally relate to specific beliefs rather than to the truths that form the core of the Christian message. Most groups would endorse the Statement of Truth adopted in 1948 by the Pentecostal Fellowship of America:

> We believe: 1) The Bible as the only inspired, infallible Word of God; 2) God eternally existing in three Persons, Father, Son, and Holy Spirit; 3) The divinity, the virgin birth, the sinless life, the vicarious and atoning sacrifice, the bodily resurrection, ascension, and second coming of Christ; 4) The absolute necessity for salvation that the sinful man be regenerated by the Spirit; 5) Sanctification, second baptism with the gift of tongues and the power of healing; 6) The resurrection of the saved, and the damnation of the lost, with the former destined to eternal happiness and the latter to eternal damnation; and 7) The spiritual unity of all believers in Christ.[6]

Two characteristics of these beliefs are worthy of note. The first must focus on theological method. Among Pentecostals these truths have not been the result of any serious theological reflection; so far their theology hardly satisfies the standards of modern scholarship. In biblical exegesis they cling to outmoded clichés and to a literalism long abandoned by the other churches. In dogma they show little or no concern for patristic thought or for the best that may be found in the Confessions or among the theological schools of the Reformation. Facts and doctrines are often given historical interpretations that are uncritical or naive. Hence few detached observers will accept without qualifications statements to the effect that: "Pentecostal sects have wielded a strong and almost immensurable influence for true orthodoxy," or that "without their faithful witness, it is questionable as to what would have become of the Church."[7] Pentecostal contributions which, as we shall see, have been positive must be searched for in fields other than a developed theology. The latter has also been handicapped by what L. Jamison calls the "principle of selective emphasis," namely, "a virtually monolithic concentration upon some limited aspects of biblical teaching, making of them the touchstone of right belief and religious acceptability,"[8] a principle—whether doctrinal, liturgical, dietary, or sacramental—that "has accounted for the most extensive proliferation of American religious groups."[9]

The second Pentecostal characteristic to be noted is the way in which these truths must be grasped either by the common people or by their preachers. Besides being apprehended by the intellect, they must be made an object of personal experience. This emotional understanding of the doctrines of faith may perhaps be traced (at least seminally) to Luther's fiducial faith. Such faith was certainly given a new emotional accent by Pietists and Wesleyans; but nowhere had it developed to the point where possession of truth became practically equivalent with an almost physical reaction. This was reserved to Pentecostals.

> We have the conviction that it is possible for people to share a definite experimental knowledge of God and salvation. It is our belief that a person can know and have a definite relationship with God. People are interested in reality, and when they are brought face to face with it, there is a response. It gives them something they can stand on. It is that basic assurance and experimental knowledge of God which has attracted people to us. Once they have that, there is the emotional reaction of joy that comes with the consciousness of the knowledge that we are right with God and that we have hope.[10]

With these introductory remarks, we are prepared to review some of the basic beliefs which, at least to a great extent, the Pentecostal groups of the West (Europe and America) hold in common with the rest of Christendom. A similar survey cannot be attempted for the indigenous African or Latin American off-shoots of Pentecostalism, either because they have not developed systems of their own or because, to the tenets and practices of the parent churches, they have added pagan or Christian elements which make it extremely difficult to visualize the specific nature of the new composite. Among the "common doctrines," we shall signalize those on which Pentecostals have taken a stand even vis-à-vis the fundamentalist groups or in which doubts have been raised about their true position. This part will be followed by a longer treatment of the specific tenets of the movement.[11]

Fundamental Tenets

In the highest order of revealed truth, Pentecostal Confessions of Faith contain a belief in the mystery of the Trinity. The official organ of the

Assemblies of God, *Pentecostal Evangel,*carries on the front page of each issue a statement which most of their people would suscribe to: "*We believe that there is one God, eternally existent in three persons: God the Father, God the Son, and God the Holy Spirit.*"But this apparently clear statement has not fully satisfied the theologians of other churches who have made, among others, the following observations: 1) Among Pentecostals "the first Person of the Trinity does not play any leading role"; 2) Many of their preachers and writers reveal an "overemphasis on the Person of Christ" (a "Jesusology") as if he were the only important Person in the Triad; and 3) Many of their theologians have exalted the work of the Spirit in the life of the Christian to the point of ignoring the role of Christ and of the Church.[12]

Everyone familiar with Pentecostals is aware of the existing confusion in their preaching and literature regarding the proper use of Trinitarian formulas. In 1915 the Assemblies of God had to reprimand a dissenting faction for identifying the Father and the Son, while others were warned not to equate Christ with the Spirit.[13] It is also true that, in many mission territories, the language of many of their pastors and evangelists does not square with the Trinitarian definitions of the great councils. How much of the ambiguity is due to the poor seminary training of their pastors and to the religious ignorance of their helpers is harder to ascertain. Nevertheless, when the main denominations (Church of God, Cleveland, Assemblies of God, Church of God in America, Pentecostal Holiness Church, and others) construct their official Statements of Faith, their Trinitarian definitions are worded in orthodox terms. In this sense, C. W. Conn is right when he concludes: "Our Movement is almost totally Trinitarian, even though one will occasionally find Pentecostal churches that hold Unitarian views. These churches are referred to as 'the Jesus only' groups, but form a negligible section in the Pentecostal Movement."[14]

When Pentecostals tell us that the doctrine regarding man holds a "Christian place" in their theology, the statement must be understood in a special context. They are not much concerned with anthropological or psychological developments. On the contrary, the "fight against evolutionism" seems to engage much of their energies. At this point their position is fundamentalist, and some of the expressions found in their writings or heard from their preachers run as follows: "There is an impassable chasm between brute and man." "We believe that the factors involved in the problem of evolution partake largely of the nature of the maybe's which have no permanent place in science." "The author of Genesis writes with an exact scientific accuracy." "Evolution undermines faith in a personal God since if man has resulted from lower material beings, he owes nothing to a Supreme Being; if he owes anything, it is to the animal kingdom from which he has evolved." "Evolutionists seek to link man with a brute creation; but Jesus came into this world to link man to God; he took upon himself our nature in order to glorify it for a heavenly destiny."[15]

Pentecostals, accepting the immediate creation of the whole man by God as well as his destiny for eternity, discourse about the components he is made of, many preferring to depart from the traditional and scriptural division of body and soul in order to insert a third element called spirit. This trichotomy, endorsed by certain leaders of the left-wing Reformation in the sixteenth century, was reasserted in the nineteenth by a well-known American Baptist, A. H. Strong, and has been adopted by a number of Pentecostal writers. They reason in this way:

> Even though it be difficult to differentiate between soul and spirit as distinct from each other in man's material constitution, strength is lent to the trichotomist view by the triads in the universe. God himself is triune: Father, Son, and Spirit. . . . The material universe is a triad: energy, motion, and phenomena. Time is also a triad: past, present, and future. . . . Personality is a triad: intellect, sensibility, and will. The human mind has imagination, memory, and judgment. . . . It is not difficult from these triads to reason that man is also trichotomic or triune in character.[16]

Man's earthly life is one of probation. The world, in addition to being made up of visible elements, is peopled with invisible beings, with which man wrestles on his way to eternity. Pentecostals live in a dualistic world "with forces of evil constantly at work and far too powerful for any human being to face alone."[17] Of all the spirits, attention is focused on the evil ones; their presence gives the Christian a chance to fight with the assistance of the "still more powerful forces of good available to help those who fervently seek such a help."[18] Pentecostal manuals give an almost detailed description of Satan and his hosts. We are told that he was the personification of beauty itself, even "with a great appreciation of music." Likewise the demons "employed under him . . . invade the world to carry his work into the lives of men . . . hinder here below the work of God."[19]

This demonology becomes one of the strongest elements in African Pentecostalism and appears at the root of its interpretation of Christianity. Divine healing and even the Person of Jesus are made to stand face to face with and to destroy the evil beings that surround us. All the urgings of man to do wrong are implanted directly or indirectly by the devil or some of his agents. But, strangely enough, anti-demonic forces are not to be found among "good spirits." Pentecostals accept the existence of "angels who assist and protect the children of God," but are not too keen about the role of "guardian angels," and prefer to warn their followers against the danger of "worshipping" them.[20] The true forces against evil, and in this they remain faithful to the spirit of the Reformation, are the Bible, which contains the whole truth, the Person of Jesus, and the protection of the Holy Spirit.[21]

The historical churches have serious doubts about Pentecostal understanding of certain basic beliefs of the Reformation. For instance, Lutherans have strong reservations about the extreme Pentecostal optimism with regard to man's capabilities in the work of his own salvation. For similar reasons they reject the Pentecostal notions on original sin and its consequences. In both instances, it seems, their suspicion is well-grounded. Pentecostals believe that, from the beginning, man was tainted by some kind of sin; a few will even use expressions that, at first sight, seem Protestant. But those admissions are a far cry from the absolutely unique place given by Lutherans and Calvinists to the original corruption of man. Pentecostals prefer to give the minutest details of the temptation of Adam and Eve rather than define the nature and depth of the sin inherited by mankind. Even the consequences of original sin are sketchily described as man's loss of communication with God, a consciousness of pollution, physical death, and banishment from paradise.[22] If we add to this their insistence on personal sin, we conclude that in this matter Pentecostals are much closer to Wesleyan optimism than to the theology of the "totally corrupted nature" of the first Reformers. Probably for this reason, one of the least developed Pentecostal theological areas is their doctrine on grace.[23] For identical reasons, Pentecostals are firmly opposed to any kind of predestinationism. "All our bodies are Arminians" (Brumback). And Pastor Riggs explains why:

> Predestinationalism limits Christ's atonement, and he died for all. It would nullify man's free will and amount to fatalism. . . . God in his all-power and all-wisdom has left men absolutely free to make their own choice. Otherwise he could not punish men for what is inevitable that they should do. God's sovereignty and man's free will are truths taught by the Bible, and both exist and operate simultaneously without contradiction.[24]

Lutherans are also far from satisfied with the Pentecostal idea of justification by faith. The insistence on sanctification (and on man's effort to attain it) renders insufficient the role of justification in the salvation process and belittles the *articulus stantis et cadentis Ecclesiae* of the original Reformation. Man seems to be fully saved only when he has received sanctification—but more on this in the following chapter.[25] On the contrary, the doctrines of redemption and atonement as taught by Pentecostals seem to follow the best Christian tradition. Sin offends divine justice and love. By sinning, man incurs divine displeasure and deserves punishment. Christ died for our sins and his death is substitutionary and redemptive. He is also the one who restores fallen mankind to divine friendship. Christ's atonement was voluntary, vicarious, self-humbling, and self-sufficient. To carry on the atonement both his divinity and humanity were needed because "without his deity, infinite value could not be obtained; without his humanity, Christ could not have taken the place of fallen man." After Christ's death and physically real resurrection, man, by accepting the atonement on his behalf, insures the honor of the law and obtains redemption.[26]

Ecclesiology.

Holiness and Pentecostal denominations are thought of in Reformation circles as having a rather jejune ecclesiology. On this point their Statements of Faith are of little help to the theologian. Some Pentecostals do not consider belief in the Church relevant enough to be included amont the "prominent doctrines" professed by the denomination. Among others the definitions are too vague and unsatisfactory. The Assemblies of God describe the Church as: "The Body of Christ, the inhabitation of God through the Spirit, with divine appointment of her commission."[27] Vagueness is also the mark in the ecclesiology of somc of their best-known writers. To Pearlman, the Church is "the company of people taken out of the world, who profess a tender allegiance to the Lord."[28] Of the Church as the universal assembly, C. P. Nelson states: "It is not an organization, but an organism pulsating in every member with the life of Jesus Christ."[29] To the question: "What is the Church," Pastor Riggs answers: "The Holy Spirit is himself the nature of the Church. He is the refining love to bind the Church together. He is flaming zeal to carry out the great commission. He is the divine power to perform signs and wonders."[30] Nevertheless, Pentecostal ecclesiology has made a fresh start with the work of E. S. Williams, former General Superintendent, General Council of the Assemblies of God, and Instructor at the Central Bible Institute, Springfield, Missouri, who has devoted a section of his *Systematic Theology* to this matter. It cannot be ascertained how many denominations in America or in foreign missions follow in his footsteps. In any case, he will serve as our guideline for this delicate but all-important theme in our ecumenical conversations.

Theologians and historians have remarked the clearly-defined pietistic origins of Holiness and Pentecostal ecclesiology. Both groups proclaim their intention of returning to the pure sources and practices of the primitive Church, where the Christian community was structurally and liturgically simple, and still unburdened by the developments of the following centuries. These denominations, Roger Mehl remarks,

> ... intend to go back to the zero year of the Christian era, not only because in their view the historical churches have failed in their mission and betrayed their message, but also because they want to suppress all tradition in the strictest sense of the word so as to be as close as possible to the sources and become the contemporary salvific event.[31]

This attempt to lessen the role of the Church in the life of the Christian is made possible only by unduly exalting the effects of regeneration and sanctification in the supernatural life of the individual. For such "wholly sanctified" persons, the Church "is no longer the community of those who have been called by the word and sacrament, but the association of the reborn, of those who earnestly desire to become Christians. To them the Church consists of small circles of pietists, the *conventicles,* where everybody knows everybody else and where experiences are frequently exchanged."[32] The man who is truly sanctified and has the Spirit with him can and must stand on his own feet. Corporate worship, sacraments, absolution, or communion have become empty words and shibboleths because "a thoroughgoing person does not need such crutches."[33] Such was the position of the eighteenth-century Pietist and it is that of the Pentecostals of our time.

The narrowing of catholicity to small conventicles *(ecclesiolae)* is at the root of the swiftness with which their leaders, often for the most trivial reasons, abandon the parent church to found new ones. No section within contemporary Christendom is so fissiparous and hopelessly divided as Pentecostalism. Again the principle of voluntariness has been carried to extremes; adult membership is not enough, but must be joined with the "born-again experience." From the same source rises the perfectionist concept of the "pure Church" as the only one compatible with the mind of Christ and the vocation of the Christian. "No wood, hay, or stubble [i.e. unregenerated material] is to be built into this wall, which is to be of silver, gold, and precious stones, the true children of God."[34]

In this hypothesis, there should be only a spiritual Church, recruited from among the saints and without a place for sinners. E. S. Williams accuses Rome of teaching a "merely external holiness."[35] Things look different, he says, when "the true Church consists only of born-again believers." Then the Church becomes "the fellowship and the means of grace through which the Spirit-filled Church (which is invisible) manifests itself," in other words, a kind of shelter in which the children of God are gathered in order to enjoy the fruits of the Spirit. To be a member of this "Holy Club," the essential condition is to have been born again of the Spirit. On the contrary, "membership in the visible Church is secondary," because the Christian has already been saved prior to and independently of the Church. "Immediately upon being saved, the believer becomes a member of the Church, and now he loves and desires the fellowship of other believers."[36] What, then, about the nominal Christians who still form the bulk of the churches? Pentecostals compare them to the "tares," in contrast with the "true, spiritual members, ... whose names are written in heaven." As a rule, they do not bother about them. One writer even says that "as far as possible, the Church should seek to extend membership only to those who are, by the new birth, members of the Church which is Christ's Body."[37] The conditions for membership in the Church are: a) repentance and faith; b) confession and witness to others in faith in Christ as manifested in the ordinance of Baptism; and c) a confirming evidence of his newly-born Christian life. The evidence can be either direct: "the witness of the Spirit in our hearts," or indirect: "the fruits of righteousness which result in the life of the believer and, as born of the Spirit, should also bring forth the fruit of the Spirit."[38]

It would seem that, under these circumstances, the Pentecostal churches are charismatically governed bodies where the initiative is left to the spiritually perfect members. On principle, however, nothing is further from the thought of their theologians. In the words of Williams:

> The visible Church manifests herself through her organization. It is impossible to function without it.... God has made full provision for that organization as he has recognised its functions as an organism. While the Spirit manifests himself and his activities through the Church as an organism, human leadership and biblical order are clearly provided for in the New Testament.[39]

The guidelines for organization laid down by the Assemblies of God follow these principles: 1) "The discipline must be exercised in the Spirit who is the head"; 2) "Organization must not supersede the organism or inward life of the indwelling Spirit"; 3) Simplicity of organization "should be the ideal"; and 4) In the New Testament "no set government is clearly defined; it is therefore the prerogative of any organization of Christians to form a government that is felt to meet the need."[40] In view of this, it seems that Pentecostals have already opted for a well-defined and uniform church structure; eliminated episcopacy as a system "not found in the Bible," and built on an organization which is a blend of Presbyterian, Congregationalist, and Baptist forms. Except for those cases in which the founder, foundress, or some dominant personality still holds the reins of power, at its top stands the General Assembly (called at times General Conference, General Convention, or Annual Conference) presided over by a General Superintendent and a number of assistants and secretaries. In some denominations the supreme authority rests in the Twelve Elders "who shall decide all matters which shall properly come before them." They shall also "try all ministers for any offence committed within the state" and "their decision shall be final."[41] Among the lower officials we find pastors, evangelists, elders, deacons, deaconesses, superintendents, and overseers. In mission countries the structures are more primitive and the churches may be ruled by a powerful chief, an outstanding preacher, or an effective healer.

Pentecostals are convinced that they have greatly perfected the role of the local congregations they inherited from the Baptists. As a miniature church, the local church is intended to be free and independent from any centralized direction. "We recognize," says one of their historians,

> ... that each local assembly has the right to self-government under Jesus Christ, its divine head, and shall have the power to choose or call its pastor, elect its official board, and transact all other business pertaining to its life as a local unit. It shall have the right to administer discipline to its members according to the Scripture and bylaws.

Non-Pentecostals are often puzzled when checking these lofty statements against actual policies that they have been able to observe. No general rule can be applied to the whole spectrum of the Pentecostal family, and cases can be adduced like those of the extremely well-organized Brazilian *Assembleias de Deus* whose strength derives to a great extent from the independence of the local congregations. Nor are all the churches governed with the stern rule with which Aimée McPherson during her lifetime (and now under her son and successor) conducted the affairs of the International Church of the Foursquare Gospel.[42] Nevertheless, considering Pentecostalism as a body that extends to many non-Western areas, it seems fair to assert that the authoritarian trend is more common than not in many of its churches. R. Wilson, writing for one of the British-born churches, concludes:

> In spite of the theoretical control by the representative conference, there can be little doubt that most of the activity of the movement is controlled and regulated by a relatively small number of administrators at central headquarters. Information, administrative capacity, experience, familiarity with the work, and various other advantages concentrate on the relatively small number of men who occupy the central positions and who, as a consequence, have a strong informal preemption upon them.[43]

There is no doubt that Pentecostal discipline, while gracious and kind to the faithful and active members of the community, can become ruthless on those individuals who do not come up to its expectations:

> Enrolled members, who shall, without cause, absent themselves from the services of the assembly for a period of three consecutive months or more, and who cease to contribute of their means to their support; or who may be out of harmony with its teachings and ministers . . . shall be considered inactive members and shall lose their privileges until they are restored to their fellowship.[44]

Even for failures which in other churches would be considered of minor importance, Pentecostal offenders may be immediately expelled from the fold.[45] In this stern discipline lies one of the secrets of the success of Pentecostalism.

Sacraments

If we divide the churches of the Protestant tradition into liturgical (sacramental) or evangelical bodies according to their emphasis on the Eucharist or on the preaching of the Word, Pentecostals definitely belong to the latter. J. B. Cobb, in his *Varieties of Protestantism,* refers to the very marginal place held by sacraments in the religions which over-emphasize religious experience and the doctrine of assurance.[46]

Roger Mehl holds anti-liturgism to be one of the characteristics of the sectarian type of Christianity, not only in the sense that they object to fixed and orderly patterns of cult, but chiefly because they conceive a down-grading of liturgy a means to stress the role of the individual in his relations with God.[47] Pentecostals are aware of this and, at times at least, seem to be proud not be counted among the "sacramentarians": "We do not regard this feature as a weakness. And most of the churches admit today that the Pentecostal Movement is much nearer to the Christian worship recorded in the New Testament than are the larger and more liberal churches."[48] The applications of these principles will be seen in their doctrines on baptism and the Lord's Supper.

Baptism. The word to specify this is "water-baptism," in contrast to the "baptism of the Spirit" to be explained in the following chapter. Baptism held a subordinate role at the beginning of the Pentecostal movement and has never risen to a central position. One can read whole Pentecostal treatises (and this is true even of some of their Statements of Faith) in which baptism is either omitted or dealt with only in a polemical way.[49] Most Pentecostals have also dropped the word "sacrament" and have substituted "ordinance." This move is not new, since that term had been already introduced by the Baptists "in order to avoid the word sacrament and the magical implications attached to it."[50]

For churches of the Catholic tradition an ordinance, as opposed to a sacrament, carries the following connotations: 1) It is not something prescribed as a *conditio sine qua non* for salvation; for instance, a person may be saved without actual baptism or by what theologians used to call baptism of desire. 2) It does not confer any internal effect on the person who receives it (cleansing and remission of sin, infusion of grace, incorporation into the Body of Christ), but always remains external in the category of a symbol of something that the candidate has already achieved through penance and fiducial faith. 3) It is, however, an action which must be performed because it was so prescribed by Christ or by the Church: "Though no one is saved through baptism, he should be baptized according to the commandment of God in obedience to his will (Mt 28:19). Baptism does not give salvation in itself, but comes after faith in Christ. Without faith in Christ and commitment to him, baptism would be in vain."[51]

In baptism, therefore, the true effects precede its reception. Repentance is an inward act of faith cleansing the soul from sin and separating man from the world. Hence, for Pentecostals, baptism is only a sign of outward obedience, signifying, it is true, spiritual death into life, but remaining always in the category of a symbol. It has also been remarked that many Pentecostals, even among those who use the correct Trinitarian formula, enlarge the words of baptism with expressions like: "I baptize you on your profession of faith," to prevent any sacramental conception of the rite and to underline the fact that the catechumen, even before the ceremony, was already Christian.

Pentecostals admit that, in taking this stand, they are contradicting the most ancient and universal Christian tradition. But they believe they have "the Scriptures on their side," adding as a reminder to the historian that the emphasis on baptism as "a saving rite" was an accretion of later times and something that took place when the Church "forsook the simplicity of the New Testament and became influenced by pagan ideas," a trend which led her to consider baptism as "something fully essential to regeneration and as such to be administered even to the sick and dying."[52] It is, therefore, enough for them that baptism should keep a twofold value, namely, that those who have been baptized have died in Christ and have been raised with him in newness of life; and while "their bodies [have been] washed in pure water as an outward symbol of cleansing, . . . their hearts have been sprinkled with the blood of Christ as an inner cleansing."[53]

Based on these principles, Pentecostals reject infant baptism, since there can be only a baptism of believers, that is, adult baptism. Any contrary practice, they warn us, is "against the word of God" and a "deviation" introduced by St. Augustine, although, in their opinion, the African bishop was soon challanged "by more enlightened Christians" because "Baptism and repentance go together; infants know nothing about repentance and faith; therefore any baptism administered to them is unscriptural."[54] Such can be the only logical position of a movement which, as we have seen, hardly accepts the consequences of original sin: even granting that infants "are not born in a state of holiness, [nevertheless] through the atonement of Christ [they are already] in a state of justification and innocence and, if they die, they will be infallibly saved."[55] This "consoling truth," which they contrast with the "gloomy views" of the Church of Rome, is deeply rooted in their churches, and has become a powerful instrument in evangelism:

> Your Pentecostal neighbor does not practice infant baptism. The child has not entered a willful act of sin prior to consciousness of evil. Therefore baptism is out of order. There is no commandment in Scripture or example that the infant should be baptized. When children were brought to Jesus, he only blessed them. . . . Pentecos-

tals believe that, because of the nature of sin in the human family, the child will sin early in life. Then he, too, after repentance and conversion, has to be baptized. But baptism is an outward sign of something else that has already taken place in the heart of the individual.[56]

Instead of having infants baptized, many middle-class Pentecostals dedicate them to the Lord, thus fulfilling the example of Jesus (Mt 19:14), and preparing them for the struggles in life.[57] In doing so, some ministers had begun to sprinkle the babies with water, but the practice has been disapproved: "Since infant baptism has been looked upon as a saving ordinance . . . and too often Pentecostal parents bring their children for dedication, but with very vague ideas as to the why," they may easily mistake one ceremony for the other.[58]

After "water-baptism" has been reduced to a mere ordinance, Pentecostals find no difficulty in prescribing it as a condition of membership to their churches.[59] In Europe, both Americas, and Asia, baptismal practice may be said to be the rule. In Africa the variety of practices is unlimited and often baptismal rites are mingled with ceremonies borrowed from pagan religions or tainted with clear ancestor cult and worship. On principle, Pentecostalism favors baptism by immersion,[60] and some of their followers look on it as a special charism of the movement:

> With amazing unanimity our Pentecostal people practice immersion by water . . . and regard all other modes as unscriptural. This is all the more remarkable as a large percentage of our people came from denominations practicing sprinkling and infant baptism. The only way to account for it is that the experience of being baptized in the Holy Spirit makes us so pliable in the hands of God that we are willing to receive instructions from the word of God on this subject as on all others as they have been loosed from the bonds of tradition.[61]

The motives behind this attachment to baptism by immersion are: 1) "Baptism should be administered according to the example set up for us in the Scriptures"; and 2) "Had sprinkling been sufficient, there would have been no need of Jesus' going into the water, or that John [the Baptist] should have been baptized in Aenon 'because there was much water there.' "[62] Similarly, Pentecostals should adopt the practice of "triple immersion." There are indeed a few groups which consider it "the most perfect form" of baptism, but the number is increasing of those who consider it "erroneous" to impose it on all as an obligation. E. S. Williams explains why:

> There are those who dip three times.... Whenever there is sincerity of heart, God accepts that sincerity, and those who practice triune immersion, honor the Father, the Son, and the Holy Spirit. ... But, since baptism signifies identification with Christ in his death, burial, and resurrection, and since the Father, the Son, and the Holy Spirit did not die to save,baptism should be a single act, signifying that "as many of you have been baptized in Christ, have put on Christ."[63]

One cannot say that the old Pentecostal controversy around the baptismal formula has completely died out. The studies being carried on about the practices of African Pentecostal denominations give us at this point a blurred picture not at all reassuring to Christian tradition.[64] But most of the better organized denominations have accepted the Trinitarian invocation of the Father, and of the Son, and of the Holy Spirit.[65] There is also, among their writers, a mild rejection of those groups who still keep the "Jesus only" formula, and thus cause "great injury to the cause of Christ and to the very doctrines for which Pentecostals stand." Some even dare to condemn it as "a most dangerous error which has been put forward for the purpose of denying the Bible doctrine of the Holy Trinity."[66]

Baptismal rites vary from one denomination to another. In the West the ceremonies are almost undistinguishable from those of the historical churches. Much stress is laid on the preparation of the candidates and in the "change of heart" they have to experience before receiving the "ordinance." The pastor is also told to impress upon all "the solemnity and sacredness of the occasion." The rite may take place either in the baptistry or in an outdoor pool or stream. Baptism is preceded by a number of questions put to the catechumen regarding the renunciation of Satan, the divinity of Christ, and the reality of his atonement. In mission territories the rites come closer to, or depart further from, those of other churches according to the degree of native influence by which they have been shaped.[67]

Eucharist. Roman Catholics, Anglicans, and Lutherans are rather disappointed at the jejune Pentecostal doctrines regarding the Lord's Supper. They wish that Pentecostals, so admirable for their love of God and neighbor, could share more of the riches of a sacrament which, from the day of its institution, has been the center of life of the Christian Church. Unfortunately this is not so. Here the Pentecostal position is among the most radical in the whole family of the Reformation. Only Quakers, Mormons, Seventh Day Adventists, Christian Scientists, and Jehovah's Witnesses may be said to fall into the same category.

Pentecostalism, deeply influenced by the Zwinglian and left-wing Reformation doctrines of the sixteenth century and heir to the Baptists in the seventeenth, has practically emptied the Eucharist of its objective content (real presence, remission of sins, and sacrificial character) to extol solely its symbolic and memorialistic aspects.

Typical of this position (and, to my knowledge, one of the few denominations which has formulated the doctrine in theological terms) is that held by the Assemblies of God.[68] From the start, the emphasis is on the value of the Eucharist as a symbol for Christian life. The "elements" of bread and wine do not undergo transformation of any kind. "Are the *emblems* actually transformed into the flesh and blood of Christ?," asks Pastor Riggs. And he answers: "No; they simply serve as object lessons to picture the spiritual blessings which Christ's death brought to us."[69] "The Lord's Supper," we read in one of their manuals, "consisting of the elements (bread and fruit of the wine) is the *symbol* expressing our sharing the divine nature of the Lord Jesus Christ; a memorial of his sufferings and death; and a prophecy of his coming; and is enjoined on all believers."[70] Hence also communion remains simply "a religious partaking of bread and wine which have been presented to the Father in memorial for Christ's inexhaustible sacrifice."[71] If some writers still refer to it as a "meal of consecration," they add immediately that it cannot be considered "as a special means for the remission of sins." A fortiori, its sacrificial character is totally absent from their thought, except, as is often the case in Latin America, when it is referred to in order to attack the "abominable superstition" of the sacrifice of the Mass.[72]

On the other hand, Holy Communion is becoming a regular liturgical feature in many Pentecostal denominations. What do they see in it that makes the ceremony worthy of reverence and reception? 1) A *commemoration* reminding us in a special manner of the atoning death of Christ which freed us from our sins; 2) An *instruction,* in the sense that the Body of the Lord, as typified in the elements, signifies "how absolutely necessary it is for our souls and bodies to be sustained by the life-giving Christ"; 3) An *inspiration* as it tells us that by faith "we may become partakers of Christ's nature"; 4) A *prophecy* leading us to look forward to the day of Christ's return; 5) A *bond of unity,* not only with Christ, but also with one another, "as a family of God, feasting together and partaking of the Bread and of the Cup"; 6) An *assurance* "that he will be gracious and merciful to the penitent"; 7) A *healing ordinance* because "if you are sick and afflicted in your body and can discern the healing virtue in the Body of Our Lord, typified by the bread, you may receive healing and strength for your body and for your spiritual nature"; and 8) An *invitation* to action and responsibility, since no one can partake of the symbols of the Body and Blood of Christ without feeling the urge "to communicate his graces and knowledge to others."[73]

Regarding the eucharistic celebration, the remarks made about Baptism are here in point. Its solemnity depends on the cultural or religious level of the congregations as well as on the type of Christianity prevailing around them. It is extremely simple in mission territories; it borrows many details from the Anglican Ordinal in South Africa, and from Catholic ceremonies in Latin America. In Northern Europe and the United States (with the exception of the colored churches which still keep their peculiarities), the tendency prevails to adopt many elements from the historical Protestant denominations. The Church of God, Cleveland, precedes communion with "a time of dedication and examination of conscience." Others consider it as a fellowship meal among Christians of the same conviction. There are also wide differences regarding the frequency of communion: from every week in one or another denomination to periods of several months in others. While unleavened bread is prescribed in some western denominations, the prerequisite is completely disregarded in many parts of Asia and Africa. Pentecostals very often practice open communion and accept not only members of other Pentecostal churches but also those from other Christian traditions, provided they are in good standing in their own denominations.

Moreover, the "unregenerates" are warned of the danger of partaking from the table in an unworthy way that will lead to damnation. Some groups strictly enjoin their ministers to recite the words of "consecration." Others leave it to the inspiration of the moment. Most of the time the pastor hands the bread and the cup to his assistants who, in turn, distribute them among the congregation. The elements may be received seated or standing. For a time no musical accompaniment was allowed, but at present the ceremony consists of community singing and thanksgiving prayers. All these details serve to show that the Lord's Supper is still far from constituting the center of the spiritual life of Pentecostals. The liturgical movement, which has influenced so many branches of the Reformation, has made little impact on Pentecostals.[74]

In certain Pentecostal groups, foot-washing still enjoys the same esteem as the Lord's Supper, or an even higher regard. Brumback reports that such was the common practice among the early members of their churches, while "real blessings attended their ministry to one another in this fashion."[75] The practice gave rise, at the beginning of the century, to a controversy. For some, foot-washing was "a true ordinance and had to be observed, together with communion, at least once a year."[76] Others, "with no desire to condemn those who sincerely practised it," rejected its obligation on scriptural grounds.[77] As usual, the controversy ended up in a splitting of congregations and the formation of new churches. At present, and in the spectrum of worldwide Pentecostalism, the situation remains fluid. To quote Brumback (who belongs to an anti-foot washing group) "the majority" of Pentecostals do not agree that the practice was "commanded by the Lord." Even in the West, however, there are important denominations (the Church of God, Cleveland, the Apostolic Faith Church, the Church of God in Christ, and others) that impose on their followers this "washing of the saints' feet." This is still more true of an increasing number of African churches which have endorsed it together with lustral purifications of dubious Christian origin.[78] The theological meaning of the practice is thus explained by Paulk: washing of the feet "is not to be viewed in the same light as the Lord's Supper, since the latter represents the death of the Lord. However, since it is a commandment of the word of God, it is to be done even as at the Lord's Supper . . . and observed in the Christian fellowship."[79]

Eschatology

Understood as the theology of the "last things," eschatology belongs to the essence of Pentecostalism. However, when we consider it in the particulars which precede, accompany, and follow Christ's second coming, it fails to hold the same central place as it does, for instance, among Seventh Day Adventists or Jehovah's Witnesses. The elements are there, but among Pentecostals, the center has been shifted to the baptism of the Spirit together with the signs that go with it. Pentecostals take seriously sin and its disastrous consequences on man. Sin is an offense against God and, unless he repents in time, the sinner will be judged and condemned by Christ. While preaching, Pentecostals prefer to dwell on the love of God or the happiness of those who are saved. Nevertheless the doctrines of God's justice to the unrepentant are also very clearly defined in the Statements of Faith and in the writings of their ministers. Death, they tell us, marks the end of man's life, but not that of his soul which, "once created, shall never die" because it can be exposed only to a "spiritual death." On the contrary, "the soul that sins against God must experience spiritual death or separation from God."[80] In the light of revelation, Christian theology has attempted to explain the status of man's soul in the interval between physical death and the second coming of Christ. At this point Pentecostals lack clarity and precision. Some like Paulk practically ignore the existence of that interval. Others, with Pearlman, after rejecting the ideas of purgatory, spiritism, and soul-sleeping, leave the reader with a rather hazy picture of that intermediate state:

> It should be carefully noted that the righteous do not enter into their final reward, nor the wicked into their final punishment, until after their respective resurrection. Both classes are in an intermediate state, awaiting that event. Departed Christians go to be "with the Lord," but do not receive their final reward. The intermediate state of the righteous is one of rest [Rev 14:13], waiting [Rev 6:10-11], activity [Rev 7:15] and holiness [Rev 7:14]. The wicked, too, pass into an intermediate state, where they await their final punishment.[81]

The fact of man's real and physical resurrection is firmly believed by Pentecostals, although "when we attempt to explain the *how* of the matter, we find ourselves in deep waters because we are dealing with mysterious supernatural laws beyond the grasping of our minds."[82] They are also convinced that the Holy Spirit will revitalize the bodies of the elect, giving them incorruptibility, glory, agility, and subtlety. The bodies of the wicked will share such prerogatives as far as they are compatible with their status of damned beings. The resurrection of the bodies will be preceded by the second coming of Christ. Where do Pentecostals stand on a matter which has been the object of heated controversies among certain modern branches of the Reformation? They begin by opposing two schools. There are the post-millennials who, putting their hopes in the capabilities of man, infer that we shall be able to preach the Gospel to the whole world, and, as a consequence, bring about "a thousand years of peace" (the Millennium). In this theory, the second coming of Christ will take place only after that thousand-year span.[83] Then there are the pre-millennials for whom man has proved to be a failure and the world, in spite of all its scientific progress, does little more than ripen for the day of judgment. Consequently, there cannot be a millennium until "Christ personally appears with the holy angels and the saints to execute judgment upon his enemies, to destroy everything that offends, every vestige of the reign of Satan and the anti-Christ."[84] Most Pentecostal groups belong to the pre-millennial school. One of their popular writers, Myer Pearlman, has elaborated the sequence of events of the "last days" as follows:

1. *We know we are living in the last days.* The signs are everywhere: Christians giving up their faith and being seduced by doctrines of evil (Christian Science, Seventh Day Adventism, Spiritualism, Mormonism, Jehovah's Witnesses); churches in a deplorable abandonment of cardinal doctrines which are being substituted by evolutionism and the worship of man; Jews returning to Palestine and forming a nation of their own; the United Nations with their theory of world-government, a preliminary of the Federation of Nations over which the anti-Christ will rule; the possession of the hydrogen bomb, the instrument of destruction of mankind predicted by John in the book of Revelation.[85] All these are a preparation for:

2. *The Great Tribulation* for which we are headed (Mt 24:21). Hence the Church's duty is to warn the world of the approaching judgment; to proclaim the coming of Christ and the gospel of grace in him. The tribulation will be accompanied by:

3. *The Rapture of the Church* when the Lord will descend from heaven and "catch away all those who are in Christ, both living and dead," in order to undergo a judgment in the heavens and to give Christians a just reward for their varying degrees of consecration and faithfulness. That judgment will be followed by the "marriage supper of the Lamb" when Christ and all those who have been redeemed will eat and drink together in the kingdom of God.[86] Meanwhile mankind will watch:

4. *The Battle of Armageddon.* We do not have many details about it, but certainly we know that it will be a battle between the anti-Christ and the armies of Christ and of his elect. There can neither be any doubt about its final outcome: "the Lord shall come forth from heaven riding on a white horse with the armies of heaven also on white horses." Anti-Christ and his followers will be utterly defeated, "taken alive and cast into the lake of fire and all the soldiers of his armies will be slain."[87] The battle will bring in:

5. *The Millennium,* whose functioning is thus described: Jesus and his followers will take the reins of world government. Its capital will be Jerusalem, "beautiful as to its situation and the city of the great king." Everything in that kingdom will be millennial: the land, the rivers, the order of worship, while the people enjoy a special outpour-

ing of the Spirit and a universal knowledge of God. But, most of all, the Millennium will be characterized by the absence of Satan who "will be bound and cast into the bottomless pit, so that he will not be able to deceive the earth's inhabitants for a thousand years." Finally:

6. *When the thousand years are over,* Satan will be released again, but only for a short time. A second battle started by God (with the use of "heavenly fire" as ammunition) will burn the enemies and cast the devil and his followers into the torments of hell. Then the Lord will purify the earth and prepare it for eternity: "The New Jerusalem will then come down from God out of heaven, and God will live in it and over his people for ever and ever."[88]

Thus the drama of the last days is unfolded, and Christ conquers the forces of evil. Pentecostals, needless to say, believe in a true heaven and in a real hell, both eternal. Sinners "will be punished with everlasting destruction from the presence of the Lord and shall have their part in the lake which burneth with fire and brimstone."[89] Regarding the happiness of the saved, Pentecostals are convinced that: "In that day we shall be like him, for we shall see him as he is; our bodies will be fashioned like unto his glorious body; we shall see his face; and he who shepherded his people through the vale of tears will in heaven lead them from joy to joy, from glory to glory, from revelation to revelation."

Such is the overview of Pentecostal theology. In spite of deviations and misrepresentations, our Pentecostal brethren have kept a large number of doctrines which, when taken together, facilitate dialogue with other Christians. From the Catholic viewpoint, their main weakness lies in the fields of ecclesiology and the sacraments. The situation might improve with a better training of their ministers and a greater familiarity with the sources.

CHAPTER FIVE

SPECIFIC PENTECOSTAL TENETS

Pentecostalism is better known for its peculiarities than for the features it has in common with the rest of Christendom. This was so at the very beginnings of the movement. "Pentecostal people," Brumback states, "were so 'different' in their conduct and worship that it would have been strange if the onlookers had not regarded them as odd visitors from another planet. After all, people who 'spoke in tongues and did a lot of crazy things' were a collection of peculiar creatures, whose antics sent shivers down your spine."[1] The most noteworthy of the differences, whether on the doctrinal or the behavorial level, were: 1) Complete sanctification, distinct from and subsequent to justification and regeneration; 2) Baptism in the Holy Spirit, often referred to as second baptism; 3) Charismatic gifts, especially speaking in tongues; and 4) The power of divine healing.[2]

At the root of these extraordinary graces stands the Pentecostal theology of the Holy Spirit, considered by many as the authentic contribution of the Holiness groups to contemporary Christianity, and raised by Pentecostalism to a kind of *articulus stantis et cadentis ecclesiae* of its denominations. According to D. Gee,

> it is no disparagement of the apprehension of the Spirit's presence by faith alone (as understood in Protestantism) to affirm as a contribution of the Pentecostal Movement to the whole Church, the desirability of having his presence made manifest by means of spiritual gifts. We dare say that this is one of the supreme purposes of God in sending the Pentecostal revival in the twentieth century.[3]

With some reluctance, the historical churches begin to acknowl edge this contribution. "If Calvinism," says F. E. Mayer, "is theocentric and Lutheranism Christocentric, then Holiness and Pentecostalism ought to be described as pneumatic."[4] Professor Van Dusen has called Pentecostalism "the body most responsible for the increased attention given to the Holy Spirit,"[5] while John Mackay attributes to the movement the "rediscovery of the Holy Spirit as a reality in the life of the Church."[6] Even Evangelicals—so often at odds with these "new comers"—accept the idea of a providential Pentecostal presence in the world. Says Billy Graham: "In the main denominations we have looked askance at our brethren, the Pentecostal churches, because of the emphasis on the doctrine of the Holy Spirit. But I believe the time has come to give the Holy Spirit his rightful place in our churches. We need to learn once more what it means to be baptized with the Holy Spirit."[7]

Whatever our personal leanings in the matter, this remains certain: We shall never understand Pentecostal beliefs and practices until we grasp the centrality of the Third Person of the Trinity in their theology and in their lives.[8] To them Pentecost is not a mere historical event that took place almost two thousand years ago, but an always renewed presence of the Spirit in the world. The Holy Spirit is now, as then, the "creator" and the "vivifier" of men. The Spirit rules the Church and cares for those who put themselves under his protection. Pentecostals see no valid reasons for restricting his power to the first centuries. The Church, they add, at present needs those gifts of the Spirit perhaps even for its own survival. In like manner, Pentecostals are persuaded that he has chosen these latter days for a special outpouring of his gifts. In confirmation they point to the spiritual and moral changes which have taken place in the lives of men and women who have been blessed by the Spirit's gifts.[9] There is in this position much that Christians of other communions might take to heart. As Carl Henry says, "the Holy Spirit is still in the twentieth century much of a displaced person" in the life of the Church. And history confirms that "absence of vital belief in the Holy Spirit has always paralleled spiritual sterility," while, on the other hand, "the recovery of the Spirit is either an evidence or a prelude to spiritual renewal founded in revitalized experience."[10] F. D. Maurice predicted years ago: "I cannot but think that the Reformation of our day (which I expect to be more deep and searching than that of the sixteenth century) will turn upon the Spirit's presence and life as [the earlier Reformation] did upon justification by the Son."[11]

Are Pentecostals the true heralds of this pneumatic message to our generation? At this stage of our research it is still too early for a convincing answer. We may begin, however, by watching Pentecostals in the act of interpreting and conveying these gifts to those who approach them. Only then shall we be in a position to discern the shape of things to come.

Sanctification

In Pentecostal theology the gifts of the Spirit are the logical consequence of the doctrine of sanctification. This, in turn, presents two facets: The action of the Spirit upon the individual, and its external manifestation. In Reformation history the term "sanctification" bears a specifically Methodist stamp. H. Lindstrom, an expert on Wesleyanism, explains the concept in these words:

> Forgiveness and sanctification are the two cardinal factors in the idea of salvation, with the main stress on sanctification. Forgiveness, based on atonement, is the ground of the Christian life and, in principle, is never overstepped. Nevertheless, it is the idea of sanctification that dominates Wesley's whole theology. The concept of salvation is determined by the idea of sanctification because salvation is seen as a process directed to the perfect, real change of the individual. . . . The Christian must prepare himself for the last judgement and the entry into heaven. . . . And the path he has to travel to reach his goal is the path of sanctification, of real, empirical change in man.[12]

In his lifetime Wesley was careful to distinguish between sanctification and the New Birth.[13] The latter was identified with the forgiveness of sins. On the contrary, the sanctified person become so perfect that, in actual fact, he did not commit sin because he loved God with his whole heart.[14] Moreover, this sanctifying action was "a direct and immediate action of God upon man. The condition to attain it was (fiducial) faith. But given the condition, man sees God acting directly to accomplish what he wishes, and by such direct action God also *extirpates* man's sinful nature."[15]

These ideas received in America a new coloring in the hands of Charles Finney and the revivalists. Finney was convinced that those who have been sanctified by the Spirit "habitually live without sin or fall into it at intervals so few and far between that, in strong language, it may be said in truth that they do not sin."[16] The revivalists made general use of the same theme in order to attract crowds and convince sinners of the practical impeccability they had acquired with their conversion and second baptism.[17] But no one developed the doctrine with the conviction and thoroughness of A. B. Simpson, founder of the Christian and Missionary Alliance, in his book *Wholly Sanctified,* which soon became the classic treatise. We are called, he said, to have a sanctified spirit, a sanctified soul, and a sanctified body, and thus to be "preserved blameless." It is "the blood of Jesus and the divine life imparted by the inbreathing of the Holy Spirit" which will purify our beings. "His pure life filling us expels all evil, and continually renews and refreshes our entire being, keeping us pure, even as the fresh oil in the lamp maintains the flame, or as the running stream washes and keeps the pebble pure which lies at the sandy bottom."[18] As explained in Chapter Two above, one of the reasons that prompted the Holiness groups to quit Methodism was the conviction that the parent church had abandoned the doctrine and the practices of what had been the bedrock of their existence. "Under such circumstances," says Kendrick, "the Holiness Movement began to exist. The people who united under this designation found their bond of union in the Wesleyan experience of entire sanctification."[19]

In our days every Pentecostal denomination places sanctification at the very center of its beliefs. Here are a few instances taken from their Statements of Faith. "The Scripture teaches us a life of holiness, without which no man shall see the Lord. By the power of the Holy Spirit, we are able to obey the command: 'Be holy as I am holy.' Entire sanctification is the will of God for all believers and should be earnestly pursued by walking in obedience to God's words" (Assemblies of God). "The Pentecostal Holiness Church believes in justification by faith as taught by Martin Luther. We believe in sanctification as preached by John Wesley. . . . Sanctification is a progressive work of grace as well as the instantaneous second work of grace" (Pentecostal Holiness Church). "Sanctification is the second work of grace. It is that act of God's free grace by which he makes us holy. Sanctification is cleansing to make us holy" (Apostolic Faith Movement).[20] Nor does this doctrine remain merely a theory. Very often, at least, Pentecostals, beginning with those coming from the lower levels of social status, are true and sincere seekers of some kind of perfection. W. W. Wood, after a careful research in the hill villages of the U. S. upper south, draws the following conclusions:

> My field observations provide abundant evidence that the Pentecostal adherent places great emphasis upon sincere seeking for spiritual blessings and holiness. At the altar, in the testimonials, in the informal discussions, this emphasis is apparent. A powerful struggle to defeat evil is likewise evident in personal testimonials, in the content of preaching, and in Pentecostal theology. Field

data indicate that the typical adherent is strongly motivated to reach the goal of Pentecostal holiness, the fruits of which are joy (even ecstasy), ethical living, control of aggression, brotherly love, and group unity in the church fellowship.[21]

The work of sanctification for Pentecostals may be twofold. Some conceive it as an instantaneous operation whose effects are not only immediate, but also have enduring—if not lifelong—consequences in the life of the individual. Denominations like the Apostolic Faith Movement, the Church of God (Tomlinson), and others are definitely in favor of its instantaneous character.[22] Experience has shown me that this concept is also widespread among a number of Pentecostals in the mission fields. Upon being questioned about the holiness they have received by joining the new denomination, they react as if they were already wholly possessed by the Spirit. Their endeavor in the future will consist, not so much in increasing as in keeping intact the blessing they have received. Other groups, among them the Assemblies of God, The United Pentecostal Church, the Church of God (Cleveland), and the International Church of the Foursquare Gospel, are more cautious or even admit the possibility of progress or the vigilance needed in the process of sanctification. "It is the will of God," say the followers of Mrs. McPherson, "that we walk in the Spirit, moment by moment, under the precious blood of the Lamb, treading softly as with unshod feet in the presence of the King, being patient, loving, truthful, sincere, prayerful, unmurmuring, instant in season or out of season, serving the Lord."[23]

Departing from the mainstream of Reformation, Pentecostals make a sharp distinction between justification and sanctification. The former, called also repentance and conversion, implies, together with the "godly sorrow and renunciation of sin," the remission of personal transgressions. It is produced "by the cooperation of divine and human activities." Some would ascribe it to water baptism provided its reception had been preceded by a "change of heart."[24] What sanctification adds to that "first work of grace" can be gauged from one of the most frequently quoted Pentecostal presentations of this doctrine:

> Justification is supposed to be the work of grace by which sinners are made righteous and freed from their sinful habits when they come to Christ. But in the merely justified person, there remains a corrupt principle, an evil tree, a root of bitterness, which continuously provokes to sin. If the believer obeys this impulse and wilfully sins, he ceases to be justified. Therefore the desirability of its removal so that the likelihood of backsliding be therefore less-

> ened. The eradication of the sinful root is sanctification. It is the cleansing of nature from all inbred sin by the blood of Christ, and the refining fire of the Holy Spirit who burns out all, when all is laid upon the altar of sacrifice. This, and this alone, is true sanctification, a distinct second definite work of grace, subsequent to justification and without which justification is very likely to be lost.[25]

The effects of this operation of the Spirit upon man are more sweeping than anything so far conceived by Christian theology. As we read in the *Manual of the Apostolic Faith Church:* "The moment any soul will make a complete consecration, God will cleanse his heart. At that moment . . . the Spirit witnesses to your heart that the work is done. The root of sin is destroyed through the perfect offering of Jesus Christ. The very nature of sin is eradicated, destroyed by the blood of Jesus Christ, the Son of God."[26] Or, as explained by one authoritative writer of modern Pentecostalism: "We believe that the Bible teaches us that [after sanctification] sin has no more dominion over us because it is our privilege to live victoriously as we reckon ourselves dead indeed to sin, but alive to God through Jesus Christ, our Lord."[27]

How can this conviction of an almost sinless life co-exist with our daily experience? There are, indeed, Pentecostals who as individuals harbor serious doubts of its reality. However, according to F. E. Mayer, the majority

> emphatically declares that their evil inclinations do not come from within, but are entirely from without, "for the heart is made pure, the enemies are without, and the fort-royal is all friendly to the king." And since the temptations allegedly are all from outside (in the main from Satan), and the "saint" overcomes them, therefore God can credit him with an obedience all the more pleasing because temptations have been so strong.[28]

Sanctification is also effected "directly by Christ without any of the self-imposed deprivations used by Hindus and Catholics alike." In the words of one of their leaders:

> The divine means of sanctification are the blood of Christ, the Holy Spirit, and the word of God. The first provides primarily absolute and positional sanctification—it is a finished work which gives the penitent a perfect position in relation with God. The second is internal, effecting the perfection of the believer's nature. The third is external and practical, dealing with the believer's practical conduct. God has made provisions for both external and internal sanctification.[29]

The second effect of sanctification is the assurance one is given of final perseverance and eternal salvation. We here face a doctrine, originally Methodist, but largely employed nowadays by eschatologists and Pentecostals as one of their powerful instruments for evangelism. In the realm of salvation it implies the full confidence and guarantee that the believer is secure of his eternal destiny. Scolfield explains that assurance is the believer's full conviction that, through the work of Christ alone, received by faith, man is in possession of a salvation in which he eternally will be kept; and this assurance rests upon only the promises of Scripture to the believer.[30] Pentecostals see this doctrine "plainly written in the pages of the New Testament" in which "doubt in a regenerated heart is everywhere condemned," while "the Epistles glow with the truth that we may know that we already possess salvation." This certitude follows the reception of the baptism with the Spirit: "All those who are regenerated by the Spirit can absolutely be certain of their standing in grace. . . . Assurance comes as the fruit of the Spirit. . . . God desires his children to have a sky without a sunset or the uninterrupted assurance of his provision and protection."[31] To simple-minded, deeply religious but superstitious people, always afraid of the onslaughts of the enemy or of the ever-present demons, these Pentecostal ideas are simply irresistible. Herein lies one of the secrets of their success in African, Asiatic, and Latin American missions. Those people are overjoyed at hearing that, once they have received the Spirit, no trials or temptations will be able to snatch them away from God. Pentecostal preachers are likewise urged to insist on this consoling message. Williams says:

> It is unwise to dwell unduly on the perils of Christian life. The emphasis should rather be placed upon the means of security: the power of Christ as savior, the faithfulness of the indwelling Spirit, the certainty of the divine promises, and the unfailing efficacy of grace. The New Testament teaches a "true security," assuring us that, regardless of weakness, imperfections, handicaps, and outward troubles, the Christian can be secure and victorious in Christ.[32]

Second Baptism

Sanctification takes place during a "liturgy" that goes by various names: "baptism of the Spirit," "baptism of fire," or "second baptism." The focal point is always the contrast between the baptismal sacrament as commonly used by Christians (and referred to somewhat derogatorily by Pentecostals as "water baptism") and a far higher ceremony, reserved to the perfect and the few, which has been claimed by certain minority groups within the Christian community, as noted in a previous chapter. Strictly speaking, neither the names nor the practice are new in the life of the Church. The Gnostics in the early centuries and the Cathars in the Middle Ages believed in a type of holier baptism. The leaders of the left-wing Reformation, following Zwingli's steps and "fearing a magical and materialized conception of Christianity, kept the visible rite [of baptism] as distinct and separate as possible from the spiritual operation."[33] The tendency was picked up by the Baptist churches because it fitted with their ideas of "adult baptism" and a "gathered community." On the other hand, Methodism was not able to stop the trend simply because Wesley himself had rather confused ideas about the nature and effects of this sacrament.[34] It is also true, as Block-Hoell remarks, that "when the sacramental nature of baptism is not believed in, the separation of water baptism from Spirit baptism becomes almost inevitable."[35] At present, the main proponents of this "spiritual baptism" are the Holiness and Pentecostal movements. The question: "Brother, have you been saved?," so often heard from our Pentecostal brethren, refers to this unique moment in their lives. Baptism in the Spirit has also become perhaps *the* cornerstone of the beliefs of Pentecostal denominations. In some of them that experience is required as a *conditio sine qua non* for membership; in others it is at least a prerequisite for holding any responsible position in the church. One may, perhaps, be saved without it, but "one who has not yet had this experience does not have full consecration or full powers for service; hence without Spirit baptism one's Christian life is incomplete and one's ministry is hampered."[36] Such is again the official position taken by their Statements of Faith. The Assemblies of God say:

> All believers are entitled to and should ardently expect the promise of the Father: the baptism in the Holy Spirit and fire. . . . This was the normal experience of all in the early Church. With it comes the enduement of power for life and service; the bestowment of gifts and their use in the work of the ministry. This wonderful experience is distinct from and subsequent to the experience of the new birth.[37]

Among Pentecostal writers, baptism in the Spirit emerges (together with the speaking in tongues) as one of the specific contributions made by their followers to the universal Church. In the words of Donald Gee:

> Unless the Pentecostal Movement keeps loyal to this its own and special witness, it has nothing to offer . . . of particular value. . . . Pentecostalism must testify particularly to the baptism of the Holy Spirit. It is not distinctive [to us] to possess evangelical zeal; neither is it peculiarly Pentecostal to believe in divine healing. There is nothing whatever Pentecostal in contending for some particular form or idea of government. . . . The true Pentecostal revival offers a testimony to a definite spiritual experience based on the significance and story of the day of Pentecost. In that distinctive witness lies its strength, its vindication, and its value.[38]

The biblical foundations for the belief are: the prophecy of Joel quoted by Peter in his sermon on the day of Pentecost (Acts 2:16-18); the promises made by Christ to his apostles (Acts 1:4-8) and applied by Pentecostals to the whole Christian community; certain episodes in the primitive Church, such as the conversion of Cornelius (Acts 10:46); the imposition of hands by Paul on some believers at Ephesus (Acts 19:1-7); and the severe warnings of the Apostle to the faithful at Corinth for their abuses in speaking with tongues (I Cor 12-14). Needless to say, these texts do not convince non-Pentecostals; and A. A. Hoekema, of Calvin Seminary at Grand Rapids, Michigan, concludes that: "there is no biblical evidence for the Pentecostal doctrine that every believer should seek a postconversion Spirit-baptism which is to be evidenced by the initial physical sign of glossolalia."[39]

As a rule, the outpouring of the Spirit is received at formal Pentecostal religious services. Only of late have neo-Pentecostals begun to seek it in private homes, hotels, and theaters. Referring chiefly to the first group, two experts from Princeton University, Lapsey and Simpson, have noticed in the Pentecostal liturgies several categories of attendants according to their attitude and preparation for the reception of the Spirit. There is first the charismatic leader who fills the role of a teacher or of a spiritual father of the congregation, and "in semi-messianic terms" becomes for his listeners "a wonderful bearer of assurance of divine favor and liberation from the power of darkness." Then comes the secondary leader or helper whose main job will be exorcising, healing, or imposing hands on those who have received the Spirit. The third group is made up of the initiates, those who have already been blessed and now act as witnesses of the experience. At times they claim gifts of prophecy and interpretation, and always appear as sponsors of the new candidates for the "gift." Fourth, there are the anxious seekers, people already familiar with the doctrines but who, having failed on other occasions to "receive the Spirit," are now trying harder to bring him into their hearts. They are most in evidence among the congregation. The "jumping, somersaulting, dancing, hand-waving, jerking in various parts of the body," observed by W. Wood, as well as the prostrations, the singing and shouting one hears during the services, are some of the signs that the Spirit may be approaching. The last group is augmented by the merely curious, whose numbers may exceed those of the other categories. Most of them have been attracted by what they have heard from friends and acquaintances. They do not remain long in that group. After a few sessions, they either leave for good, or join the instruction classes as a preparation for the second baptism.[40]

Until recent years, there was practically only one set of religious services to "receive the Spirit," inherited from the founders of the Pentecostal movement.[41] That original pattern has not changed in Pentecostalism at large, and can be observed in the poorer sections of the United States, and among all the Pentecostal communities of Asia, Africa, and Latin America.[42] E. T. Clark has given a realistic description which re-creates what I have observed in many other parts of the world. The event takes place in a small Pentecostal chapel during an evening service:

> The congregation is composed of men and women from the lower ranks of culture. The evangelist preaches on the gift of the Holy Spirit, stresses the possibility and privilege of the Pentecost outpouring for present-day believers, relates experiences thereof, perhaps now and then he breaks out in ecstatic jabbering of strange phrases, and points out the barrenness of those who have never been so blessed. The enduement is held out as God's supreme grace.... All the tricks of rhythm are employed, and gradually the mass melts into what Pratt calls the "psychological crowd." For a more or less extended period, this is continued before the desired effect is secured.... At last, conditions become ripe. Seekers come forward in anticipation of the gift. Confessions are made. Excitement runs high. Various blessings in the form of emotional reaction are secured. Some cry out, others fall in trances or wave their hands and bodies rhythmically in near ecstasy. One feels unduly blessed and rises to testify. He begins speaking faster and faster, words fail, there is a muttering in the throat, and the subject breaks out into a flood of words that have no meaning to ordinary individuals. The Pentecostal power has fallen, the blessing has been received, hallelujahs ring out, persons gather about the fa-

> vored saint, and a wave of emotion, perceptible even to the unbeliever onlooker, sweeps the company like an electric charge.[43]

Of late, however, things are taking a new shape among the middle-class European or American Pentecostals, as well as among the wealthy industrialists and businessmen enrolled in organizations like the Full Gospel Business Men's Fellowship International (FGBMFI), who are ready to raise Pentecostalism from the humble status of its beginning to the more honored position required by the times. The case applies also to those individuals who have grouped around certain Episcopal, Lutheran, and Presbyterian pastors in order to restore to their communities "the charisms of the primitive Church." Among all of them the "receiving of the blessing" is done in different settings and by different methods. The religious services often take place in the ballrooms of plush hotels—in which the business conventions are held—while participants sip their morning coffee, or lounge in comfortable chairs listening to the testimony of those who have already been blessed. At a given moment, the emotion-filled audience begins to sing in the Spirit. Tears of joy flow from many eyes. People intone the hymn *Praise to the Lord,*which alternates with softly spoken prayers and ringing hallelujahs. A few speak with tongues while others testify to the healing they have received from the Spirit. The session is closed with a final prayer in which the leader (often an ordained minister) exhorts the group to "go forth in power." On occasion, true "miracles" seem to accompany those who take part in the gathering. An Episcopalian writer, John E. Sherrill, tells one of those amazing stories. The recipient was the wife of a Baptist minister:

> This lady had been born with one leg a full two inches shorter than the other, and all her life had worn a built-up shoe on that foot. On the night she received the baptism of the Spirit, she felt a burning sensation in this leg, but paid no attention in the intense joy of the moment. She sat for hours on a sofa, tears of happiness streaming down her cheeks. But when at last she stood up, she stumbled. The next step was the same. After she had tripped and hobbled the length of the room, she realized what had happened. Her short leg had grown two inches. The built-up shoe was making the legs unusual. The healing, she added that Saturday, looking down to two shapely shoes, was permanent.[44]

Of the two categories of religious services to "get the blessing," just mentioned, the first is by far the most common and, one might add, the only one which meets the approval of orthodox Pentecostalism. Our comments will therefore center on it, and only occasionally shall we refer to the services of the neo-Pentecostal groups.

In Pentecostal theology and practice, the second blessing constitutes the fulfillment of God's promises to mankind and the climax in the spiritual experience of the Christian.[45] Through this dispensation of the Spirit, they believe, Pentecostalism has been able to re-establish a very important missing link between the modern Church and "original Christianity."[46] Furthermore, the second baptism has become in their hands not only a powerful missionary weapon, but also an eschatological sign (in the sense of the Latin *signum)* that the days of the world are counted and the second coming of Christ, of which they are the heralds, is at hand: "While not minimizing," says Brumback, "the splendid achievements of contemporary non-Pentecostals, we thank God for Pentecostal baptism that has been the gateway through which have poured thousands from the farthest reaches of the earth. And it is our firm conviction that the effects of this mighty enduement are just beginning to unfold."[47] The baptism of the Spirit may be obtained "by tarrying in faith as the first apostles did, continually pressing and blessing." Its emotionally felt effects are: "love, joy, peace, long-suffering, gentleness, faith, goodness, meekness, and temperance." The Holy Spirit assists those whom he has blessed, guides them in personal matters, and even gives them "the ability to teach, to exhort, to be generous, to rule, and to show mercy." Enjoying a peace which no evil or temptation can destroy, Pentecostals believe they possess riches that far exceed anything this world can offer.[48]

To non-Pentecostals the doctrine and practice of the second baptism appear scripturally and theologically doubtful and its imparting to the candidates for the gift extravagant or shocking. The most severe criticism comes probably from one of the great German experts in *Konfessionskunde,* Konrad Algermissen: "Any normal person who has been present at a Pentecostal gathering when the Holy Spirit has been poured out, or has witnessed the baptism of the Spirit, the so-called speaking with tongues or the driving out of the devil, is bound to conclude that it is not divine but demoniac, or, at least, morbid and psychopathic powers that are at work.[49] Few who have attended enough of such sessions can be so apodictic. Many will probably continue to harbor serious doubts about the supernatural origins of the phenomena or try to find more down-to-earth explanations for them. They will also, together with some progressive Pentecostals, dislike jerkings, dances, and other bodily distortions of doubtful taste. "I consider it a heresy," says David Du Plessis, himself a prominent Pentecostal,

> to speak of shaking, shouting, and such like actions, as manifestations of the Spirit. These are pure human reactions to the power of the Holy Spirit, and often hinder more than help to bring forth genuine manifestations. There are far too many Christians who are satisfied with such emotional reactions and do not seek to grow in grace and to become channels through which the Holy Spirit may manifest his gifts for the edification of the Church.[50]

But unfriendly criticism, in addition to being usually unfair, only contributes to stiffen the attitude of Pentecostals who attribute such opposition to the schemes of the devil. In the words of S. H. Frodsham: "There is no doubt that the enemy of souls today hates this [Pentecostal] revival which is taking away so many from his kingdom, and is seeking to destroy the work in every way, to belittle it, and to bring it injury. But the more the enemy seeks to destroy, the more the Lord pours out his Spirit and continues to bless."[51]

An effort therefore must be made to evaluate the benefits Pentecostals derive from that conviction and to understand the special situation of those who seek God "in the Pentecostal way": the generally low, or even primitive, socio-cultural level of the seekers; the depth of their religious yearnings, never fully satisfied (or perhaps never adverted to) by the historical churches; the group pressures they have been subjected to by their leaders; the spiritual satisfaction, release of emotions and freedom from fear and damnation they have acquired in the new experience; and finally, the atmosphere of brotherhood and mutual help they have found in the new community after years of having been despised by other nominal Christians. All these count for their final decision. "Highly valued in Pentecostalism," concludes Wood, "are religious fellowship, absence of conflict, and contact with the Holy Spirit. Fervently sought after is a personal condition of holiness, a condition free from evil influences of Satan which can affect persons through misfortune or illness as well as through character and personality defects."[52] A more delicate issue is that related to the "abuses" and "moral turpitudes" which some observers have attributed to certain sessions for the second blessing. We know that, on occasion, excesses accompanied the revivals preached by Finney, Cartwright, and others.

> In the backwoods of Lincoln county, Herndon found people at revivals hugging each other and singing in ecstasy [songs] that were half-religious and half-sexual. . . . It became necessary to post guards to prevent affected couples from going into the woods. . .

. In their hysteria, some women threw themselves to the ground, tore open their clothes and hugged and kissed every one around them.... With some basis, but probably with unfair exaggeration, some cynics concluded that "more souls were begotten than saved."[53]

A few years before World War II the *China Christian Year Book* reported the existence of sexual disorders during the night-long Pentecostal meetings in some provinces of the interior.[54] There are sporadic indications of unbecoming conduct among certain African Pentecostal groups.[55] In Latin America I have heard from trustworthy witnesses reports of actions committed by certain native pastors which would certainly be disapproved by their parent churches in the United States.[56] From these instances—even if they are exceptions—one conclusion is clear: the urgent need for responsible leadership and responsible congregations. Illiterate and rude men, raised to ministerial positions on the sole merits of the baptism of the Spirit, cannot but show these and other weaknesses. Incidents of the kind reported contribute also to the low opinion that, rightly or wrongly, other Christians have of many Pentecostals and their leaders.

The last effect of the imparting of the Holy Spirit in the second baptism is seen in the charismatic gifts bestowed upon the receiver. It seems doubtful that Pentecostals have developed in a systematic way anything that could be termed a theology of charisms. They have, however, made a supreme effort to revive them and to show their relevance for contemporary Christianity. Pentecostals would accept the first part of the definition of *charism* given by Christian exegetes: "a particular type of spiritual gift which enables its receiver to perform some function in the service of the Church," "a visible sign that a new force, a new spirit" is at work in the world. But they will reject its "temporary character" or the "pretension" that charism was something that "did not endure once the Church was securely established in the communities."[57] Pentecostals accept the ninefold division of gifts: wisdom, knowledge, faith, healing, miracles, discernment of spirits, tongues, interpretation, and prophecy. Their reception is subjected to the following rules: (1) God is sovereign in bestowing them, and no human pressure can force him to grant the gifts; (2) God regularly requires in the recipient certain conditions, such as submission to his will, a holy ambition and desire to obtain the gifts for his service, faith that he will give them; (3) keeping these prerogatives intact, Pentecostals are convinced that God makes the gifts available, hence they cannot be considered a privilege of the few, but rather a property which, as far as the Almighty is concerned, may be shared by every true member of the Church.[58]

Of all the charisms with which the first Christians were endowed, Pentecostals make a claim to two or, at most, three: divine healing, and glossolalia (speaking with tongues) to which is attached also the gift of interpretation. The purpose of this restriction seems to be mainly missionary, in other words, the efficacy of these extraordinary manifestations to win new members to their churches. "In the heathen lands," says Gee, "the missionary is facing almost identical conditions to those of the early apostles. . . . But the healing of the sick does have a great power to arouse the indifferent, convict of sin, attract to the Gospel, and lead to genuine conversions."[59] The gifts also strike the imagination of the masses more than any other "testimony of the Spirit" and thus serve to prove the heavenly origins of the message given by the preacher. Yet the fact that charisms are enjoyed in our days by more people than at any other time—except that of the primitive Church—are a sure sign that the great day of Christ's victory is at hand, a thought which may not affect the lukewarm Christian but fills with unbounded exultation the members of the Pentecostal communities.[60]

Pentecostals realize the dangers involved in the actual exercise of the gifts and are aware that what Paul denounced at Corinth repeats itself too often in their own congregations. But they insist that "the pandemonium of Corinth was due to a lack of knowledge of spiritual manifestations" (Pearlman), and, more generally, they recommend that those who "are carried by the Spirit" never lose control of themselves but use common sense, be orderly in everything, and remember that the Holy Spirit, the great designer of the beauty of the whole universe, certainly will not inspire anything disorderly or disgraceful to the community of Christians. How far these prudent guidelines are followed in the actual operation of the gifts will be discussed in the next two chapters.

CHAPTER SIX

SPEAKING WITH TONGUES

Speaking with tongues (glossolalia) is the most dramatic and spectacular of all the signs in the Pentecostal movement. It is at the same time the "counter-sign" by which, for more than half a century, Pentecostals "have been ridiculed and often classed with pseudo-Christians and auto-soteric cults."[1] Pentecostals were not the first in modern churches to make use of it. The Great Awakening itself gave rise to manifestations of this type, and glossolalia became rather frequent during the revivalistic campaigns of Finney, Moody, Dowie, and Torrey. In the nineteenth century, "tongues" occurred among the members of the Catholic Apostolic Church (Irvingites) and in various Lutheran and Evangelical churches in southern Germany. In 1904–1905 the converts of the Welsh Revival, who ordinarily spoke little or no Welsh, sometimes broke into fluent Welsh prayers.[2] The phenomenon, however, remained uncontrolled, and only "in modern Pentecostal movements has a context been founded which was sufficiently stable to embrace glossolalia into theology, devotional practices, and church organization."[3] From a different viewpoint, glossolalia may be called a peculiarity of Protestant America. Kelsey writes:

> It is in the nineteenth-century United States that the speaking with tongues has come to its own and become a significant movement. In this country glossolalia is found among three different groups: among the Pentecostal churches; among certain fundamentalist communities; and, in the past few years, among the clergy of the large and well-known Protestant churches.[4]

But here a distinction must be made; among the fundamentalists and historical denominations glossolalia is not only an isolated phenomenon, but is repudiated by the communities as a whole, while for Pentecostals it remains one of the basic tenets and practices of the church. "It waited for modern Pentecostalism," comments B. R. Wilson, "before glossolalia was fitted into an ordered pattern of Christian life. Orthodoxy had always ignored the gifts, considering that they had been withdrawn from use, or accepted them as evidence of human faculties. . . . Pentecostal teaching has returned to a radical and revelatory explanation of the gifts."[5]

Pentecostals have often tested the faithfulness of their followers, as individuals or corporations, by their stand on the theology and practice of glossolalia. As mentioned above in chapter two, it was a controversy over tongues that sundered Pentecostals from the Holiness denominations. The latter were not, on principle, opposed to glossolalia and many of their preachers made full use of the "angelic language," generally in their evangelistic campaigns. But the Holiness movement was also quick to perceive the dangers inherent in its uncontrolled use, and thought the time had arrived to take a stand on the matter. The first move was the dramatic statement (1907) of A. L. Simpson, founder of the Christian and Missionary Alliance, that the manifestation of the Spirit of God could not be limited to one experience; he also advised his followers against the hallucination of thinking that glossolalia was the necessary or normal result of having received the second baptism.[6]

Following this, in 1919, the Church of the Nazarene purposely dropped the word Pentecostal. "This was primarily a move to disassociate in the public mind any connection with the other radical Pentecostal groups which taught or practiced speaking with tongues."[7] The third rebellion took place in the same years when one of the Pentecostal preachers, F. Bosworth, returned his credentials because he did not believe that all, once baptized in the Spirit, had to speak in tongues. The matter was taken to the General Convention of the Assemblies of God and Bosworth was expelled from its ranks. The resolution ran:

> This Council considers it a serious disagreement with the fundamentals for any ministry among us to teach, contrary to our distinctive testimony, that baptism in the Holy Spirit is regularly (but not *always*) accompanied by the initial, physical sign of speaking with other tongues as God gives utterance. We consider it inconsistent and unscriptural for any minister to hold credentials with us who attacks as error our distinctive testimony.[8]

The lesson was clear: Pentecostal belief about speaking with tongues could not be challenged. "We shall cease to be worthy of being called a Pentecostal Movement at all in the true sense," D. Gee wrote later, "if we cease to have any speaking with tongues in our midst."[9] And the Statements of Faith of their various denominations leave little doubt about this conviction. The few dissenting voices (especially in neo-Pentecostalism) could not prevail against the common trend.[10] To the Church of God, Tomlinson, "the receiving of the Spirit is always evidenced by the speaking of the tongues." The Assemblies of God affirm that baptism of believers "is accompanied by the initial, physical signs of speaking with the tongues." The International Church of the Foursquare Gospel teaches that baptism in the Holy Spirit "should be attested by tongues-speaking." Basically the Pentecostal Church of America, the Apostolic Faith Movement, the Pentecostal Holiness Church, and the Church of God in Christ share this same conviction. In the words of James L. Slay, the "preachers' preacher" of the Church of God, Cleveland, Tennessee: "Not only does the church believe that the baptism of the Holy Ghost is subsequent to a clean heart; we also affirm that speaking with other tongues, as the Spirit gives the utterance, is the initial evidence of the baptism of the Holy Ghost."[11] Latin American Pentecostals are known for their "lenguaje celestial," and the Brazilian "crentes" practice the same gift, although both these segments of Pentecostalism attach more importance to divine healing. Tongue-speaking, accompanied by "prophesying" and interpretation of dreams, continues to be one of the characteristics of African Pentecostal denominations.[12] What might be called the official stand of the movement was taken at the World Pentecostal Conference of 1952:

> Over and against all objections, the Pentecostal Movement affirms a baptism in the Holy Spirit accompanied, as at the beginning, with scriptural evidence of speaking with other tongues. . . . Even if very few groups avoid dogmatism on tongues as the initial evidence, the whole Movement is unanimous in affirming that baptism in the Holy Spirit is marked by an immediate, supernatural manifestation of the senses.[13]

The Nature of Glossolalia

The issue of tongues becomes more perplexing as we look for a definition of the gift or for an explanation that satisfies those within and without the movement. Etymologically, *glossolalia* derives from two Greek words: *glossa* (tongue) and *lalein* (to speak). Professor Behn, in Kittel's *Theological Dictionary of the New Testament*, defines the phenomenon as a "spiritually effected speaking" addressed "not to men but to God"; its value being "for the individual concerned rather than for the community"; an utterance of "mysterious words, obscure both to the speaker and to the hearers"; a speech of "inarticulated sounds as of an instrument played with no clear differentiation of notes," thus "leaving the impression of speaking in foreign languages."[14] It became a powerful instrument of spreading the Gospel and witnessing to the risen Christ in the primitive Church:

> Like other ecstatic phenomena in early Christianity, glossolalia is more than a tribute to the century of its origins. In the Spirit the young community learned by experience "that decisive experiences begin with a powerful act as with an upwelling spring." But the first enthusiastic surge quickly assumed fruitful forms of spiritual activity. Ecstatic egoism was harnassed to general edification [Paul]. We can thus see that the divine power of the Spirit did in fact rule in the community. Any subsequent phenomena of glossolalia in Church history can only be hollow imitations of this first springtime of the Spirit.[15]

In vaguer terms the *Encyclopedia Britannica* had defined glossolalia as "the abnormal or inarticulate vocal utterance, under stress of religous excitement, which was widely developed in the early Church circles and has parallels in other religions."[16] Pentecostals, of course, flatly reject any definition that attempts to equate their most precious and supernatural gift with a mere human and often abnormal phenomenon. Hence their search for explanations which will fit with the theological concepts they have already assigned to that blessing. Of a number of definitions proposed by Pentecostal writers, that given by W. H. Horton in *The Gifts of the Spirit*[17] is typical:

Speaking with tongues, he avers, is:

> 1) The supernatural utterance by the Holy Spirit, 2) in languages never learned by the speaker nor understood by the hearer; 3) it has nothing whatsoever to do with linguistic ability, not with the mind or intellect of man; but, 4) is the manifestation of the mind of the Spirit of God employing human speech organs; hence, 5) when man is speaking with tongues, his mind and intellect and understanding are quiescent, and it is only the faculty of God which is active; man's mind is certainly active, but the Mind that is operating is the Mind of God through the Holy Spirit; finally, 6) tongues speaking is a sort of miracle; the mentality is God's; it is a vocal miracle.[18]

Before we proceed further, a few distinctions are in order. Pentecostals find in the Bible three glossolalic experiences. One is the "sign tongue," given at the baptism of the Spirit; the second is the "tongue spoken in a meeting," usually interpreted by someone present; the third is the "tongue spoken in private devotions."[19] In world Pentecostalism—as well as in Protestant literature—the first and the second receive the greatest attention. The third appears to be, at least to a certain extent, an addition made by neo-Pentecostals to avoid the objections that have been raised against their brethren in the faith.[20] Experts distinguish also several modes of Pentecostal glossolalia. One of them consists of "inarticulate sounds or utterings"; another is made up of "articulate sounds or pseudo-language"; the third would correspond to "articulate and combined language-like sounds" (which some have suggested could be those of my native Basque tongue!); while the fourth is "an automatic speech in a real language," although unknown to the speaker himself and to the audience.[21] It is said that Pentecostals have made use at times of all four kinds.[22]

My own experience does not go further than those of the first and second type. The "languages" I have heard consist in completely unintelligible bubblings of sound and words which not even the Pentecostals around me (and some of them had already been blessed with the gift) were able to grasp. This seems also the conclusion of several experts who have studied the phenomenon in various parts of the world. Thus Douglas Webster, after protracted research of African Pentecostalism, writes: "We are bound to conclude that, almost certainly, the tongues are utterances in no known languages, and therefore untranslatable. The general gist of them, however, can be interpreted if someone is present with the complementary gift of interpretation."[23]

Here, again, Pentecostals would not agree with our version. Speaking with tongues, says Kelsey, "is a supernatural gift of a foreign, non-human language, given at the time of the breakthrough of the Holy Spirit into an individual's life."[24] Being a gift—a *gratia*—it cannot be obtained through human effort. "Do not make the mistake," Dalton warns, "of trying to work yourself into an experience or of struggling hard in prayer to induce God to give you the blessing."[25] "Such gifts," says Du Plessis, "are not operated; they are manifested by the Spirit. . . . They are his miraculous and instantaneous manifestations."[26] Or, as summed up by Conn:

> As on the day of Pentecost, God speaks with the tongues of those endued with the Holy Spirit. The unknown tongue is not the stammering of excited vocal organs, but rather the clear utterance of

the spiritual ecstasy. When the Spirit speaks through you, it will be exalted praise or convincing exhortation. It will not be dead, pompous, monotonous, or pointless verbiage. When the Holy Spirit wills to speak through lips of flesh, it will be in praises of exalted, errorless meaning, as the language of the Bible, for he is the author of it too.[27]

As indicated in the previous chapter, glossolalia has become for Pentecostals "a sign for them that believe not" as well as an instrument of conversion. Oral Roberts testifies to the efficacy of tongues for evangelism when he writes:

> Power to be witness to Jesus Christ is the basic purpose of the baptism of the Holy Spirit. This baptism provides an inner power that becomes an outward force to bring the reality of Jesus Christ to others. To help release this power, the Holy Spirit gives the believer a new tongue. This is one of the most revolutionary experiences that can happen to a believer.[28]

Glossolalia seems to Pentecostals to be among the "solidly-grounded" biblical doctrines. It is true that most exegetes part ways with them, but Pentecostals find no reason to falter:

> Most recent expositors and writers tend to give up as hopeless any attempt to account for the phenomenon of speaking with tongues on any grounds that could be palatable to modern lines of thought, and either dismiss the record as an illusion, or else attempt to draw spiritual lessons from it. Some of the latter are of value, but they do not justify a quiet neglect of the simple facts as given in the New Testament.[29]

Of these "simple facts," some are, even to Pentecostals, more convincing than others. In the four Gospels, only Mark (16:17–18) speaks of tongues as one of the "signs which accompanies missionaries in the work of evangelization," but this is an isolated text which cannot resolve the problem. Most of the Pauline writings are also silent about the gift. But, replies Pearlman, this is due to the fact that "their largely pastoral instructions were addressed to established churches where the power of the Holy Spirit with outward manifestations was considered to be the normal experience of the Christian."[30] The matter, adds the same author, "must be settled first by the Book of Acts which records many instances of people's receiving the baptism of the Spirit, and describe the results that followed,"[31] and by the rich glossolalic doctrine contained in the First Epistle of Paul to the Corinthians.

In Acts 2:4–21, the gift of tongues accompanies the coming of the Holy Spirit upon the Apostles. Likewise the "gift of the Spirit," mentioned by Peter (Acts 2:38) as destined to empower the apostles in their work of witnessing to the Gospel, should be applied to "tongues." "Since it is the business of the Holy Spirit to convict the world of sin, and since he operates principally through believers, it is imperative that he empower all believers in order to work through them more effectively."[32] The episode of the deacon Philip and that of Peter and John in Samaria (Acts 8:4–24) provide Pentecostals with another "key text." Glossolalia is not mentioned explicitly there; but they see the gift hidden in the bestowing of the Spirit itself.[33] For doubtful cases like this, Pentecostals have recourse to parallel texts, and they find one in the conversion of Cornelius and his household (Acts 10:44–46). "The instance of Cornelius remains a blessed proof that it is possible for God to sweep a new convert instantly into the fulness of the Spirit."[34] The criterion applies to what one author labeled "the most baffling of all passages in Acts associated with glossolalia," namely, Acts 19:1–7. Paul arrives at Ephesus to find a number of disciples who are completely ignorant of the Holy Spirit. He instructs them and, after baptism and the imposition of hands, the Holy Spirit comes upon them, and "they spoke with tongues and prophesized."[35]

We face similar problems with the Pauline concept of glossolalia in 1 Cor 12–14, "the only section," according to an author, "where this topic is discussed in detail." For Pentecostals the words and lessons intended by Paul are clear:

> At least three chapters of Paul's First Corinthian Letter are related to the use and abuse of the "tongues" phenomenon and charismata of spiritual gifts. If such spiritual endowments were to be only for those who lived in apostolic times, why would the Holy Spirit allow such information to be included in his work? Why should we be told in such precise terminology about the regulations of a gift if it were not in the plan of God for us to be given as much? Why tell the children of a pauper how to spend the inheritance of one who has left them nothing?[36]

The tendency among the commentators from the historical churches has been, very often at least, to play down the relevance of speaking with tongues in the primitive Church. They point to Paul's "marked ambivalent attitude" to that gift, or to its omission from the other list of supernatural blessings (Eph 4:11–12; Rom 12:6–8). The troublesome community of Corinth, they maintain (a true "problem child" for the apostle), could not be presented by him as a model community to the other churches. Cerfaux remarks that the Christian community of Rome, perhaps alarmed at the events in Corinth, preferred to ignore the existence of that gift. For these authors, glossolalia remains not only the last but also the least of the supernatural blessings and something useful only to those who were immature in the faith. Douglas Webster goes even further and asserts that: "Tongues are basically primitive, belonging to an early stage of growth and development among unselfconscious people with no advanced intellectual training."[37] Hence the conclusion: "One certainly does not get the impression that tongue-speaking is the *sine qua non* of mature Christianity, the gift which is indispensable for vibrant, personal devotion, warm and fervent intercession, or full-orbed victorious Christian living."[38]

And yet, these reticent and half-negative attitudes hardly solve our real problem or, for that matter, seem to square with the contents of the Bible narratives. Glossolalia played its role in the formation and religous life of the primitive Church. "Those wonderful manifestations," says Prat, "verified the prophecies, proved visibly the continued presence of the Holy Ghost in the bosom of the Church, and symbolized the great catholic unity and universality of the Gospel which was destined to speak all languages and to gather together all men in the profession of the same faith."[39] In the Epistle to the Corinthians, adds Cerfaux,

> Paul speaks extensively of this gift which is dissociated from baptism and takes place during the liturgical celebrations. . . . The gift of tongues held an important place in the formation of the Christian. . . . In the Book of Acts Luke has seen in it a symbol of the universality of Christianity which will be expressed in all the languages of the world. Paul does not point to such an idea. He accepts glossolalia as a fact in the Church and tries only to convince the Corinthians that it is something else than a spiritual sport for entertainment.[40]

Regarding the glossolalic passages of the First Epistle to the Corinthians, we are at an impasse. As already noted, the exegetes who wrote before the present-day controversy, usually tended to minimize the role of that charism in the life of the Christian, insisting more on its dangers than on its positive values. Under the present claims of Pentecostalism, both sides tend to be apologetic and defend the positions already taken by their respective churches. Ervin refuses to acknowledge that because glossolalia comes last in St. Paul's listing, its importance is thereby belittled. Paul's advice, "desire earnestly the greater gifts" (1 Cor 12:31), does not refer to the charisms, but to the order of offices such as "prophets" and "apostles." Again, "it was not tongues, it was teachers that introduced division into the assembly of Corinth." No one will say, he surmises, that Paul downgraded the value of tongues because he counseled restraint in its use. Ervin argues against the "arbitrary explanations" that have been given to this passage, and asks "a more sympathetic and objective appraisal than the critics of tongues have so far been willing to concede." "In summary," then:

> The evidence indicates that Paul did not depreciate tongues as a lesser charism. Used in private devotions, he thanked God for the full measure of the gift in his own life, for therewith he edified himself.... In the use of tongues in public worship, he counseled restraint for the sake of the uninitiated or the catechumens, and that all the other gifts might receive equal emphasis.... It cannot justly be deduced, therefore, that Paul simply "honed an ax" in these chapters against the gift of tongues.[41]

But those in the other camp are not moved by this reasoning and continue to claim that Pentecostal glossolalia cannot be based on solid biblical grounds. After a long analysis of the texts, Gromacki concludes that "the gift of tongues must be viewed as a minor gift which was necessary to the infancy of the Church, but which ceased within God's purpose when God's revelation was complete."[42] Staggs speaks of a "threat of tongues" against which Paul rebelled at Corinth. Glossolalia, he says, had become to the outsider madness, to the neophytes meaningless and at worst an argument that the Church was fostering insanity. The conduct of the speakers in tongues had become disgraceful. On the other hand, "it is not defensible to identify the tongues at Corinth with what Luke describes at Pentecost." Pentecostals should also remember that, according to Paul, the fruits of the Spirit were "love, joy, peace, patience, kindness, goodness, faithfulness, gentleness, self-control." "These are marks of maturity and purpose . . . not the confusing babblings of ecstatic egoism."[43] Regarding the contemporary scene, these opponents conclude:

> The modern tongues movement reflects a confusion and ignorance of Biblical doctrine. It has its basis in Arminianism and in spiritual immaturity. Many of their experiences simulate the crisis encounter of Barthian neo-orthodoxy. All kinds of doctrinal foundations are accepted by them as long as the person has had the proper experience.... Their emphasis upon extra-Biblical revelation and

phenomena (visions, dreams, healings, tongues) is unhealthy and contrary to the witness of the Holy Spirit through the Word. Their doctrinal concepts of the baptism of the Holy Spirit and the "latter rain" fulfillment must be rejected.[44]

For the time being, at least, the scriptural road seems to be closed. Both sides claim the same authorities: God's revealed word, and invoke the presence of the same Holy Spirit. It may be the basic question about glossolalia must be sought elsewhere: How do we know that, in God's providence, the phenomenon was destined to remain until the end of time with the People of God (at least with a number of individuals) as a living testimony of his presence among us? Pentecostals insist that Paul is on their side; that speaking with tongues was a common feature in the communities founded by him; that the limitations imposed on its use, while valid then and now, do not derogate the benefits derived for the individual and for the Church; and that, even in the Pentecostal tradition, love of God and neighbor always retain the primacy: "While the gifts of the Spirit," says Pearlman, "are important and should be coveted and given proper place in the Church and in the Christian's lives, yet love is far more important and must be maintained at all costs."[45] Here the answers offered by writers from the historical churches are unconvincing. To say, for instance, that Paul did not allow women to speak in tongues, while Pentecostals do; that tongues belong to a primitive stage in human history; that neither the Reformation nor the different revivals within the English Church knew glossolalia; or that in Christianity the first and imperfect manifestations of the Spirit have given place to a more quiet and disciplined method of prayer, thus interiorizing and perfecting the gift of tongues, are far from decisive. To Roman Catholics the living magisterium brings an assurance that this is not the ordinary way Christ wants his grace present in the Church, although our Protestant brethren do not share the same conviction.[46]

The Mechanics of Glossolalia

From scriptural "proofs" we turn to study the mechanism of glossolalia. First of all, let some prominent Pentecostals express for us their feelings with regard to this experience of Spirit-possession resulting in the speaking with tongues. The descriptions are often couched in terms that are hardly scientific, but, perhaps for that very reason, reveal better the original thoughts and the cultural-theological standards of the recipients of the gift. To the question: "What do you feel when you are prompted to speak with tongues?" the answers are:

"When the Holy Spirit fills a person, all his limbs are under His control, but mostly the tongue. This is the evidence that He has gained control over man: he begins to speak with tongues" (Mrs. McPherson, foundress of the International Church of the Foursquare Gospel). This infusion of the Spirit "is like a power within a person. It rises up within one and takes control of one's vocal organs. An utterance comes out which does not come through the mind. It is an ecstatic utterance" (J. R. Flower, Secretary General to the Assemblies of God). "When a man speaks with tongues, his inner being transfers from this area up here [the mind] to this area down here [the inner being]. One of our problems is that we try to think our way through to God by our argumentative minds; but, the more we think, the more we get involved in ideas and thoughts and theories, when the truth is: God is a Spirit and, as Spirit, he must be discerned. Our discerning center is our soul center, and probably it has a lot to do with the innermost being which is sometimes characterized as belly. It is perhaps in this inner being that God moves us when our intellect gets in the way" (William E. Reed, Episcopal minister). "It is significant that it is in the believer's innermost being that the desire to speak to God in tongues originates. In our deepest selves, where our needs really are, the Holy Spirit floods up like a mighty river and starts flowing upward toward God. Our objective thinking processes slip into the background for a few moments; and, out of heart or spirit, we begin to speak to God and as it comes to our tongue, it becomes a *new tongue* whereby our spirit speaks to God and is edified and released" (Oral Roberts).[47]

In recent years neo-Pentecostalism has entered the scene and some of its representatives have given more elaborate accounts of the experience. As a rule, the candidates in this category come from educated backgrounds. In describing the experience, their aim seems to be to prove to their contemporaries that Pentecostalism, far from being a despised religion limited to the fringe sectors of the population, can make sense and even fulfill some of the innermost longings of the men and women of the twentieth century. Few have succeeded in the attempt so well as the already-quoted J. L. Sherrill. He is describing his own experience in tongues. The event takes place in a room of a large hotel in Atlantic City, New Jersey. He is joined by other neo-Pentecostal friends who earnestly convince him that he should now ask for the gift of tongues. The group moves closer and closer to him "as if they were forming with their bodies a funnel through which was concentrated the flow of the Spirit that was pulsing in that room." They all pray, sing, and entreat the candidate to go ahead. The "tongues" will swell in a crescendo that is "musical and lovely at the same time." He opens his mouth and tries to speak. But nothing happens. Then they order him to look up, to raise his hands and to cry out with all the feeling in him a great shout of praise to God. And, lo:

> A hot, angry flush rose and flooded me. . . . I shouted: "Praise to the Lord." It was the floodgate open. From deep inside me, deeper than I knew voice could go, came a torrent of joyful sound. It was not beautiful like the tongues around me. I had the impression that it was ugly. I didn't care. It was healing, it was forgiveness, it was love too deep for words and it burst from me in wordless sound. After that one shattering effort of will, my will was released, freed to soar into union with him. No further conscious effort was required of me at all, not even choosing the syllables with which to express my joy. The syllables were all there, ready-formed for my use, more abundant than my earthly lips and tongue could give shape to. It was not that I felt out of control of the situation: I had never felt more truly master of myself, more integrated and at peace with the warring factions inside myself. I could stop the tongues at any moment, but who wanted to? I wanted them never to stop. And so I prayed on, laughing and free, while the setting sun shone through the window and the stars came out.[48]

There is no need to recount once again what Pentecostals believe about the "heavenly origins" of their speaking with tongues. The gift is rated almost as a first immediate step toward mystical union with God: "As we humble our proud spirits and allow the Holy Spirit to speak through us in a language unfamiliar to our rational minds, we are making a step of consecration towards God. We are allowing him to have his way with us rather than having our own way. . . . The relinquishing of our tongue to God is, then, the first step toward the Spirit-directed life."[49] They recognize that "untaught Spirit-filled believers sometimes bring confusion into public worship by the exercise of the unknown tongue" while their reactions "do not edify others." But, they add, "because misuse is evident in some is not sufficient reason for rejecting and turning aside from the blessing which the Bible reveals to be associated with such supernatural bestowment."[50]

Non-Pentecostals are not ready, as a rule, to accept such explanations. They discount the supernatural character of glossolalia and try to find for an experience which is certainly extraordinary (if nothing more) explanations based on theological arguments, on theories of psychoanalytic, or "demoniac" character, or in a combination of several of them. Most theologians deal harshly with these Pentecostal "pretensions." Here are some typical statements. "The theology of this 'gift of tongues' displays ignorance and perversion of Scripture. It subordinates the great facts and truths of the Christian revelation to the subjective experience of the Christian."[51] "This [speaking with tongues] is not due to human thinking, but is the consequence of an entirely different operation (diabolic possession)."[52] "The cessation of signs and wonders after the first generation of Christians has given occasion for counterfeit manifestations. . . . The usual belief that all supernatural manifestations arise from God gives Satan the opportunity to confirm in the minds of many his misrepresentations of doctrine."[53] "Modern glossolalia is in an entirely different category from the glossolalia of the day of Pentecost and true glossolalia in the Gospel in the Pauline age. It is not so much that I do not believe that God could not act along the same lines today. But for several reasons unknown to us, it would seem that God very possibly does not choose to act thus through the miraculous in these days."[54]

Recently, psychoanalysts have turned their attention to glossolalia. Their investigations should be welcomed on one condition, namely that they do not discard a priori any supernatural elements simply because they cannot be explained in purely scientific and experimental terms. G. B. Cutten, of Yale, was one of the first to study the tongues phenomenon from a clinical stance. Among other elements intervening in the strange experience he pointed to the following: hysteria and the ecstasy based on a lack of control; the taking over of the speech-center, not by the higher cortical centers, but by those controlled by the subconscious; the presence of visual and auditory hallucination; the tremendous power of suggestion the Pentecostal leaders have over the candidates to glossolalia. All these can result, after a protracted period of training, in the production of sounds that are unintelligible to the speaker and to his audience.[55] After Cutten, other experts have stressed further aspects of the phenomenon. According to A. Mackie, glossolalists exhibit "personality or neurotic disease, as well as an unstable nervous system." Andrew L. Drummond, who has studied glossolalia among the Irvingites, believes that the "speakers" fall into a kind of "hypnotic state" which, in turn, supposes "the loosening of control in the speech centers." As a consequence, "a subconscious which is soaked in religion relates the confused speech to religion, and the person feels motivated because the indwelling Holy Spirit is laboring to get free through him to others." D. Bess insists on the "mentally unhealthy climate of glossolalia" and sees in it "a great deal of unleashing of sexual energy, hysteria, exhibitionism, and latent psychosis." Elmer T. Clark attributes glossolalia to the excitement of the cerebro-spinal system:

> Persons given to these reactions are nearly all ignorant, in whom the lower brain centers and spinal ganglia are relatively strong, and the rational and volitional powers residing in the higher centers are relatively weak. Rational control is never marked in such individuals and it completely vanishes under great emotional excitement. They are reduced to something like a primitive mental and nervous condition. Impulsive feeling rules. The stimuli never reach the higher centers, but are stopped by the lower ones and shunted immediately to the muscles. In the cases of glossolalia, the subject breaks out in speech which is entirely divorced from thought, resulting in the jargon of unknown tongues.[56]

J. N. Lapsey and J. H. Simpson of Princeton Seminary, under clear Freudian and Jungian auspices, have also taken up the study of glossolalia, mostly among neo-Pentecostals. They notice among those who seek the "gift" the presence of "uncommonly troubled people" exhibiting "more anxiety and instability than non-Pentecostals of the same socio-economic background," even if the authors refuse to catalogue them as "mentally ill in any clinical sense." They are, moreover, "persons who have enough credulity to be able to reduce all their problems to the one global problem of the battle between good and evil." Pentecostals have also "an apparently universal concern with demons and demon-possession," and hence attribute "all kinds of difficulties, no matter how trivial, to the activity of the satanic power."[57] these authors explain away glossolalia in terms of Jungian psychoanalysis:

> If we regard the conflict as being due genetically to the unconscious attachment to parental figures, characterized by strong feelings of both love and hate, neither of which the individual can express directly, thus producing tension, then glossolalia may be viewed as an indirect, though powerful expression of primitive

love toward the parent, and the demonology a projection of the hate and fear in that childhood relationship.[58]

Thus glossolalia presents two facets from the psycho-motor viewpoint. On the one hand, it appears to be "like trance states, somnambulism, mediumship, and automatic writing in which the conscious centers of the psyche are bypassed in the production of these behaviors." On the other hand, speaking with tongues is also "like automatism in that it only involves a specific set of muscles, but like a massive disassociation in that it seems to come from *beneath* without ever having been consciously learned."[59]

Glossolalia is discussed at length by M. T. Kelsey, who introduces himself as a non-tongue-speaker, but as the Episcopalian rector in a Californian church "in which there is a group of tongue-speakers." "I have been able," he says, "to observe the practical results of glossolalia in my own parish and to assess the psychological development of many of those who have had experience both in glossolalia and in psychotherapy."[60] Kelsey makes a sharp—and a historically dubious—distinction between the Aristotelian-Thomistic concept of the Gospel and of the Church on the one hand, and "the attitude of Plato, the New Testament, the Fathers, and Eastern Orthodoxy and, in our times, of the Pentecostals" on the other.[61] With regard to glossolalia his mentors are Freud and Jung whose ideas about the unconscious, repressed memories, subliminal perceptions and archetypes he uses in order to prove the nature of Pentecostal glossolalia.[62] In Kelsey's opinion, "most of Jung's followers have sustained the view of tongues as a genuine invasion into consciousness of content from the deepest levels of the collective unconscious."[63] He finds this view confirmed by the studies done among South African Pentecostals by another Jungian, Dr. L. M. Van Eetvelt Vivier, for whom glossolalia "can be understood as an experience of theHoly Spirit" and as a "prime evidence of the reality of religious experience."[64] The rest of Kelsey's treatment of the problem is devoted to answering criticisms of speaking in tongues. Glossolalists have been labeled schizophrenics by Bishop Pike. Kelsey admits that "occasionally it does occur along with serious mental illness," but denies any but "casual relation between them," to conclude that "if any large number of the two million Pentecostals in this country who have spoken in tongues were schizophrenic, one would hear from them in public, because lack of control is one characteristic of this disease."[65] For similar motives he refuses to link glossolalia with hysteria which is "a sickness which puts the mind and often the body as well out of commission, while tongue-speaking is a religious experience which, from the evidence we have, seems to lead to a greater ability to function in the world."[66] On the contrary, he is more ready to accept the relations between glossolalia and the world of dreams: "The experience of tongues is automatic and one has no more conscious control of the words that come to his lips than the dreamer does of the image which comes to him. . . . Tongue-speaking is a kind of somnambulism while awake, a sleepwalking with one's vocal cords while still conscious."[67] This connection, however, is nothing to be ashamed of, since dreams have played such an important role in the Bible and in the life of the Church. Consequently, . . .

> if God (or some archetypal element of the collective unconscious) speaks through dreams, why not through a similar experience of tongues? The same significance can be attributed to tongues as is attributed to the dreams. A religion which values the dream can equally well value tongue-speech. And a psychology which sees the dream as a meaningful contact with the realm of the unknown will see tongue-speech in the same light.[68]

Interpretation

Pentecostals confirm the ultra-mundane character of the gift of tongues by another "scriptural blessing" found in the First Epistle to the Corinthians (14:5), namely interpretation. The gift was not very common at the beginning of the movement, but it was introduced in order to cope with the criticisms leveled against the indiscriminate and troublesome use of tongues. At present it forms an integral part in the teaching and practice of glossolalia. To Pentecostals interpretation is a gift of the Spirit and, therefore, supernatural in nature. It "comes directly from the Spirit"; it is "vastly different from ordinary interpretation"; it "does not imply the slightest natural knowledge by the interpreter of the language spoken in tongues."[69] Interpretation must also be distinguished from translation. The latter is "seeking to give the exact meaning of every word spoken; interpretation is giving the meaning or sense of the message as a whole."[70] In the category of gifts this one ranks highest. Many, according to Du Plessis, can speak in tongues, but few become good interpreters; many churches have more glossolalists than interpreters.[71] At the same time, interpretation may be very effective "when a person speaking in an unknown tongue under the power of the Spirit immediately follows this in the known language, giving the sense of the utterance in the tongue."[72] Some Pentecostals have almost equated interpretation with the infallible word of God, thus causing a real scandal among the biblicists in the fundamentalist churches:

> Interpretation is the supernatural power to understand and utter the significance of the mysteries spoken in diverse kinds of tongues. . . . It enables him who speaks in an unknown tongue to speak not only to God, but also to men. . . . Unlike tongues, interpretation involves the understanding, for his words are in a known tongue and thus it is clearly understood by the interpreter and congregation. . . . Interpretation does not originate in the mind of the believer, but in the mind of the Spirit of God. Even the words themselves are the result of an immediate inspiration of the Spirit rather than a calm selection by the interpreter. In this respect, *interpretation of tongues bears a resemblance to the manner in which the infallible* Word of God came into being.[73]

Our knowledge of the nature and techniques of this gift is minimal. The gaps may be due to several factors. Even in our days, mainly in mission territories, glossolalia is not accompanied by interpretation, or the latter consists simply in endorsing approvingly the preacher's ideas with joyful "Amens" and "Hallelujahs." On the other hand, the words by which its technique has been transmitted remain shrouded in poetic expressions like those of the foundress of the International Church of the Foursquare Gospel: "The next meeting where a message in tongues was given through the brother, I yielded to the Spirit who seemed literally to lift me to my feet and spoke to me in English the interpretation of the message which had been given in tongues. I was amazed how easy it was."[74] Unfortunately Sister Aimée was better known for her imagination than for the accuracy of her descriptions.

On principle, interpretation may take different forms. 1) After a person has spoken in tongues, the interpreter gives a comprehensive idea of what has been said. 2) The interpretation is limited to a general outline of the message given by the speaker. 3) The interpretation includes a number of sentences of the preacher's sermon. 4) The interpretation is done *verbatim,* in the exact words used by the speaker.[75] In actual fact (and here there is almost a consensus which, so far as I know, has not been effectively challenged by serious Pentecostals), "the two first forms of interpretation are the most common" (Bloch-

Hoell), if not the only ones. There is hardly anything as vague, commonplace, or matter-of-fact as the interpretations given by Pentecostals. Even Sherrill admits that "more often than not, it is a stereotyped exhortation 'to stand fast in the latter day,' to 'walk in the ways of the Lord,' " and similar expressions."[76] And D. Gee confesses that "usually, if interpretation is given, it is something which the preacher would almost certainly have said in the ordinary course of the sermon."[77] Perhaps for these reasons Brumback tells us that this gift is something like a free translation made "to catch the spirit of the original rather than its exact meaning." Hence, when judging interpretation, "we must not question its genuineness solely because it is shorter than the utterance in tongues. . . . Its purpose is to interpret the meaning of the mysteries. It is not necessary to translate literally the unknown tongue."[78] The difficulties non-Pentecostals experience in accepting interpretation do not arise from the shortness of the version given by the interpreter, but from the vagueness of its contents for which no special "gift" seems necessary.

The preceding discussion leads to a final point: What is the Christian value of glossolalia as practiced and taught by world-Pentecostalism? The assessment is difficult and cannot be solved by calling upon witnesses from one or the other camp. The attempts to prove "scientifically" the reality of speaking with tongues by appealing to psychoanalytic findings, convincing to some neo-Pentecostals, is flatly rejected by those of the older school. "Speaking with tongues," C. W. Conn says, "cannot be explained psychologically, but must be understood in terms of the supernatural."[79] On the other hand, the purely "experimental" testimony, especially when it comes from persons considered somewhat subnormal in their behavior, will not be accepted by those who reject its objective value. And to insist that all the benefits enjoyed by the Pentecostal faithful (peace of soul, transformation of their lives, a new sense of personal value and destiny) derive solely from speaking in tongues is to overstress the value of the blessing. The peace is a consequence of many other factors, among others the sense of community that the one who has been "baptized in the Spirit" finds among his brethren of the new faith. Kelsey has made an effort to evaluate the gains and losses that can be found in the phenomenon of tongues. He concedes that to non-Pentecostals glossolalia looks like an unattractive, irrational, automatic, non-conscious phenomenon that often intrudes upon the devotion of the congregation, hinders the worshipers, and gives the impression of being a meaningless gibberish.[80] "No wonder," he adds, "that the experience is viewed with such horror by most rational Christians."[81] The practice is also divisive and often leads its possessors to overzealous claims of power, or to despise those who have not been blessed by the same gift. Such self-conscious holiness has caused serious moral misgivings among certain leaders. On occasion, tongues have become a liability to physical health.[82] Nevertheless, in Kelsey's opinion, the advantages far outweigh the embarrassments: "All who have written of their first experience of speaking in tongues call it one of the most valuable and transforming experiences of their lives. . . . New doors opened in life. . . . They had been knocking, seeking, asking, and now they had found what they were looking for. . . . Everyone felt that his life had been changed, and that many fruits, both visible and invisible, came from the experience."[83] There are, moreover, in certain Protestant denominations "some people for whom the sacraments and belief of the traditional church transmits very little, or nothing at all, and these men and women clamor for life and some of them find it in the experience of tongues."[84] For these reasons, Kelsey rather injudiciously, in my opinion, sides with the glossolalists:

> Speaking in tongues . . . is a true Christian phenomenon. It is one entrance into the spiritual realm; by giving access to the unconscious, it is one contact with non-physical reality which allows God to speak directly to man. As a spiritual gift, it is given to some and not necessarily to others, is neither to be forced. . . . For one who has been caught up in a totally materialistic point of view, this experience gives a balance which only religous experience can give. . . . As a spiritual gift, it has value not only for the individual who speaks in tongues, but for the whole group. One of the greatest values of tongue-speaking is that it forces us to consider the possibility of direct contact with non-physical or spiritual reality. . . . Glossolalia can be a regenerative influence with relatively few dangers within a Christian community in which there is understanding of the mysterious spiritual levels of the human psyche and of the God who touches men at those levels.[85]

Even such a glowing interpretation of glossolalia, however, does not settle the matter. Other elements must also be kept in mind. Whether they solve the puzzle about "tongues" is more than can be said at this stage of research. We must first know, for example, more about Pentecostalism as a world phenomenon before we assess its values or shortcomings. As of now, our psychological and psychoanalytical knowledge of glossolalia reveals too many lacunae and is founded on too many suppositions to be called anything but embryonic. A further challenge is the closer study of the only level on which glossolalia is placed by the majority of Pentecostals: the supernatural. Bloch-Hoell, for example, after weighing his reasons against the Pentecostal position, admits that there "might in some cases be a demonstration of divine influence" in the speaking with tongues. But, for a Christian, these must fit into the framework of the Church. It is extremely hard to endorse as "Christian" a system that practically rejects the essential role of Church and sacraments in the life of the Christian. The scriptural proofs in favor of the continuation of glossolalia in the contemporary Church seem very shaky. Church history and tradition forbid one to accept such a statement as "every person who is baptized in the Holy Spirit will always signify this by speaking in tongues." Nevertheless, one must be impressed by the strong faith, the good works, the mutual love, and the missionary zeal of Pentecostals. Thus it may come about that, by ways that seem mysterious and puzzling to us, the Spirit may lead them to the unity he desires for all the children of the Father.

CHAPTER SEVEN

DIVINE HEALING

In Pentecostal theology divine healing has constituted from the beginning a new sign of the presence of the Spirit in the individual and in the community. C. F. Parham, for example, was called "the divine healer" and credited with "miraculous powers." In Galena, Kansas, he preached in January, 1904 for several weeks. "During the services," he recounts, "there have been as many as fifty people at the altar at one time seeking to be restored in soul and body. Here people who had not walked for years without the aid of crutches have risen from the altar with their limbs so straightened that they were enabled to lay aside their crutches, to the astonishment of the audience."[1] That early tradition remains solidly anchored among the leaders of the movement. As we read in the Minutes of the 1966 General Conference of the Church of God, Cleveland, "People will believe when the church fully witnesses to the power of Christ and his Gospel. Every healing, every miracle, every spiritual manifestation is a witness, a testimony to the power of Jesus Christ our Lord. We must continue to witness by miraculous works in order to be a full gospel church."[2] In Pentecostalism, concludes D. Gee, "There is no spiritual gift more frequently desired than the gift of healing."[3]

Pentecostals realize that this power has not always been evident in the Church. The Reformers in general were set against it and often accused the Church of Rome of attributing miraculous powers to its saints or shrines. Wesley, who was not against it on principle, had become convinced that Christians had lost these powers through "unbelief." Among Protestants the systematic teaching of the "Biblical view on divine healing" began during the last part of the nineteenth century. A. G. Gordon, the Boston Baptist and theologian; Andrew Murray, the saintly missionary to South Africa; and A. B. Simpson, the Presbyterian who founded the Christian and Missionary Alliance, may be counted among its forerunners. "It was not," concludes an author, "until the mighty outpouring of the Holy Spirit in this century that the number of witnesses became large enough to attract the attention of the general public."[4] Simpson's effort to give a theological basis for or even to popularize the doctrine was outstanding. He had blind faith in the power of healing:

> In spite of the cool and conservative and sometimes scornful unbelief of many, this doctrine is becoming one of the touchstones of character and spiritual life in all the churches of America, revolutionizing, as a deep and quiet movement, the whole Christian life of thousands. It has a profound bearing upon the spiritual life. No one can truly receive it without being a holier and more useful Christian.[5]

Simpson was also the first to take a pledge which has remained as an example to the other groups who practice divine healing. It read in part: "As I shall meet Thee solemnly on that [last] day, I solemnly agree to use this blessing for the glory of God and the good of others, and to speak of it or minister in connection with it in any way in which God can call me, or others may need me in the future."[6]

This heritage, taken directly from the Holiness denominations, has become one of the "cardinal doctrines" in Pentecostalism, and perhaps "the most widely loved doctrine of its churches." In the words of P. C. Nelson: "The Pentecostal people, one hundred per cent strong, accept the doctrine of divine healing, and nearly all of them have proved it in their bodies."[7] Your Pentecostal neighbor, adds Paulk, "is one of the strongest believers in God's power to heal today. Pentecostal churches around the world believe and practice the power of God to heal."[8] This position is fully endorsed in the Statements of Faith of the denominations. Glancing only at a very incomplete list, divine healing is officially endorsed by the International Church of the Foursquare Gospel, the Christian and Missionary Alliance, the Apostolic Faith Movement, the Church of God in Christ, the Pentecostal Church in America, the Church of God, Anderson, Indiana, the Fire Baptized Holiness Church, the United Pentecostal Church, Inc., the Assemblies of God, the Pilgrim Church, the Church of God, Cleveland, Father Divine's Peace Mission, the Catholic Apostolic Church, the Calvary Pentecostal Church, and others. The stand taken in this matter by Mrs. McPherson, one of the most "gifted" persons in faith healing, may serve as an example:

> We believe that divine healing is the power of the Lord Jesus Christ to heal the sick and the afflicted in answer to believing prayer; that he who is yesterday, today, and forever has never changed but is still an all-sufficient help in the time of trouble, able

> to meet the needs, and quicken into newness of life the body as well as soul and spirit in answer to the faith of them who ever pray with submission to his divine and sovereign will.[9]

It is true that divine healing has been played down, at least in practice, by a number of middle-class Pentecostal congregations in Europe and in America. The same may be said about neo-Pentecostalism among the wealthier groups in some of the historical churches. One gets the impression that both the affluent society in which they live and the education they have had incline them to put more faith in doctors and medicines than in the supraterrestrial remedies offered by the unsophisticated preacher who expects everything from above. On the contrary, faith healing is being raised to first place in missionary territories, above all in Africa. Lutheran Bishop Sundkler has said that while Catholicism offers grace through the sacraments and Protestants rely on teaching and preaching, some of the African independent churches look like institutes for healing. The appeal of the healing message springs from the social milieu where ill-health, malnutrition, and child mortality take a terrible toll.[10] "Faith healings," adds Hans W. Debrunner,

> by the laying on of hands and by prayer, wherever in the world these works are mentioned, act like a magic spell, most particularly in Africa. Illness is conceived in Togo as something evil, caused by demons. The wrath of an offended guardian spirit, or of one's own soul, can produce illness. But, even worse, people can become witches, i.e., their personal soul can detach itself from their body like a ball of fire and suck out the life-force of other people like blood.[11]

The leaders of the independent churches proclaim this prime purpose: "We are here to heal," said one of them to Dr. Baeta. "This is not a church, it is a hospital," answered one of the prophets of a Zionist congregation. R. C. Mitchel concludes:

> The truth of these statements has been borne out once again by experience. The direct healing of man's physical and mental illness by Almighty God, often without the use of medicine, either European or traditional, is proclaimed as of the essence of the Gospel and is perhaps the most characteristic of the Aladura or Zionistic type of the independent African Church. . . . The important and definitive aspect for this group *is not belief in a creed, but the experience of deliverance through a restored relationship with God in Jesus Christ.* The emphasis is more that of Luke than of John, of Acts [of the Apostles] rather than the Shorter Catechism

[of Luther]. This deliverance is claimed in the present, and the victory over sin and sickness is thought to be complete, not partial or ambiguous.[12]

To a lesser extent, the rule applies to Asia and Latin America. In Brazil and Chile divine healing constitutes one of the secrets of Pentecostal advance. "Physical healing," D. Gee concludes in a more general way, "often opens the door of the heart to the message of the Gospel as nothing else will do." Several historical churches realize this, and concern was voiced in 1963 by the Pan-Africa Congress of Christian Churches: "Healing," they said, "is becoming one of our grave issues. We have seen that healing in independent (mostly Pentecostal) churches stresses the reality of the spiritual world, the basic unity of man and the profound inter-relation of religion and healing, in a way which has met the previously unsatisfied needs of many African Christians."[13]

The Theology of Healing

Before we go further, it is useful to clear up certain basic concepts related to Pentecostal vocabulary on this matter. Pentecostals make a distinction between faith healing and divine healing. Faith healing, they say, takes place in the body of the individual because of his mental attitude or because of his faith. The presence of an outsider is not needed in order to win this favor from God. On the contrary, divine healing is a "direct work of God in the body of the afflicted." It is usually effected in response to faith, but in cases of insensibility, infancy, and so on, where there can be no faith on the part of the patient, God alone performs the cure. As a rule, a healer is necessary as the agent of the cure. Strictly speaking, therefore, Pentecostalism should accept only divine healing. We shall see, however, the insistence put by their most famous healers on the absolute need of prayer and faith in order to win the divine favor.[14]

Pentecostals adduce a variety of theological explanations for divine healing as they practice it. They fall under three main headings: 1) Disease is from sin and from Satan; 2) Christ atoned for our sins and infirmities, and his atonement is always available to us; and 3) Healing is a gift from the Holy Spirit and given to all those who surrender completely to Christ.[15] A few comments will illustrate these notions.

1. The nature of sickness has received much attention from their

writers and preachers and, in spite of slight differences, the basic concept is the same for older and modern Pentecostals. "Sickness is of the enemy." "Not God, but the devil is the author of disease." "Sickness is not a blessing but a curse." "God does not send disease; it comes through disobedience to the natural laws. . . . It may also come through the devil." "God willed happiness and health of mankind; the devil, as the enemy of God, desires our destruction and would put upon us all kinds of afflictions of soul and body." One could continue without end in the same vein. Two longer quotations, one from the early Pentecostal movement and another from a pastoral manual issued in the last years by the Assemblies of God, will show their stand:

> According to A. B. Simpson, sickness is named among the curses of Deuteronomy which God was to send for Israel's sin. Again it is distinctly connected with Satan's personal agency. He was the direct instrument of Job's sufferings, and our Lord attributed the diseases of his time to direct Satanic power. It was Satan who bound the paralyzed woman "for these eighteen years"; and it was his demoniacal influence which held and crushed the bodies and souls of those Christ delivered. If sickness be the result of a spiritual agency, it is most evident that it must be met and counteracted by a higher spiritual force, not by mere natural treatment.[16]
>
> According to Luke (13:16), it is Satan that binds God's children. God brings diseases to the ungodly. But nowhere in the word do we find him putting sickness upon his obedient children. Sickness is the result of sin. Satan is the instigator of sin and afflicts the sinner with sickness. No; God does not put disease upon his own; he removes it. Not only does he take it away, but in this verse he says it should be taken away.[17]

This is, indeed, a gloomy theology of Christian suffering, based on shaky foundations and repudiated by the whole tradition of the Church. Nevertheless it is a concept that finds a deep echo in pagan attitudes toward the sufferings of millions upon millions of innocent victims within and without the Christian fold. Pentecostals seem ready to exploit among the ignorant masses of the world such sufferings, attributed to a malevolent divinity and not seen as trials permitted for our sanctification by our Father in heaven.[18]

2. The "biblical proofs" to confirm the satanic origins of sickness and God's power to cure it are taken from the two Testaments. The choice of texts is always the same: one from Genesis, two from Exodus, another two from the Book of Numbers, and three each from

Deuteronomy and Kings. The Psalms and certain sections of Isaiah, interpreted in a spiritual sense by biblical scholars and constant Christian tradition, are understood by Pentecostals literally and applied to bodily disease. In the Gospels and Acts, Pentecostals dwell on the diseases miraculously cured by Christ or his apostles (and always attributed to the devil), omitting all the other passages that can harm their theories. Apparently St. Paul does not provide them with new evidence, but they are convinced that St. James is "on their side" since he does not recommend medicines or the help of doctors for the sick, but prayer and the laying of hands, so that by confession, "the Lord may raise him up." In conclusion, the Bible "clearly" teaches the following truths: "God has always healed; he promises to heal; he declares he does heal; he has made provisions for our healing; he sent his Word to heal us; he tells us to ask him to heal; he tells us this is his will; he says we ought to be healed; and, through Christ, he has already healed us."[19]

Thus, using Gospel truths which Christians have always accepted, but mixing them with many half-truths interpreted contrary to all sound exegesis and in a way contrary to consistent Christian tradition, Pentecostals are able to lay "biblical foundations" for divine healing and to conclude that "no man, church, king, or potentate has any authority to countermand the Lord's orders."[20]

3. For Pentecostals divine healing is the heavenly gift they receive at second baptism and is a consequence of Christ's sacrifical death. "Jesus bore our sickness. He has purchased healing for both soul and body. The sacrifice on Calvary was for our bodies as well as for our souls."[21] Some have warned their followers against an excessive assurance that they possess the gift or against the conviction that they can invariably heal all cases of sickness. "There are no indications that, although certain members of the early churches undoubtedly possessed the power to super-naturally heal, they therefore went around healing everybody without exception . . . because then, as now, there were only *some* healings."[22] But such voices are not heeded by the majority. The average Pentecostal member who has received through the Spirit the healing ministry that was once given to the apostles and to the seventy is persuaded that it is available to each individual in the Church. "Healing is not a fad, nor is it an idealism. It is firmly established by the word of God. If we belittle the word of God, we do so at our peril. To limit the Holy One of Israel is a fearful thing."[23] Healing should rather be conceived as a kind of participation in the healing power of Christ among those who have been blessed by his Spirit:

"When the soul is walking in harmony and obedience, the life of God can fully flow into the body. . . . The living, physical Christ must come into our life sharing his physical life with you in a union which is nearer than the connubial life, so near that the very life of his veins is transferred into yours. . . . The sanctified Christian receives the healing in Christ's body by faith and as he abides in Christ's living body."[24]

From these premises, Pentecostals proceed to define divine healing. As with glossolalia, they do it in two stages: one negative, namely, by showing what this gift is not, and another positive, by declaring its supernatural characteristics. Divine healing is not:

1. Medical science, "which can be learned by sinners who have never had the Spirit of God" (Grant); "God has not prescribed medicine" (Simpson). If medical science is good at all, "it gives glory to man, something that God will never permit." Even "medical missions" should be shunned. They are, after all, concerned with healing by natural means. Pentecostals cannot allow such achievements—magnificent as they might be—"to befog the testimony of the Scriptures." It is not:

2. A metaphysical cure, such, for instance, as the one attempted by Christian Science. This deals with disease from the natural point of view, and is anti-Christian in denying the reality of disease and even of the body of Christ. Mrs. McPherson was totally opposed to the cures of Mary Baker Eddy: "I would prefer," she said, "to be bedridden all my life than to be cured by such deceit." It is still less:

3. Spiritism, which must rather be counted as one of the inventions of the devil and, as such, reserved for the last days which will precede the anti-Christ. Seemingly it cures the body, but "the trouble only moves around over the body, leaving the patient possessed with many more troubles than at the beginning, and bringing him to an early death." It is not, at least for orthodox Pentecostals:

4. *Healing prayer.* Hence their followers are reminded that the only effective prayer is that of Christ himself; that it is Christ in person who comes to the sick with his holy touch, and that, consequently, it is neither the human healer nor his prayer, but Christ who "directly" does the healing. "It is always God and God alone who heals; therefore, the less you rely on prayer, faith, or any other means, the better prepared you are to receive the blessing."[25]

Pentecostals present their own understanding of divine healing in the following positive terms: "It is the divine and supernatural power of God overflowing on the human bodies, renewing its forces and replacing its sore members with the life and power of God; it is nothing else but the touch of divine omnipotence over us, that same power which rose Lazarus from the sepulcher."[26] Its purpose is manifold: "to deliver the sick and to destroy the works of the devil in the human body"; "to establish the resurrection of Jesus"; "to draw people within the sound of the Gospel"; "to convince unbelievers of the truth of God's words"; and to show the world "God's love for us." "The end," says D. Gee, "is the preaching of the Gospel of Christ and the kingdom of God, aiming at the planting of local churches where the converted are gathered to be established in the faith, and then, in their turn, become centers of Pentecostal evangelism."[27] Critics have at times accused Pentecostals of stressing almost exclusively the supernatural aims of healing to the detriment of that human compassion which was also present in the miracles and cures performed by Christ. Pentecostals seem to the historian akin to those spiritualists of the school of Origen for whom the human body was more a burden than a companion and a help on our earthly pilgrimage. We are in any case far from the authentic ascetics of the best in Christian tradition.[28]

Pentecostals, accordingly, engage in a running fight with modern medicine. At the beginning of the movement, the tendency was to forbid medical advice and service as something contrary to belief in divine healing. To consult a doctor was to betray a lack of trust in God, and vice versa, doctors were not needed when the all-powerful God had already intervened. At present, however, the denominations are not unanimous on the matter. Some continue openly to reject recourse to any medical care: "Doctors can be a great blessing to sick people; but the Bible does not say: 'go to the doctor when you are sick'; the Bible tells us to take our needs to the Lord in prayer" (Riggs). "We must most emphatically state that modern medicine is not the legitimate fulfillment of Jesus' command 'to heal the sick'; it is the negation of it. . . . Medicine and surgery is the world's way. God's way, the only way revealed in the Word, is healing by supernatural, divine power. These two ways are entirely opposed: medical healing is not, as some say, 'God's second best'; it is entirely of the educated world; God has no second best."[29] This trend is gaining ground among the Holiness and Pentecostal churches in Africa, where, according to J. W. C. Dougall, the situation is as follows:

> One curious feature which is common to many of these churches is the rejection of Western medicine. In Nigeria both foreign and native medicines are forbidden in these churches. . . . "Jehovah has revealed to me that I must not be healed by medicine, but only

through his word," said Shembe, one of the best South African Zulu prophets. To many of these Christians, dependence on medicine is equivalent to the worship of Satan. One of the independent churches in Uganda is called the Society of the One Almighty God. ... Its principal feature was its rejection of medicine for man and beast.... For Mugena, the founder, "to combine Christianity with medicine was to worship God and Mammon at the same time.... " His rejection of medicine insisted—whether rightly or wrongly—that this ideal had been distorted by a purely Western acceptance of the cult of health, "a cult which might readily oust faith in the One Giver of health." This rejection is all the more remarkable when we give due weight to the overwhelming effect of the white man's technical achievements on Africans and the insistence on health and hygiene in schools."[30]

Other Pentecostals are less apodictic. "Elim's [Foursquare Gospel Church] attitude towards the medical profession," says Wilson, "is not free from ambiguity. Officially it is never suggested that medical treatment is wrong, but the sick one is exhorted first of all to turn to God in prayer.... The ultimate choice is left to the believer, but the tenor of all commentaries is to urge believers to seek for divine healing first."[31] This seems to be the more common pattern adopted in modern times by Western Pentecostals, among others by the Assemblies of God, the International Church of the Foursquare Gospel, and the Church of God, Cleveland. This insistence on divine healing, comments C. W. Conn, "does not disparage physicians and medical science. God can and does work through human agencies. Medical science does a commendable work, but for those who believe, there is healing at the hand of God for every disease and affliction. God does with ease and readiness what other powers cannot do when we come to him in faith."[32]

The Healer

Almost every important Pentecostal church has one or more healers who, even though unknown to the general public, have a specific mission to perform within the community or towards neighboring Christians. Their "power" is not exercised in a permanent way, but only on particular occasions. Some are pastors or elders who have devoted their lives to the service of the congregation. In mission territories women also may perform the "gift," although exclusively among persons of the same sex. All these persons firmly believe they have been blessed with healing power in order to alleviate the corporal ailments of their fellowmen. They regularly visit the homes of the sick or the wards of hospitals, read the names of the afflicted during religious services, or lead to the altar those who have been already cured so that they may proclaim in testimony their thanksgiving to the Almighty. These healers have always given me the impression of being sincerely convinced of their vocation and of relying for their cures at least as much on the faith and prayers of the sick persons as on their own supernatural gifts. The healing is done by the imposition of hands, accompanied by imploratory prayers, the "handling of the handkerchief," exorcisms, and other techniques. As a rule, such healers shun publicity and are satisfied with the relief they have brought to others.[33]

Besides these individuals, Pentecostalism has professional healers: men and women who travel from city to city (or from country to country) to conduct healing sessions for large groups. Usually they work for some Pentecostal denomination, but may also be borrowed by fundamentalist churches in order to "warm up" their revivals. The presence of these healers is especially requested for evening meetings when everything (darkness not excluded) can make the sessions more dramatic. For years, Latin America has been one of the favorite showplaces for such performances.[34] The names of the successful healers are legion. Some are attached to regular churches and operate with the blessing of authority. Others prefer the way of free-lancers. In mission territories (especially in Africa) the healers may become founders of new denominations, and, if they are consulted by kings and chieftains, acquire great political influence and even succeed the rulers. "In the modern world," says Sundkler about Africa, "the influence of the chiefs is dwindling fast. Here is the prophet's (and healer's) opportunity, brought about not by calculating opportunism, but by the logic of events. When chieftainship falls into limbo, there follows a vacuum of power and authority, and the separatist church leaders step in."[35] A similar phenomenon seems to be developing in Brazil with Manoel de Melo, a former preacher in the Church of the Foursquare Gospel, and at present a successful healer who, through his *Tendas Divinas* (Holy Tents), has attracted the working classes of São Paulo and surrounding districts, and by announcing "miraculous cures" over the radio station, has become "the right hand of some of the great political figures of the country."[36]

In the West the number of professional healers greatly increased during and after the two world wars. Among the best-known figures we mention the following. Jack Coe is a Pentecostal who claims to have "the largest tent in the world" and publishes a magazine which goes into "hundreds of thousands of homes monthly." William Branham, the revivalist "called by an angel to the healing career," asks his patients to believe in him as a prophet. After World War II he visited South Africa and staged enormous healing campaigns in several of the big cities. Tommy Hicks has figured for a time among the most spectacular healers in the American continent. His favorite field of action has been the Southern hemisphere. Magazines reported that his Buenos Aires audiences had reached the 200,000 mark and quoted his presence as a further proof that "Protestantism was spearheading deep into the nominally Catholic countries South of the border." Mrs. Agnes Standford, the wife of an Episcopalian minister, is, according to one of her admirers, "the member of the laity who is wielding the most widespread influence on the revival of healing." Her books have gone into many editions. Now, together with her husband, she runs "a teaching center for spiritual healing . . . to help clergy and ministers to a better understanding of how they can aid their people in illness, depression, alcoholism, emotional disturbances, and guilt complex."[37] T. L. Osborn started his campaigns in Cuba and has carried them into Europe and the Far East. From his headquarters at Tulsa, Oklahoma, he has organized branches in many parts of the world and, through his magazine, *Faith Digest*, helps with money and preaching material the members of a healing group known as The Association for Native Evangelism.[38]

President Tubman, of Liberia, sent his personal invitation to conduct an "Inaugural Revival and Healing Campaign" to Ralph Byrd who, with his anointings and miraculous cures, has become one of the popular healers of that part of Africa. "God blessed him so marvelously that a presidential citation was read at the close of the campaign which rejoiced that God had used Byrd in 'healing the sick, restoring sight to the blind, causing the dumb to speak, the lame to walk, through the power of Jesus Christ, the Son of God.'"[39]

England and the Commonwealth seem to have become, after the United States, the promised lands for divine healers. Dorothy Kevin was, until her death in 1961, one of the great faith-healers of the Church of England. Having been miraculously cured from tubercular meningitis, she became conscious of a spiritual presence within her, and decided to devote her life to alleviate others. Bishops gave her favors and protection and in the year of her death presided over a special thanksgiving service at St. Paul's Cathedral, London. She founded a Chapel of Christ the Healer in a Kent valley where, under the auspices of the Burswood Fellowship, healing services are held regularly.[40] There is also in Great Britain a National Federation of Spiritual Healers, made up of members of different churches. Harry Edwards, G. Mowatt, Alex Holmes, Cameron Paddie, Margaret Lyon, and others appear often among its best-known healers. "Some time ago," H. Edwards states, "the BBC carried out an extensive national audience survey and, while its findings have never been published, it is known that ninety-three percent of those interrogated expressed belief in spiritual healing."[41]

No faith-healer, however, surpasses the popularity and wide influence of Oral Roberts, the Pentecostal minister of "miraculous" powers. His story has been told, by himself and his admirers, many times over. He was dedicated by his mother three months before his birth; bedridden and almost an agnostic at sixteen, he was cured instantaneously from tuberculosis and favored by a vision from Christ in which a Voice, the miraculous companion of his many wanderings, told him: "Son, I am going to heal you, and you are going to take my healing power to our generation." Finally, after much fasting and prayer, came the long "revelation" of God and his "anointing" to preach to the world the Gospel of healing.

The rest is contemporary history. Brother Roberts' headquarters in Tulsa, Oklahoma, occupy a fifteen-story building that matches any of those of the prosperous oil companies in the city. The Oral Roberts Evangelistic Association is a huge organization. Over 300 secretaries handle 150,000 letters a month—"fifteen thousand of which contain testimonies of having been cured by the healer." After a careful screening process, these letters appear in his magazine *Abundant Life,* with full-sized pictures of those who have been blessed by his action. Oral Roberts claims "the salvation of millions of souls in less than three years," and is in constant demand by Pentecostal and fundamentalist churches for revival campaigns. He is also the founder of a World Outreach Ministry, which aims at "winning a million souls every year." This purpose will, in turn, be accomplished by the training of young men (American and foreign) at the Oral Roberts University, also in Tulsa, and certainly one of the best-equipped educational centers of its type. This twenty-five million-dollar project, with a gigantic Prayer Tower in the center, has been completed thanks to the generous contributions of a number of American politicians and business leaders. The university will train young pastors and evangelists from the whole world who will be sent by Roberts as faith healers "to preach the gospel of deliverance for the whole man."[42]

The Techniques of Healing

In order to describe the techniques of these professional healers, I have chosen those of Oral Roberts. Few of the sessions I have witnessed in mission countries and in South America can compete with those conducted by him. But most of them display features common with those of Brother Roberts, and the ideal of the lesser healers is to have at their disposal the means of the famous healer and to imitate his secrets for attracting the masses.

In Roberts' campaigns the most important part is its preparation. The arrival of the healer is preceded by weeks of work on the part of experts who are in charge of the preliminary details. The preparation is two-fold. First, the anticipated audience (and even the whole local population) is keyed up to the desired psychological state. This build-up is often worked out in collaboration with fundamentalist groups more familiar with the local situation. For this purpose they make extensive use of the press, radio, and other means of communication. This propaganda pressure is often resented by some of the population, as can be seen in the letters to the editor printed in the newspapers. But the simple people who expect so much of the healers are on their side. Second, individuals who apply for reception of the healing during the religious sessions are "reved up." Here the directives given by Pentecostals are concrete: "All those who come for the healing line should be at the services several days to hear the Word of God, to see people healed before their eyes, and to hear the joyful testimonies of those who have been healed. . . . Those who come forward for healing should fast and pray before coming up and get everything distracting out of their minds."[43]

These precautions extend to the healing session itself which requires an excited, almost hysterical, audience. To attain it, congregational singing is specially recommended. The rest will be obtained when the healer himself tells his audience of the blessings other people have already received, and the greater ones waiting for those who are now stirred to hope. The healers are also known for their extraordinary mastery of the spoken word and make full use of it. "The healing sects," comments Scherzer,

> and their leaders appeal to the masses, and are ingenious in reaching them. They are successful in mass psychology and offer the people something tangible in the way of healing. They appeal to emotions and prepare their patients to expect healing. The masses

> are awed by the mysterious and dramatic, and overwhelmed emotionally by supernatural manifestations. They expect the Lord to do something extraordinary for them and regard spiritual leaders as individuals who have special influence with . . . the Lord who works through them."[44]

There is likewise a careful screening of the individuals who will be admitted for the healing. A little familiarity with the techniques of the sessions shows that the individuals who "take the line" are well-known to the organizers, while others are excluded or postponed. If the organizers forget this important detail, the healer is told which are the difficult cases in order not to lay hands on them. The reasons given for the refusal may be various: the patient requires "further personal attention," or "his faith is not strong enough for the blessing." This "gift" receives the name of "discernment."

> The healer does not ordinarily accept the rank and file of all cases submitted to him, nor undertake to heal them without discrimination, but a careful selection of the patients must be made. He regards some as improper prospects and culls the cases aside, working only upon the most promising and likely ones. This is why applications must be made in advance. The patients must be also personally interviewed and many are rejected.[45]

Pentecostals have drawn up a list of hindrances to or requirements for the reception of the gift. The conditions exacted in our days, as can be seen in Oral Roberts' book *If You Need Healing, Do These Things* (1965), do not greatly differ from those demanded at the beginning of the century by A. B. Simpson or Mrs. McPherson. They can be listed as follows: 1) "Know that it is God's will to heal you and make you a *whole* person" (Roberts). "You must be so sure that this is part of the Gospel and the redemption of Christ that all the teachings and reasonings of men cannot shake your faith" (Simpson). 2) "Remember that healing begins from the inner man" (Roberts). "Be careful that you are yourself right with God" (Simpson). 3) "Use a point of contact for the release of your faith . . . and release your faith now" (Roberts). "Act your faith. . . . Begin to act as one who has been healed" (Simpson). 4) "Close the case for victory. . . . Look up toward God and believe him every step on the way. Burn every bridge between you and the old affliction" (Roberts). "In receiving supernatural healing, the first thing to learn is to cease to be anxious about the condition of the body, because you have committed it to the Lord, and he has taken responsibility for your healing" (Simpson).[46]

On the other hand, the following *hindrances* indicate the causes why some candidates for healing are not cured. A person will not receive healing if he "consciously violates natural laws"; if he "is not willing to give up his sins"; if "he does not obey God"; or "does not want to live for the glory of God." Lack of blind faith may ruin the whole process: "unbelief will keep you away from getting the desire of your heart." Such will also be the case if "you listen to the devil's doubts and discouragements." Finally, "God cannot heal a person who thinks the time has come for him to die; when a person is in this frame of mind, he simply cannot exercise faith for healing."[47]

Pentecostal literature is full of narratives of healing sessions and sensational cures. It was probably S. H. Frodsham who led the way with his book, *With Signs Following* (1926), still widely read in Pentecostal circles. According to Gernster, "healing is one of the most conspicuous features of religion in the past decade," while Russell finds that "more material, both in articles and books, was published [on this topic] in any month in 1949 than in the last 50 years of the last century and the 25 first of the present."[48] Healers claim fantastic successes: everything from cancer, thyroid, blindness, lameness, goiter, peritonitis and arthritis, to dispepsia, paralysis, and ulcers seems to yield to their marvelous powers. The healing sessions reach their climax when, after long preparation, the healer shows up before his audience and makes the call, while those who want to be cured line up in order to receive the blessing, and put themselves under the powerful, and at times electrifying, influence of the "man of God." Let Oral Roberts explain for us this facet of the operation as it took place in one of his 1964 revival campaigns in India:

> In my message I told them of a vision seven years ago in which a man from India had appeared before me saying: "Oral Roberts, when are you coming with the word of God to India?" "I am here," I said, "in answer to that call for help. This is a moment ordained of God, therefore we can expect miracles and can see God work as never before. . . ." I could see flashes of receptivity on their faces, a new world was opening to them. . . . The next amazing thing was the call to the unsaved. . . . Literally thousands stood and for the first time received the Lord Jesus Christ. I looked at Bob and Tommy, both were in tears. . . . We had prayed about how to hold the healing services. What could three men do with crowds up to 50,000? . . . The Lord spoke to my heart to have the 1,000 pastors

> take up the stations in the audience and, as I directed them from the pulpit, to lay hands on each one. I told the audience what to expect and hoped for the best. It happened! A wave of prayer swept up like roaring waters, the power of God came like a shock of electricity. It was so strong on the platform I cried to Bob and Tommy, "It's like we'll be translated." Healing began to happen here, there, and all over, as wave after wave of the Spirit swept over us. In two hours we were through and still there was perfect order. Not a one demanded more. Tired, but happy, we returned to the hotel. . . . [Another day] there were people everywhere, in the stadium and all around it, sitting and standing patiently. I spoke on "Christ, A Mighty Savior from Sin, Disease, Demons, and Fear." Again another large response to accept Christ. In the healing service that followed, I was again deeply moved by the Spirit of God like in a tidal wave. A woman was so crippled she crawled on hands and knees, and was instantly straightened. A tremendous miracle! A man with a heart beating like a pounding fist in his breast, felt Christ say, "Peace, be still," and found his heart beating normally. . . . [Then] I began the last lap of my trip which had taken me more than 25,000 miles for souls and touched nine countries. Several thousand precious souls had accepted Christ, many others were healed, and vast numbers had heard the Gospel preached by men anointed by God.[49]

Such are the stereotyped narratives published by the great healers for the benefit of their readers and admirers. No hagiography of the past (even that of the medieval *Golden Legend)* contains anything to match them, either in the number of miracles performed by these "men of God," or in the glorious tones in which the performances are described by the thaumaturges. There is, however, a difference: the saints of the past used to hide themselves from the crowds and shun the publicity that followed their wondrous deeds. Oral Roberts and his associates have been accused by critics from European churches of displaying a typical American form of commercialized religion. One may wonder if that is the proper term. It seems rather that we face here a common Pentecostal pattern, even if it may vary somewhat according to situations.

Criticisms

As mentioned earlier, a full-scale verbal battle has been raging for some time between Pentecostal healers and medical doctors, who are usually supported by non-Pentecostal writers. The Pentecostal viewpoint is simple: the healers have been, in diverse ways, anointed by God and possess healing powers, not only as part of Christ's missionary command (Mt 28:18-20), but also as a sign of the last dispensation, namely, the second coming of Christ whose preaching has been especially entrusted to the movement. In this they follow the way of the Master which included liberation from sin and from all bodily ailments:

> There is only one way to reach the world for Christ today, and that is to bring this mighty power of deliverance to them by faith. We must have revivals to bring healing to the whole man. The power of God must fall upon us, the power of the Lord must be presented for our deliverance. The hurts and ills of humanity must find deliverance in our prayer of faith. Dare we fail God and the suffering people in this crucial hour of the world's need? . . . The only kind of revival conducted by Jesus, the seventy disciples, the deacons, and missionaries of the early Church was to heal men in soul, mind, and body. They did then. Why not now? Let us raise the roof of victory![50]

Others, while fully aware of "Christ's methods" and of the needs of our suffering mankind, are not so sure of the validity of such a simplistic approach. Most of them seem also to discern in Pentecostal healing certain elements that are hardly compatible with sound biblical exegesis and Christian theology, with the results of medical research, and, at times, even with sheer common sense. Here is the gist of the main objections:

1. It is not true that Jesus healed all the diseases he came in contact with. This principle must also hold true of his present-day followers. Consequently that "whole Gospel" which Pentecostals claim as their own must have a deeper meaning than the one they attribute to it. Moreover,

> the alleged scriptural argumentation for the healing theory is based to a great extent on the use of figurative language. . . . In most cases the word "heal" does not refer to physical but to spiritual restoration. . . . And, more basic still, faith healing ignores the true nature of sin and thus vitiates the true value of Christ's redemptive work. The demonic power which Satan exercises over men is not so much physical ailment as rather an eternal separation from God.[51]

Lastly, there are startling differences, if not contradictions, between the miracles reported by the Gospels and the healings performed by Pentecostals. The latter are often unsuccessful, liable to relapses, restricted to functional diseases, preceded by conspicuous build-ups and publicized to the four winds by the performers.[52]

2). Medical science is familiar with diseases that spring from psychic or psycho-pathological disturbances. In such cases of functional infirmities, Pentecostal healers, psychiatrists, spiritual directors, and gifted counselors can obtain results which, although astonishing to simple folks, do not fall into the category of miraculous healings. Many such ailments "are attributable to a neurosis.... We must also give due consideration to the dynamic force of such basic emotions as joy and fear. Such emotions can be engendered by endlessly repeating such refrains as: 'I come, I come'.... Crowd psychology is another valuable ally to the divine healers. The crowd not only restricts the individual's freedom, but also serves as a reservoir of individual courage."[53] Besides, many Pentecostal healings, when subjected to analysis and medical observation, turn out to be non-organic, temporary, superficial, i.e., not going to the root of the disease, or simply false. These statements can be confirmed by accurate medical records when they are available, a practice strongly opposed by healers, unless those who supply them have already been won over to their side. It can also be confirmed that the percentage of those who relapse is very high, and even Oral Roberts has reported that he would be glad if twenty-five per cent of his cases were permanently cured. As a matter of fact, it is rather common to find in the healing sessions men and women who were once "cured," perhaps by a less famed preacher, and are now back with the burden of their disease in the hope that this time the healing will be final.[54] In such cases, the action of the healer had "an anesthetic effect rather than a real cure."[55] Finally, "medical and psychological experts agree that strong and persistent suggestions and impressions modify the patient's functional dispositions. An abnormal mental state invariably affects the patient's metabolism and his entire physical condition.... Furthermore, a large percentage of ailments is attributable to neurosis. ... With these, we can understand the success of divine healers."[56]

Here we may close the account of divine healing among Pentecostals. Both theologians and medical specialists have a long way to go in order to solve an extremely complex problem. Neither the totally negative position (often taken by Protestants of the liberal tradition) that all miracles and healings ceased with the apostles in New Testament times, nor the excessive credulity of many popular sectors within Catholicism which have multiplied the number of miraculous cures, can lead in the right direction. At present, the concrete case of Pentecostal healings remains unsolved. The deeper one goes into a study of it the more confused one becomes regarding its supernatural claims. Those humble healers whose deep spirituality and love of God and neighbor are a shining example of dedication to suffering humanity are to be admired. On the contrary, the flagrant publicity-seeking methods of many of their best-known professionals make one suspicious of ways and means never employed by Christ or his saints, and it is impossible to see how Pentecostals can with such credulity claim many cures which, to the eyes of detached observers, seem faked or unfounded. Such stubbornness has impelled many to deny *en bloc* the plain honesty of their actions. At the same time, a Christian cannot agree with those who deny flatly even the possibility of divine intervention upon human diseases—a position often taken by the members of the medical profession.[57] We must admit that the Holy Spirit moves as he pleases and bestows his benefits even outside the institutionalized Church—or organized medical science. The Second Vatican Council has referred to those who "honor sacred Scripture, taking it as a norm of belief and of action, who show a true religious zeal . . . [who are] consecrated by baptism, through which they are united with Christ. . . . We can say that in some real way they are joined with us in the Holy Spirit, for to them also he gives his gifts and graces, and is thereby operative among them with his sanctifying power."[58]

Perhaps our Pentecostal brethren may be included in this description. In any case, the frontiers of the *au delà* are too distant for us to decide on a complicated case like this of Pentecostal healings.[59]

CHAPTER EIGHT

PENTECOSTAL MISSIONS: A SURVEY

The systematic missionary effort of the churches of the Reformation began only at the end of the eighteenth century. For various reasons missionary thought and effort remained from 1517 to 1792 something alien to the mainstream of Protestantism:

> Mighty as were the changes wrought, and far-reaching as were the influences exerted by the Reformation, it is to be borne in mind that the movement was not missionary in its character. It was a battle against ecclesiastical abuses, moral corruption, and the veritable heathenism within existing Christendom. And so absorbed were the Reformers with the struggle for freedom from the papacy, and with the establishment of new communities in the faith, and developing the church life of these, that the needs of the outside world were forgotten. Indeed there is abundant evidence that most of the leaders of the Reformation . . . seem to have had no serious sense of responsibility for direct mission effort in behalf of heathen and Muslim.[1]

During the last century and a half, however, Protestant missions have constituted "the most notable outpouring of life, in the main unselfish, in the service of alien peoples which the world has ever seen," and a "Christian-inspired effort to redeem life in its wholeness."[2] During this span, Protestant missions have witnessed periods of phenomenal growth, of stagnation, and of painful setbacks. One of their serious crises occurred in 1926–1932, and centered in China. The controversy affected the theology and missionary strategy of the sending churches, splitting them, as well as the missionary body itself, into conservative (evangelical) and liberal factions. As a consequence, says Bishop Sundkler:

> Traditional theological categories, such as "natural religion" and "general revelation" were re-interpreted and deprived of their eschatological elements. . . . The religions tended to be interpreted as manifestations of a deep-seated human instinct. The evolutionism of the late nineteenth century in its religious application regarded Christianity as the end and goal of all religious

> development. . . . The most fully developed of this liberal approach was that of the American theologian, William Hocking, in his much discussed book *Rethinking Missions*.[3]

We are not concerned with these issues as such. But it must be stressed that the crisis served to enlarge the gap between the fundamentalist and historical churches and their corresponding missionary societies. Moreover, the clear decline of missionary activity in the historical churches and the boom of conservative missions owe, if not their beginnings, at least their impetus, to the radical conclusions of the Fact Finding Commission which the historical churches had sent to the Far East. The conclusions became the guidelines to the older churches, and anathema to fundamentalists. At present, thirty-five years after the event, we begin to envisage the depth of the rupture: seventy per cent of the Protestant missionary endeavor is already in the hands of conservative denominations. Further, if this trend continues, the day may come when the burden of missions will have shifted from the main churches of the Reformation to the eschatological and holiness denominations.[4]

Pentecostals are among the late-comers into the mission field, and it is not accurate to say with Perkin-Garlock that Pentecostalism contributed to the beginnings of the missionary movement in the Reformation churches. Their work was on foot a century before the appearance of the Holiness and Pentecostal groups. On the other side, there is no doubt that missionary ideals found a well-prepared ground in the theology and the temper of the Pentecostal movement. As remarked by S. H. Frodsham:

> The Pentecostal revival has been decidedly missionary from the beginning. The Spirit-filled have heard the word of the Master: "Go ye into the world," and they have responded to this call. They went forth in simple faith, trusting God for all their support, and as a result, there have been gracious revivals in every part of the world. . . . The stories of the outpouring of the Spirit in different lands read, as someone has said, "like the twenty-ninth chapter of the Acts of the Apostles."[5]

Meanwhile, in the last four decades their progress has been simply fantastic. Pentecostal missions may be found in every corner of the earth. The number of their missionaries from the West, mainly America and Europe, has probably reached the six thousand mark, a mighty force when we recall that the forty million Lutherans in Germany contribute no more than a thousand missionaries to the field. In per-capita contribution to missionary support, Pentecostals rank among the highest. The Assemblies of God in the United States, with a membership of 508,602, gave to missions in 1961 more than six million dollars.[6] World evangelism is also becoming the test by which the "supernatural and charismatic gifts" claimed by their leaders can be recognized by mankind.[7] One may therefore understand the pride of certain Pentecostal writers at seeing what was often thought of as an introverted and provincial American revival that might have died in obscurity turned into a powerful, world-wide movement. "The religious world," Brumback comments,

> is well aware of the impact of the Pentecostal missions. A stubborn refusal in the past to print any news concerning Pentecostal advances has given way to a grudging admiration of the amazing growth of the Assemblies of God and other Pentecostal organizations. Periodicals, ranging from the most liberal to the most conservative, today publish eloquent testimonials from eminent churchmen who have found that Pentecostal statistics are fully confirmed by facts. In a number of countries the Assemblies of God is the largest Protestant church, and in association with other Pentecostal groups, the largest single evangelical force in the whole continent.[8]

If, as a working hypothesis, we assume for the over-all Pentecostal community some twelve to fourteen million followers, we must conclude that at least four-fifths of the total live outside the boundaries of the United States. Few other examples can be adduced of an American-born Christian denomination (or rather movement) which has attained, in such a short time, a similar world-wide importance. In early Pentecostalism, missions constituted a piecemeal undertaking often left to individual or group initiative. Some of the smaller communities still operate in this way, but the larger denominations long ago abandoned that policy. By 1915 the Assemblies of God had reserved to themselves the right to choose, support, and withdraw missionaries from the field,[9] and these rulings have been perfected and tightened in recent years. Among the Holiness denominations, the Christian and Missionary Alliance may be considered the most effectively organized. The Assemblies of God also have reached a high degree of efficiency. Through a powerful Foreign Mission Department "flow millions of dollars annually; materials and equipment are purchased for the fields, transportation is arranged for missionary families . . . missionary rallies and itineraries are scheduled, and missions are promoted in every way."[10]

There are two possible ways of analyzing the strength of Pentecostal missions: to survey the mission field country by country, or to look more closely at those territories where their advance has been outstanding, even spectacular. The historian is almost forced in the present conjuncture to choose the latter road. The Pentecostal movement as a whole does not run a central office for statistics or any clearing house where one may apply for information. Referring to Brazilian Pentecostalism, for example, W. R. Reed says: "Information about these active churches is difficult to get. They are so busy that they have not had time to bring their statistics up to date, write detailed histories, or explain why they are growing so fast."[11] Furthermore, when the task is left in the hands of native church officers, the material produced is often unreliable or even contradictory. However, there are a few world regions in which the Pentecostal advance has assumed such proportions that the historical churches, struck by the phenomenon, have begun to evaluate with all the means at their disposal the depth and characteristics of the thrust. These somewhat detailed studies provide us with a better picture of the meaning of Pentecostal expansion in the contemporary mission field. It is the method we shall follow in our journey from Asia through the Pacific Islands and Latin America.

The East and Middle East

The Muslim Middle East. Muslim Pentecostals have made strenuous efforts to penetrate the predominantly Muslim countries of this area. Numerous missionaries of the Assemblies of God were at work in Egypt before World War I and have been engaged ever since in educational (training schools) and philanthropical fields. The Assemblies, together with several Churches of God, are present in Lebanon, Iraq, Syria, and Israel. In some of these countries they have carried out extensive refugee work among the Arab population. Pentecostals, however, have never expended much energy in evangelizing Muslims, but have been able to attract a fairly good number of individuals from the deeply divided and extremely poor communities of orthodox (mostly non-Roman) Christians, a tactic denounced by the Eastern Patriarchs at numerous ecumenical gatherings. At present, most of the Pentecostal churches are concentrated in the United Arab Republic where the Assemblies of God have 138 places of worship and 15,000 members, while the Pentecostal Church of God, Cleveland, speaks of approximately 5,000 followers. In the other Near East countries, their congregations are negligible.[12]

China. The Chinese Pentecostals of the pre-Mao years had been recruited from the ranks of different Protestant denominations, chiefly the Presbyterian, the Methodists, and the Anglicans. Chinese Pentecostalism seemed to be deeply influenced by Buddhist and Taoist mysticism, and was marked by a primitiveness which, more than once, degenerated into excesses condemned by other Christian bodies. The provinces of Shantung, Kiangsi, and Swechwan were the most affected by the movement. There was a Jesus Family group, inclined from the beginning to communalism, which has in recent years easily been absorbed by the Communists who have presented it as a model of a Marxist-Christian "denomination." Others, like the Bethel Bands, devoted their time to public preaching and to the distribution of Christian literature. To win converts, Pentecostalism laid much greater stress on divine healing than on glossolalia, which was reserved for the more solemn religious services. Pentecostals never had a great following, perhaps because the Chinese have never been by nature inclined to emotionalism in religious matters. Since the Red takeover the outside world has lost track of the fate of Pentecostalism behind the Bamboo Curtain. Its missionaries, however, have continued their activities in Formosa and Hong Kong. The British Colony, with its unending flow of refugees, has offered them a particular opportunity to increase their total community to 15,290 people distributed between the American and Canadian Pentecostals, the Foursquare Gospel, and the Assemblies of God. In Formosa their advances have been more modest.[13]

India and Pakistan. Under the leadership of American, British, Canadian, Australian, and Swedish missionaries, Pentecostals have, since the early 1920's, challenged the historical churches at work in the Hindustanic peninsula. Pentecostal communities flourish mostly in southern and central India (Maharasthra, Andra Pradesh, and Kerala); there are fewer in the North (Calcutta and vicinities), and among the aborigines of the Northeast. Indian Pentecostals have shown contemplative and mystical tendencies in their approach to prayer. Tongues-speaking is not prominent, and easily gives way to the attraction of divine healing, especially, as seen in a previous chapter, when the country is visited by American healers of world fame. In recent years the leadership of the local communities has been in the hands of Indians, leaving to foreigners the overall planning and the extensive financial assistance. According to the last *World Christian Handbook* (1968), the most prosperous Pentecostal denomination in India is the Church of God, Cleveland, which has 35,932 members (a remarkable growth from the 10,000 of 1962); there are two Indian denominations: the India Pentecostal Church of God (30,000), and the Pentecostal Church of God, Andra Pradesh, with 20,000; while the Swedish Pentecostals have a membership of 26,275. The Assemblies of God have a following of 19,859 in the South and 6,571 in the North. There is also the Church of God with 15,000 members.

These totals, when considered in the light of the efforts made by Pentecostal missionaries, or compared with the results achieved by other Christian churches and denominations, are not spectacular. In the nation as a whole, the Pentecostal impact has been rather light chiefly because of its neglect of educational institutions. On the other hand, Pentecostals deserve praise for their work among the needy masses. Another extremely delicate problem is whether Pentecostals, with their blunt approach to evangelism and conversion, so contrary to the Hindu temper and the prevailing legislation of the republic, are in the long run going to foster the common cause of Christianity. Most missionaries of the historical churches do not believe so. Pentecostals have published glowing reports on "outstanding revivals" carried out among outcast Hindus and among the Muslims in East Pakistan, and have even spoken of the existence of 5,000 Pakistani Pentecostals. The sources at hand seem to be less optimistic. Between the Assemblies of God and several Churches of God, Pentecostals run 52 places of worship and have a total membership of 2,376.[14]

Japan. Here the task force of Pentecostalism came from the United States and Scandinavia. No great advances were reported before 1937, and the years of the push for "Greater Asia" and those of World War II brought the work to a standstill. The enterprise was resumed after 1945 and the Japanese response seemed encouraging. The number of foreign missionaries increased to 240, and the economic boom of the fifties seemed a good omen for the future. The best-known Pentecostal denominations are represented in the field: American and British Assemblies of God, the Church of God, Cleveland, the Pentecostal Church of God in America, the International Foursquare Gospel, and one Swedish and two or three Japanese denominations. Bible schools have been built for the training of converts and the preparation of native workers who have already begun to take over some of the religious and administrative responsibilities. The mushrooming of Japanese sects of every type, which in some of their techniques (for instance faith healing and ecstatic prayer) have imitated the Holiness churches, could have favored the prosperity of the latter. Yet the results do not confirm such hopes. The only denomination that fares better, and has even doubled its membership in the last eight years, is that of the Assemblies of God with 11,875 followers. The numerous other Churches of God have a membership of less than a thousand.[15]

Philippine Islands. Here we have a different phenomenon: a country with a massive population of baptized Catholics, and a fairly well established Protestant community. Pentecostals are represented in the archipelago by three main bodies: the Assemblies of God, the Church of God, Cleveland, and the Pentecostal Churches of God. Their main field of expansion has been the island of Luzon whose countryside, long neglected by the Catholic Church, is dotted by Pentecostal and Holiness chapels and elementary schools. Of late their work has been extended to Mindanao and Negros Occidental. The Assemblies of God claim 49,464 members; the Church of God, 6,281, and the Pentecostal Churches of God a thousand. Filipinos seem to be more attracted by their own brand of dissent, such as the very influential Manalo Church which, in spite of its charismatic features, cannot be included among the Holiness and Pentecostal bodies.[16]

Indonesia. Among the Asiatic countries none has been so ready to accept Pentecostalism or to produce an indigenous version of it as the former Dutch East Indies. The movement was introduced by two American missionaries of the Bethel Church in the island of Bali. From there it moved to Java proper where it was received and preached by Dutch converts. Growth was very slow before World War II. But the Japanese occupation of the islands unleashed religious forces and prompted the churches to put themselves completely under native leadership, a trend that continues up to the present. The arrival of a number of American Pentecostal groups after 1945 has not really changed the picture. In spite of their strenuous efforts, the Assemblies of God have only 10,141 followers, and the Pentecostal Church of God must be satisfied with a similar total. On the contrary, native Pentecostalism seems to be catching fire all over the country. It is represented by two main bodies: the Geredja Pentekosta di Indonesia with 250,000 members, and the Geredja Bethel Indjil Sepenuh with 150,000. Other denominations are the Sidang Aliah, the Geredja Pantekosta, and the Geredja Isa Aimasih, which serve an additional 500,000 members.[17] It is extremely difficult to check the accuracy of statistics provided by native agencies and coming from thousands of scattered islands.[18] Two things, however, seem clear: the rapid advance of Pentecostalism, and its almost total indigenization in leadership and finances. The following points have also been made to account for the rapid growth: the parallel advance experienced during the last decades by other churches in Indonesia; the spiritual warmth Pentecostals have been able to offer to candidates coming from the ranks of the rigid Dutch Reformed Church; and the rather common Pentecostal policy of permitting their new recruits to retain many ancestral elements (some of them religiously innocuous) regarding belief, worship, and moral practices.[19]

Oceania

Under this heading we include the Australian Commonwealth, New Zealand, and the numerous islands of the Pacific east of Hawaii. In the Australian continent, Pentecostalism does not seem to be a vigorous spiritual force. Several of its bodies were amalgamated in 1927. Ten years later they decided to join hands with the Pentecostal Church for a united action in order to map out missionary work among the aborigines, or in India and Japan. These hopes, however, have not been fulfilled. The *World Christian Handbook* lists only the 7,000 members of the Assemblies of God.[20] Relatively speaking, the results seem more promising in New Zealand where the Associated Churches of Christ have 10,585 members. Of the Pacific Islands, New Caledonia, Cook Islands, and New Hebrides yield no statistics on Pentecostal members; Gilbert and Ellice, Guam and Marshall Islands show communities of less than 500 members. The Fiji Islands have 8,562 members of the Assemblies of God.[21]

Africa

The study of African Holiness and Pentecostal movements remains today as fascinating and puzzling as ever. At a time when world-ecumenism is apparently on the move, Africa has become the home of the most fissiparous Christianity. Years ago Sundkler spoke of the existence of 2,000 separatist Christian bodies in South Africa.[22] But, as

Parrinder remarks, a similar fragmentation is taking place in other parts of the continent. "There are," says G. B. Gerdener, "sectarian outbursts all over Africa, and prophets everywhere, in whom a veneer of Christian truth is overgrown by non-Christian excrescences, including anti-white rebellion and animistic survival."[23] The latest survey contains "an analysis of *six thousand contemporary religious movements,*" a great percentage of which is of Christian origin.[24]

A puzzled historical Christianity has sought the causes of such proliferation. Here are some of the answers offered: 1) Almost without exception, the new off-shoots are direct descendants of the missionary churches.[25] 2) With a few and recent exceptions springing from Roman Catholicism, the independent sects have split off from Protestant denominations. According to D. V. Barrett, Anglicanism has given rise to 39 splinter groups, Presbyterianism to 37, the Baptist Churches to 32, Methodism to 22, and Lutheranism to 20.[26] 3) "Most of these movements are strongly based on a literal, uncritical interpretation of the Bible. Even the visions and dreams that spurred prophetic activity were usually based upon Scripture passages."[27] In other words, the denominations are a product of misguided personal interpretation of the Bible. 4) The reasons for joining the new churches are varied. In certain individuals it is the way to legitimize moral behavior disallowed by the Western Churches. Some want to practice an enthusiastic and evangelical commitment which was not allowed by the missionaries. Others are trying to escape from formalism and looking for a more immediate contact with Christ.[28] Many others feel the need of integrating religion with everyday life and work, and believe that this can be achieved more easily in their native framework than in the western way of Christian life.[29] 5) Among the immediate reasons for the separatist insurgence, Africans concur in blaming missionaries for their lack of acculturation and for trying to impose on their converts ways and techniques which, besides being foreign, only serve to delay their autonomy. "The greatest part of prophetic movements in Africa is the expression, even bloody expression, of economic and political revindication. At the same time they are the cause and consequence of the passage of a tribal conscience to that of a national conscience."[30]

The historian does not have at his disposal the means of discerning which of these separatist movements belong to the Holiness-Pentecostal family. The question cannot be solved by referring to those denominations founded and still financed by Western Pentecostalism. Nor can we be too strict in applying our standards of what the "essence" of

Pentecostalism is in its African off-shoots. Even in the matter of "charismatic gifts" we have no right to exclude those African groups which, while experiencing trances, do not regularly practice glossolalia, but accept divine healing, interpretation of dreams, prophetism, and other means of "proving" the presence of the Spirit among them.[31]

Well-known Africanists like H. W. Turner, Dom Guariglia, F. Koppers, and B. Sundkler are busy listing the separatist movements. A first division is made between *secessionist* and *prophetic* movements, the former being the result of the separation from an already existing church, the second the product of an outstanding personality known as the prophet.[32] A further classification looks at them from the viewpoint of doctrines, worship, polity, and ethos. Thus we have Ethiopian churches, i.e., groups in which the emphasis is on independence from any western influence, while retaining many of the pre-existing church patterns;[33] and the Zionistic or Aladura churches which stress the importance of ecstatic prayer among their followers.[34] Sundkler has described the latter as syncretistic movements in which healing, speaking with tongues, purification rites, and taboos constitute the main expression of faith. Their worship makes ample use of dancing, drumming, and hand clapping. Believers' baptism is stressed and the Lord's Supper is often omitted and seldom emphasized.[35] Their ethos is distinguished by "a morality which is often legalistic and rigorist, stressing the necessity of tithing, fasting, sabbath-keeping, observing the hours of prayer, and avoiding alcohol and tobacco."[36]

Although these characteristics closely resemble those of Western Pentecostalism, it is still hard to assess how many of the Zionistic African churches belong to the movement. Research to date hardly justifies general conclusions, although some groups are clearly identifiable. The African Israel Church, founded in 1927 by D. Z. Kivuli during an "outpouring of the Spirit," is certainly Pentecostal. Its Quaker-Holiness origins, its doctrinal tenets and liturgical expressions, as well as the charismatic gifts bestowed upon its followers during its noisy assemblies, make of it a model of what Pentecostalism can become when transplanted to a completely different milieu and allowed to absorb an unlimited amount of indigenous accretions.[37] Barrett speaks also of a God's All Times Association, founded by students in Addis Ababa, Ethiopia, which lays major emphasis on healing, exorcism, glossolalia, and evangelism.[38]

Grundler has also compiled a list of some ten African denominations which belong to this category.[39] On the other hand, African expert C. G. Baeta refers to three other Ghanian denominations: the Church of the Twelve Apostles, the Musama Disco Cristo Church, and the Ethodome Prayer-Healing Group which proclaim healing as their first concern and contain certain other Pentecostal elements.[40] Four of the Zionist churches in South Nigeria, the Christ Apostolic Church, the Christ Army Church, the Cherubim and Seraphim Church, and the Church of the Lord, stress divine healing, and practice in their liturgy "rolling, whirling around until one falls in dizziness" and the like.[41] Another powerful African movement, the Kibangu or Eglise de Jésus Christ sur la terre par le prophet Simon Kibangu, in the former Belgian Congo, displays a great number of Pentecostal features, including bodily shaking, prophecies, and healing.[42] The same may be stated of certain separatist movements in South Africa, the cradle and still the most thriving land of Zionistic churches. Unfortunately, the study and the cataloguing of these independent bodies is still too incomplete to allow us any definite conclusions.[43]

Regarding "imported" Pentecostalism, Africa's picture is similar to that of Asia. Generally speaking, the territories dominated by Islam tolerate little or no action by foreign missionaries. There are no statistics of Pentecostal work from Sudan, Morocco, Mauritius, Niger, Libya, Gambia, Guinea, French Somaliland, and even from Brazzaville in the Congo.[44] Swaziland has only one Pentecostal body, the Full Gospel Church of God. Other African countries with one Pentecostal denomination are: Senegal—the Assemblies of God, with 1,698 members; Rwanda—the Swedish Pentecostal Church, with 9,201; Madagascar—the Pentecostal Church, with 9,000; Malawi—the Assemblies of God, with 4,337; Mali—the Gospel Missionary Union, with 2,500; Ghana—the Assemblies of God, with 14,490. Lehshoto, Togo, and Dahomey—with the same denomination, with a total community of 22,043, of which two-thirds belong to Togo; Tunisia—the Eglise Pentecôte, with 20; and Gabon—the Eglise Evangelique de Pentecôte, with 1,000.[45] Most of these territories formerly belonged to French Colonial Africa. In contrast, Pentecostalism has advanced more in the old British possessions. Nigeria has six churches and shows, mostly in its Biafran sections, a large Pentecostal community of 132,000 members.[46] The Kenyan Pentecostal population is 137,000.[47] Rhodesia has four denominations, and there are groups in Tanzania, Sierra Leone, and Botswana.[48] Liberia gives shelter to several churches with 36,647 members; Burundi, whose Christian population is one of the highest in Africa, to 158,725.[49] Our information regarding the former Belgian Congo remains scanty and unreliable. According to official statistics,

Pentecostals there have 1,820 places of worship and 205,725 followers. But the Kibanguistic church boasts of having 200,000 members, and one wonders if, in the débacle of the latest political events, there have not appeared religious movements of the holiness and political type. The situation in any event is not clear.[50] For different reasons, our evidence regarding South Africa is also fragmentary. The most important Pentecostal bodies of foreign origin are: the Full Gospel Church of God with 141,000 members; the Apostolic Faith Church with 100,000; the Assemblies of God with 20,000; and the International Church of the Foursquare Gospel with 5,611.[51] Taking these totals at face value, or even adding the 200,000 members reported by the rapidly growing Zion Christian Church (in case this should be rated among the Pentecostal bodies) Pentecostalism would still not figure as the leading group among the three and a half million Christians enrolled in the South African independent churches.

On this note of uncertainty, due chiefly to the present lack of reliable information as to the character of the independent Christian bodies, the writer must take leave of Africa. On the basis of the *World Christian Handbook* (1968), African Pentecostalism has well passed the one million mark. The movement is taking deep roots in some of its countries, and becoming fully indigenous, even with the adoption of doctrinal and cultural accretions which remain totally unacceptable to most other Christian churches. Their existence, as a typical autochthonous African phenomenon, is composed of the following elements: 1) the central confession of Christ as Kyrios (using the vernacular term for chiefship) and of the Holy Spirit as the agent of man's healing and sanctification; 2) a marked resurgence of traditional African customs and world-wide views and of categories of morality which had been rejected by the Western churches; 3) a strong affirmation of their right to be both fully African and Christian, independent of foreign pressures; and 4) a new quality of corporate Christian life and responsibility, a *koinonia* of warmth, emotion, and mutual caring in the Christian community, together with a new philanthropy towards all.[52]

Latin America

A modern sociologist has predicted that "Pentecostalism, the youngest off-shoot of the third Reformation, has dealt a decisive blow to Catholicism in Latin America."[53] Metaphors apart, there is much truth in the fact that nowhere in the world has the Pentecostal thrust gone deeper than in that hemisphere. Its advance has overshadowed in a few decades the progress of all other historical Protestant churches and become, in union with other fundamentalist groups, the true representative of the Reformation in Latin America. Its indigenization process has not everywhere reached the same level, but the tendency is clear. Pentecostalism also presents to the Roman Catholic Church in this area pastoral problems of serious renewal which, however, go beyond the descriptive purpose of this chapter.[54]

Mexico. The main American Pentecostal bodies entered the Republic at the height of the religious persecution against the Catholic Church.[55] Their progress has ever since been uninterrupted and is marked by two features: the desire to reach the lowest and religiously more abandoned strata of the population, and the systematic effort to build up a truly self-supporting Mexican Pentecostalism. To attain this aim, it has made large use of Mexican-American converts, has established Bible schools for the training of native leaders, and organized a program of distribution of the Scriptures and religious literature. The most important Pentecostal bodies at work are: the Assemblies of God, with 630 places of worship and 39,948 followers (more than double that of 1962) directed entirely by nationals; the Church of God, Holiness, with 512 chapels and 33,542 followers; and the Church of God, Cleveland, which directs 377 places of worship with 33,480 members. The other Pentecostal denominations, the Church of God, Prophecy, the International Church of the Foursquare Gospel, the Pentecostal Holiness Church, and the Pentecostal Church of God, have a much more limited following.[56] Pentecostal work is concentrated in the poorer sections of Mexico City, Veracruz, Tamaulipas, Chiapas, Tabasco, Nueva León and Coahuila, and in the thousands of places in the hinterland which have for so long been deprived of priests.[57] Nationally, however, the Pentecostal impact is lighter than that of the historical Protestant churches; the 115,715 Pentecostals cannot compare with the 1,500,000 in the total Protestant community.[58]

Central America and the Caribbean. For unknown reasons this large area is bypassed by many chroniclers of Pentecostal missions. Nevertheless, its global importance, especially when added to the English-speaking territories of the Caribbean, far exceeds that of Mexico. Here are the highlights of their activities in each one of the republics.

Guatemala has 40,785 Pentecostals, more than half of them enrolled in the Assemblies of God. Neither the Church of God, Cleveland, where missionaries have seen "a miraculous duplication of the day of Pentecost," nor the Church of God, Prophecy, have fared so well. The large Indian and spiritually abandoned population offers Pentecostals a well-prepared ground for their action.[59]

Nicaragua is being worked by the Assemblies of God, which has the largest community, 4,939; the Church of God, Cleveland, which has been working through converts from El Salvador and the Dominican Republic has 2,709; the Church of the Foursquare Gospel is small, although its missionaries report that "in every place the Gospel is planted so that truly the heathen hearts are without excuse as the light of the Gospel is being spread abroad."[60]

El Salvador may be said to have been "invaded" by the Assemblies of God which have there no less than 1,088 places of worship and 41,291 members. To them must be added the 4,499 converts made by the Church of God, Cleveland, and the 10,000 assigned to another rather amorphous body by the name of Pentecostal Churches.[61]

Costa Rica. Here again the leading group is the Assemblies of God, with 3,600 members, followed by the Church of God, Cleveland, with 1,054, and a few other denominations. The Foursquare Gospel speaks of "outstanding revivals" and miracles witnessed as the Lord confirmed the Word with signs, but its community, ignored by the last edition of the *World Christian Handbook,* seems to stay around 499.[62]

Honduras. The outlook is as follows: the Assemblies of God have 459 members; the Church of God, Cleveland, 2,743; the Church of God, Anderson, 6,675; and the Church of the Foursquare Gospel, 1,000.

Panama. The capital's barrios have been from 1928, the year of the arrival of Dr. and Mrs. Arthur F. Edwards, the fief of the Church of the Foursquare Gospel. Signs and wonders, they are convinced, followed their ministry. From a tent they moved to a garage and later on to an old church building. The work continued with giant strides until they have now more than a thousand preaching points throughout the country. That church, the largest among Protestant denominations, has a total membership of 9,000, and is moving into the region of the Choco Indians for whom its missionaries have translated the Gospel of Mark. The Church of God, Cleveland, has a community of 1,000 members.[63]

In several Caribbean countries Pentecostalism is meeting with more than ordinary success.

Haiti. In this country the most rapidly advancing denomination is the Church of God, Cleveland. At one time, its chapels were closed by government orders because a visiting missionary had made derogatory remarks about the regime. But the persecution ceased in 1943 when the "people back home" aroused public opinion, and requested the U. S. State Department and several Senators to intervene in their behalf.[64] Now the church has 185 places of worship and 54,121 followers. The Church of Prophecy has also gathered 33,650 members into its fold. These two denominations are followed at a distance by the Pentecostal Church of God, with 9,000 members, and the Assemblies of God, with 7,050.[65]

Puerto Rico has been from the beginning a fertile mission for Pentecostals. The island is dotted with their chapels, and the initiative in administration has already passed into the hands of natives. The Assemblies of God report a total community of 35,000, and the Church of God, Cleveland, 17,505. The other denominations are represented by a few hundred converts. Nevertheless, in order to be fair, we would have to remember the presence of many thousands of Puerto Ricans who, mostly in the New York City area, but also in other great American cities, are active members of Pentecostal churches. Most likely they outnumber their Borinquen brethren.

Dominican Republic. The most active group here is the Assemblies of God with 341 places of worship and 10,436 members, followed by the Church of God, Cleveland, with 2,539, the Church of God, Prophecy, 2,000, and the Church of God, Anderson, 1,300.

Cuba had a sample of all the important Pentecostal groups of American origin, with the Assemblies of God on the top of the list. They have important mission stations in the poorer sections of Havana. But their most important activities are with the *campesinos* of the great sugar plantations.[66]

Others. Among the former or present British possessions mention must be made of Jamaica where the outstanding work has been carried out by the Church of God, Cleveland. At the beginning, the missionaries were too strict in demanding of prospective converts a life of holiness for which, because of their social and moral environment, they were not prepared. A change of policy brought better results and the membership has risen from 3,269 in 1935 to 67,598 at present. The Assemblies of God report 8,728 members. There is also an unspecified Church of God with 6,000 followers, and the Church of God, Anderson, with 3,480. In Barbados the Church of God, Cleveland, has 12,533 members. The total Pentecostal community of Trinidad remains at 7,854. Pentecostals are more numerous in the Bahamas: 40,124, with the Church of God, Cleveland, leading the way (18,130), followed by the

Church of God, Anderson, with 11,949. Neither Bermuda nor British Honduras have Pentecostal communities of any size, and the same may be said of the French colony of Guadeloupe. Nevertheless, adding the partial results of the just mentioned territories, we get for the Central American and Caribbean areas a total of close to half a million members of the Pentecostal churches.[67]

Andean Republics. Pentecostalism is at work in all of them. In Colombia the Assemblies of God report a membership of 5,731, the Church of the Foursquare Gospel, and the United Pentecostal Church an "estimate" of 20,000. The other denominations have a much smaller following.[68] The statistics regarding Ecuador are incomplete: the Assemblies of God with 556 members, and the Church of the Foursquare Gospel with 3,402 followers. The same must be remarked about Venezuela where certainly there are more than the 9,000 members assigned by the statistics to the Assemblies of God.[69] The pioneer work in Bolivia has been done by the Foursquare Gospel Church, but the results do not seem startling. Here the Assemblies of God (American and Swedish) have 5,680 members. The former run biblical institutes at La Paz and Montero. In 1960 they complained that national pastors had not yet experienced the "revival" of the Spirit. Peru has been specially cultivated by the Assemblies of God. They have stations in the outskirts of Lima as well as among the Indian population. If the information at hand is reliable, their progress has been outstanding: from 93 places of worship and 7,000 followers in 1957, to no less than 322 chapels and 26,264 converts. There are also other smaller communities. Briefly, Pentecostalism, with only 84,514 followers in a population of forty-three million baptized Christians, cannot be called a strong force.[70]

River Plate Republics. This is a region where Pentecostalism started its work at an earlier period of its expansion in Latin America. In Argentina the missionaries of the Assemblies of God were at work (mostly through Italo-American converts) from the beginning of the century. They have been joined by Canadian and Swedish missionaries. Their approach to the Argentinians has been carried out on a higher level, through Biblical schools, and with less emotionalism than in other countries. Even their liturgical services are more sophisticated than elsewhere in the Southern Hemisphere. It must be said that these efforts have met with success, as shown by their 417 places of worship and no less than 82,016 members. On the other hand, the Church of God, Cleveland, has gathered 19,424 members.[71] The Church of the

Prophecy and the Pentecostal Holiness Church have each a few hundred followers. The Church of the Foursquare Gospel, in spite of its glowing reports, has no more than 3,380 members.[72] In Uruguay the Pentecostal gospel has also been preached by the American and Swedish Assemblies of God. But their fruits have not been as rewarding as in Argentina: 3,000 members. The Church of God, Cleveland, claims a following of 4,332. These same denominations are at work in Paraguay. Much of their work is concentrated in and around the capital, Asunción, but some ministers are moving inland. The total membership is 4,512.[73]

Chile. The story of Pentecostalism in this country has been told by different authorities. We have the original version of Pastor W. C. Hoover: *Historia del Avivamiento Pentecostal en Chile,* 1931, and the more recent studies of R. Muñoz and I. Vergara.[74] Its initiator was an American missionary of the Methodist Church, W. C. Hoover, who at the beginning of the century was working in Valparaiso. Having read what the "Spirit" was doing in India, he suddenly felt the same call. In 1909 he summoned some of his "hermanos" for a meeting in his house where they began to pray for and received the blessing. Soon the congregation of Valparaiso and Santiago experienced strange reactions: the brethren danced, had spiritual visions, spoke in tongues, and prophesied. The Methodist authorities intervened and tried to call them to order, but the answer was that they had to obey the Spirit and not men. In the following year they were expelled from the mother church. They then formed a denomination which received the names of First and Second Methodist Church, both under superintendent Hoover.[75] The movement proved from the start to have popular appeal and expanded throughout the country. But its unity did not last long. Internal discussions split the ranks, pastor Hoover was accused "of vituperable conduct whose seriousness was beyond any doubt," while his colleagues were charged with ambition. That rupture of 1932 resulted in two denominations, the Iglesia Metodista Pentecostal, under Chilean pastor Umaña, and the Iglesia Evangélica Pentecostal, which remained faithful to Hoover. In time other separations occurred either from these two churches, from Methodism, or from other Protestant denominations. Here are some of the most important products of the splits:

1. The National Wesleyan Church, founded in 1928 by Victor Mora, a Marxist who believes there is no opposition between Marx and Christ. The church accepts baptism in the Spirit, but without consider-

ing it or the subsequent charismatic gifts essential parts of its tenets.[76]

2. The Evangelical Church of Emmanuel, with headquarters at Concepción, is clearly Pentecostal regarding charismatic gifts, mostly divine healing.[77]

3. The Evangelical Corporation of Vitacura has 10,000 members and follows the doctrinal statements of the Apostolic Mission, Oregon, U.S.A.[78]

4. Iglesia Pentecostal de Chile is a splinter group of the Methodist Pentecostal Church and fairly well spread through the country. Its congregations are made up of people of humble origin who are extremely devoted to the cause to which they often leave their modest properties in their wills. This was one of the Chilean Pentecostal branches accepted in 1961 at New Delhi into the World Council of Churches.[79]

5. The Iglesia Evangélica Metodista Pentecostal Reunida en el Nombre de Jesús had the same origin as the former church. The split took place in 1950. At the death of its founder, José Mateluna, the denomination had 155 places of worship and 60,000 members. But it has already suffered several internal disruptions, among others the Misión Cristiana and the Iglesia Evangélica Pentecostal.[80]

6. The Pentecostal Church of South Chile directs its activities from Valdivia, and is under the leadership of "pastora Berta," widow of the founder. It is a small but typical South American Pentecostal group made up mainly of *campesinos* and people of humble origin.[81]

7. The Iglesia Pentecostal Apostólica which works regularly among convicts in prisons.[82]

8. The Iglesia Pentecostal Apostólica, which in 1960 had 137 places of worship and some 60,000 members, presided over by "bishop" Arturo Espinosa Campos.[83]

The foreign Pentecostal contribution of Chile is made up of a number of American denominations. The Assemblies of God arrived in the country in the early 1930's and are organized into three districts. At Santiago they run a Bible school for the training of ministers and publish a periodical, *La Voz del Aire.* They sponsor campaigns of divine healing, have 60 places of worship and 6,064 followers. The Scandinavian branch of Pentecostalism has adopted in Chile the name of Asambleas de Dios Autónomas; it has 22 chapels and 4,500 members. The Church of the Foursquare Gospel arrived in 1945; it has two missionaries, 35 native pastors and 74 (or 17 according to other sources) places of worship, with a membership which varies between 905 and 1,800.

There is also an unspecified Church of God with 3,663 followers, and the Church of God, Cleveland, established in Chile in 1953 and purporting, if the statistics given are true, greater totals than all the other American branches taken together: 41,829 members.[84]

The attempts to evaluate statistically the true strength of Chilean Pentecostalism have not been, so far, very successful. Vergara speaks of 459,000; Coxill's estimates for 1968 are 700,000; in different publications it is becoming common to speak of the "one million" Chilean Pentecostals. One point, however, remains unchallenged: Pentecostals in Chile make up eighty per cent of the Protestant population of the country, and constitute a numerous, active, and proselytizing body.[85] Pentecostalism is there a popular movement, made up of the so-called "rotos," or tenant farmers, and lower-class workers in the industrial areas of the country. Few of their leaders have received higher education and still fewer are familiar with theology. Intellectual training has been shunned as a hindrance to the action of the Spirit, although at present there is talk of opening a well-staffed theological seminary, and even a Pentecostal university in order to prevent contamination by the State and Catholic universities. Doctrinally, Chilean Pentecostals have remained relatively untouched by the paraliturgical practices of the Catholic Church. They adopt the main tenets of Holiness and Pentecostal theology, but in practice they seem to be more indulgent in their interpretation. As in Africa, personal revelations and interpretations of dreams are taken seriously and have even been the *raison d'être* for new denominations. In a country so often visited by earthquakes, millenarist ideas are not given much attention. Glossolalia, accepted and practiced in all their churches, is not considered an absolute prerequisite for membership (some would say, not even for the pastorate), but becomes a super-added blessing for those who have attained perfection. Divine healing has retained in Chile much of the "precatory" character of the "prayers for the sick" in the Catholic, Orthodox, and Anglican churches.[86] The appeal of Pentecostalism to Chileans seems to be founded on these realities: the sense of *koinonia,* togetherness and belonging for the average member who, in the mother church, had been "condemned" to be a non-entity in the mass of believers; the experience of being filled with the Spirit and in immediate contact with the *Totus Alter* for men and women to whom a symbol-laden and ritualistic Christianity had ceased to be meaningful; the realization that, whatever their social status, Pentecostals have an apostolic role of witness and action to play with their countrymen; and, finally, the realization, attested by government officials, that the Pentecostal message can be an effective antidote against deep-rooted social evils (for instance, alcoholism) and an instrument for building an honest and industrious population.[87]

Brazil. The largest of all Latin American nations has also become the fastest growing Pentecostal section in the hemisphere. The glowing Pentecostal reports speak of people being saved, healed, and filled with the precious Holy Spirit who confirms with signs and wonders the message of the Word; and of indigenous churches mushrooming all over the country with revivals that call to mind those of the early days of the movement.[88] This description fits still better the branches of Pentecostalism we are now going to consider: the Assemblies of God, the Congregacao Crista do Brasil and the movement known as Brasil para Cristo.

The Assemblies of God. Their missionaries arrived in Brazil in 1934 and are at work in the states of Paraná, Guanabara, Espiritu Santo, Amazonas, Maranhão and Pernambuco, and in the great cities of Rio de Janeiro and São Paulo. Street preaching, together with a systematic house-to-house visitation, remain their best means of expansion, but they also promote a dynamic literature and print a multiplicity of books and leaflets. "Specialties are also radio, Bible schools for the training of lay leaders, city-wide mass meetings for evangelism which have been instrumental in the establishment of new churches, orphanages, and homes for the aged, day schools and medical dispensaries."[89] The Assemblies have experienced an amazing progress. In 1952 Monsignor (now Cardinal) Rossi assigned to them 2,382 pastors and native helpers, and a total community of 600,000, an increase of two hundred per cent from the time of their arrival. The statistics of 1962 spoke of 6,172 "workers" and 960,000 followers, of which no less than 650,000 were communicants. In the *World Christian Handbook* of 1968 the figures are: 4,250 places of worship, 19 foreign missionaries, 5,000 ordained and non-ordained native helpers, 1,400,000 communicants, and 1,700,000 members in the total community.[90]

Assemblies of God (Swedish). Two Swedish missionaries from the United States, Gunnar Vingren and Daniel Berg, came to Para in 1910 in order to conduct an evangelistic campaign.[91] Their publications have spoken of "miracles" to explain their fantastic Brazilian expansion. To the outside observer the so-called "Swedish Assemblies" are a puzzle. At times they seem to represent small American congregations of Swedish origin, but on occasion they are identified with the

Svenska Fria Mission or Swedish Free Mission.[92] In Brazil the number of their missionaries has always been small and consists at present of 5 ordained ministers, 14 lay men and 5 women. The church leadership is, therefore, overwhelmingly indigenous, which explains the rapid increase of the congregations: from 60,000 in 1942 to 450,000 in 1957 and to no less than 1,300,000 (800,000 communicants) for 1968. These Assemblies work principally at Rio de Janeiro, and in the states of Refice and Manaos. Those immense regions, where Catholic priests were not able to reach the faithful for a long time, have been the scene of ceaseless migrations of peasants who, drifting into the big cities, establish themselves in the large slum areas. Pentecostals have been at hand to meet them and to offer them the material and spiritual help they could afford. Their present success is to a great extent due to such Christian concern.[93]

Congregacao Crista do Brasil. In 1912 an Italo-American Pentecostal from Chicago arrived at São Paulo and began to preach the "gospel of salvation" to the thousands of Italian immigrants just settled in their new country. These had left on the other side of the Atlantic their families and religious ties, and had not been accompanied by their own priests on their journey to the New World. A hymnal in Italian provided the songs for the religious services. The message was well received and the conversions came in. Their numbers increased during the internal migrations of Italians from the hinterland to the cities. Francescone, who died in 1964, made eleven trips from Chicago to Brazil and remained the patriarch of his spiritual clan. Those who embraced the Pentecostal faith transmitted it to their children or spread it among relatives and friends. As the Italo-Brazilians of the second generation bettered their economic and social position, the Congregacao Crista became a middle-class Pentecostal church, a rather rare spectacle in South America. Its headquarters are at Bras, São Paulo, with a temple which has achieved the rank of a semi-basilica frequently visited by its devotees. They have mission stations in Minas Gerais, Mato Grosso, Bahía, and Goiás. Their religious services are a blend of Pentecostal enthusiasm (verging but seldom into glossolalia) and the exuberance of an Italian festival, including 100-piece bands, testimonies for favors received, petitions for graces, an apostolic blessing imparted by the Elder (anciao) and even a kiss of peace among people of the same sex. Much importance is given to water baptism for whose reception no instruction or preparation is required at all, only a confession of faith.[94] The members are permitted to "prophesy," and the church has kept the anointing of the sick which, with the laying on of hands, often takes the place of divine healing. What with all these peculiarities, some observers have wondered how pentecostal the Congregacao can be. The organization overlooks the Bible and stresses the role of personal inspiration. The church has no trained ministry, and the preaching is entrusted to volunteers whose zeal "is commendable, but often void of sound doctrinal orientation."[95] Hence the fears of Professor Léonard that, in a few generations, its members might drift into Spiritualism, the plague of contemporary Brazil. But the danger does not seem imminent at present. The Congregacao is growing: from a few dozen followers in 1910 to 45,805 on the eve of the Second World War; to 297,578 in 1960; and a total community of 700,000 in 1968. The church is organized on the basis of elders, deacons, and voluntary leaders whose services are taken care of by a special fund. There is no tithing. Its members have been impressed with missionary ideals, which may explain the vitality and progress of the congregacao.[96]

In addition to the "great three" in Brazilian Pentecostalism, mention must be made of some of the less powerful branches. Uppermost among them is the movement known as Brasil para Cristo (Brazil for Christ), started in the late fifties by Manuel de Melo, a former preacher of the Church of the Foursquare Gospel. He is a powerful orator able to sway the masses of São Paulo and surrounding cities. Melo has made large use of broadcasting and refers also to many "miraculous cures" effected through that medium. In the opinion of his admirers, he has already made more conversions than "all other evangelical denominations put together." His Monday night services in a storehouse which seats 5,000 have become very popular. Unfortunately, Pastor de Melo, who fights under the banner of anti-Communism, has become more than once the unwitting tool of shrewd politicians who use him not precisely for religious aims. Thanks to the generosity of friends and converts, he is erecting "the greatest Christian temple in Brazil" with a capacity of 25,000. The figures of his progress—1,600 places of worship and 500,000 members—have to be taken very cautiously.[97] The movement has retained some of the sensationalist aspects of Pentecostalism, but perhaps not all of its deep and sincere Christianity.[98] There is also a Church of the Renovation, formed by disgruntled Baptist ministers and lay people. Since they have already adopted a number of Pentecostal beliefs and practices, it seems that the new congregation can be numbered among the off-shoots of the movement.[99] A similar initiative is taking place among Presbyterians, Baptists, and Congregationalists of Rio de Janeiro who have founded a Church of the Restoration which emphasizes "prophetic dreams, utterances, and ecstatic pronouncements in tongues, regarded as a medium of revelation equal or above that of the Bible." The São Paulo Methodists are engaged in a biblical revival with special emphasis on divine healing. Some evangelistic bands, sponsored by the Church of the Foursquare Gospel, have started a Cruzada Nacional de Evangelizacao.[100] Three small Pentecostal denominations, Igreja Evangelica do Provo, Igreja Evangelica Crista Unida, and Igreja Evangelica das Maravillas, have amalgamated into an Igreja Evangelica Pentecostal Unida which is said to have 10,000 members. The Pentecostal Assemblies of Canada claim 5,000 followers, and the Church of God, Cleveland, a late-comer into the field, 4,257 members.[101] In 1964 twenty-five Pentecostal denominations, headed by the movement Brasil para Cristo and the Church of the Foursquare Gospel, founded a Federation of Independent Pentecostal Churches. Adding up all the Pentecostal churches and denominations so far studied, the Pentecostal force in Brazil would be close to, if not over, 4 million followers, of which at least 1,800,000 would be communicants.[102]

Our long, dry, and statistic-laden journey through mission lands thus comes to an end. It has, however, proved at least one thing: Pentecostalism is not a passing phenomenon in history and furthermore its advances outside of its birthplace have turned it into one of the most powerful and dynamic religious movements of our day.

CHAPTER NINE

MISSION AND ECUMENISM

The world-wide progress of Pentecostalism, the ready and enthusiastic acceptance of its message by millions, and the solid build-up of its structures require some explanation. We shall attempt this, although the available documentation is somewhat scarce.[1]

To the question: *Why be a missionary?* Pentecostals give answers worth recording as an indication of their religious temper:

1. Pentecostals have been called in the Church to proclaim the truth of the presence and action of the Holy Spirit, long forgotten by other denominations. "The baptism of the Holy Spirit, with its immediate manifestation of speaking with other tongues, is the basis of the entire Pentecostal contribution. . . . Restoring this experience to 'as many as the Lord shall call' was the purpose for which God raised this twentieth-century band of believers."[2] Hence "anyone who is filled with the Holy Spirit must be a missionary, not only in theory, but also in practice, with a purpose of heart to take the same light to those who sit in darkness and the shadow of death. This fellowship is and must remain just an agent to spread the Gospel to the ends of the earth."[3]

2. The spiritual needs of the world lead Pentecostals to action. Usually the world picture is drawn in the darkest colors so as to encourage members to work in the missions. "Our main task," says W. H. Horton, General Overseer of the Church of God, Cleveland,

> is urgent because so many are still without Christ. . . . Sixty per cent of the world has never heard a real Gospel message, and people of 1,789 languages have neither a Bible nor a missionary. There are six hundred thousand towns and villages in India alone that have never heard the footsteps of a missionary. Many are sitting in darkness here in America. Modernism, with its leadership of liberals and ultra-liberals, is making rapid inroads into the minds of masses of church-going people of today. . . . God help us to get the Gospel message to all the people as fast as possible, using all means and methods at our disposal.[4]

3. Pentecostals are driven by their belief in the imminence of the Second Coming of Christ. From a number of passages (e.g., Jn 14:13; Acts 1:11; Mt 24:44; 1 Cor 15:51; Rev 1:48), Pentecostals gather that "Christ is coming in an hour when people are not looking for Him; He will come like lightning, suddenly . . . as never before has there been so much distress, frustration, [so many] riots and revolutions as there are today." The saints in the Church know that there is only one way to escape these calamities: "the way of the Rapture." But this "has to be prepared by the preaching of Pentecostal salvation to the world."[5]

These are the ideals, but how does the average Pentecostal missionary compare with those from the historical churches? He is characterized generally by a blend of excellent virtues and of mediocre preparation. He is full of zeal for the salvation of "precious souls" which he considers lost unless they are brought under the influence of the Spirit. But his disregard for the "good elements" preserved by the other Christian traditions is absolute. *A fortiori,* he knows nothing of what modern missiology calls the "natural dispositions of pagans for the faith," or of the "anonymous Christian" who may be hidden in the pagan soul. The pagan is simply "the unsaved" who must be brought to salvation. The days are gone when Pentecostals would respond to the "call of the Spirit" and, without more ado, embark for the missions, but even now, at least in many denominations, the selection of missionaries fails to meet the minimal standards set by the boards of the historical churches. The theological preparation he gets at home is extremely superficial. In the mission fields his linguistic attainments have long been poor, although a more systematic effort is now being made to learn local languages before he is sent to the mission station.[6] Cultural anthropology (that much used and abused concept of our day) has little meaning to him. Pentecostal pastors and families remain aloof from the rest of the missionary body—even if the fault is not always theirs. To balance these rather negative characteristics, we must recognize some excellent qualities. Since neither his salary nor his standard of living are those of other American missionaries, the Pentecostal pastor is not seen playing tennis or golf in the company of affluent local friends. The people come to notice and praise this when they see him chatting with his neighbors, hurrying to the hut of one of his converts, or attending the sick who flock to his dispensary: as they remark in Latin America, this is a strange way for a "gringo" to live!

Missionary Strategy

Pentecostal missionary strategy, like that of most fundamentalist bodies, differs from that of the historical churches. The latter, at least generally, have understood Christ's missionary mandate as addressed to populations which have neither received the Gospel nor have been baptized in the Lord. Their missionaries in pagan lands have committed themselves (either by means of "comity pacts" or other "fraternal agreements") to respect the mission territories already "occupied" by other groups. The rule has been more widely applied in recent times as a sign of good-will among the denominations and as a preparation for the "comimg greater ecumenical church." Here Pentecostals are convinced that they hold a special position: as missionaries, they have been endowed with "miraculous powers" and may perform "marvels of conversion" where others have to rely heavily on "human instruments"; in their interpretation of the requirements of salvation, they have set the "baptism of the Spirit" as a goal which every individual must attain. The historical churches may acknowledge the "water baptism" of other denominations, or even the possibility of salvation outside their own fold. Such suppositions do not fit into the Pentecostal mold. As a consequence, their mission field extends beyond the horizons of paganism to all those communities of practicing or nominal Christians which have not received the "baptism of the Spirit." Most Pentecostal activities are carried on among those who, through baptism and profession of faith, already belong to some Christian church or denomination.[7] Pentecostals have accordingly been accused of "sheep-stealing" and branded as disruptors of the already badly shaken unity of mission lands.[8] The Pentecostal reaction has been swift and unequivocal. As stated by Brumback, it may be summarized as follows:

1. Pentecostal missionary work aims at the salvation of all men. But "salvation" must be understood as something indissolubly connected with the "baptism of the Spirit." There are, they say, only two classes of people: "the saved and the lost." Therefore God cannot be offended "if a *lost* soul is led to *salvation* and induced to leave a congregation pastored by an unregenerated man where no saving Gospel is ever preached."[9] Therefore, "international niceties that are observed at the cost of the eternal damnation of souls do not reflect the spirit of Golgotha."[10]

2. Given the dichotomy of *salvation* and *damnation,* the ecumenical argument loses much of its vigor for the Pentecostal. "Any attempt to persuade the believer to leave one good church and join another merely because of a minor variance in doctrine, ritual, or polity, should not be tolerated." It would be a clear case of "proselytizing." But this cannot be true when the problem is "to be or not to be filled with the Spirit." God cannot but add "his blessings to the testimonies and invitations of those who are seeking to lead believers into a full New Testament experience."[11]

The Pentecostal case, therefore, is clear, and their missionaries act according to principles they have held as basic for the interpretation of Christianity. If the historical churches continue to reject their claims and consider their missionaries and followers to be fanatics, the rejoinder is at hand:

> The so-called extremists of history, the men who have not always been possessed with the desire for balance, tolerance, and feeling for others, the men who have hammered on the theme—these are the men who have contributed that which is significant. Pentecostalists would have been "disobedient to the heavenly vision" if they had not been almost fanatical in their zeal to persuade believers to seek the fullness of the Spirit.[12]

With a few exceptions, the candidates for conversion to Pentecostalism are drawn from the lower strata of society. Their social and economic lot is not enviable: migrant farmers flocking into the great urban centers, or other uprooted people who have found refuge in the poorest sections of industrial conglomerations. Had they been reared in an agnostic milieu, they might have turned to Communism, but being deeply religious and practically abandoned by priests and ministers of the historical churches, they are overjoyed when they meet, possibly for the first time in their lives, men and women who greet them as brothers and offer them the salvific message of the Gospel. People like this need no pre-evangelization. Neither have Pentecostals anything that corresponds to a regular religious course or catechumenate. Some learn of Pentecostalism from friends or from reading their religious literature; others become acquainted with it in a more "existential" way: in personal conversation with the "brethren," listening to the emotional sermon of the pastor, rubbing shoulders with the members of the congregation or watching "the work of the Spirit" in their midst. The preparation need not be long; some have even advocated that it should be cut short lest the primitive fervor die before it has blossomed to the full. The candidates already possess a smattering of

Christian doctrine and continue some practices of the mother church. The theology of holiness and perfection, which could deter them, is made easy by insistence on the "work of the Spirit" as seen in the lives of their friends and acquaintances; glossolalia and divine healing are learned not by lectures but by experience.[13]

Observers search for the ties that keep Pentecostal converts strongly attached to their communion. One of them is, of course, the experience of the "baptism of the Spirit." However we interpret the phenomenon, there is no doubt of its effects in their hearts. The conviction that the "Spirit" is within him accompanies the Pentecostal at work, in church, and at home. To the outsider he may give the impression of being obsessed or "brainwashed," but he could not care less about such an opinion. Pentecostals have also found in their new denominations something of the attachment the ancient Fathers expressed when they referred to *Mater Ecclesia.* This sense of belonging, as a living member, to the Body of Christ, is an experience Pentecostals missed in their original churches. Two other peculiarities arise from this. The first has been described as "philadelphia" or "group solidarity." Its presence and effects have been specially noticed in tribal societies, but they can be also found elsewhere. Historical churches, by paternalism or negligence, had failed to stress it; Pentecostals, by restoring it to people who are in greatest need, have found in it one of their strongest appeals for conversion.[14] The other characteristic, "philanthropia," is the practical result of the first. Pentecostals are known the world over for the help they give each other in times of prosperity and of need. Their congregations delegate special persons (at times deacons or the pastor himself) to take care of the derelict, find jobs for the unemployed, and visit the sick. One of the touching moments at a Pentecostal religious service is that of "testimonies," when those who have recovered from sickness or have been beneficiaries of special favors thank God and the brethren for the support received.[15]

Mention has already been made of the missionary spirit of each true Pentecostal. It is a feature stressed in every report from mission lands. "The Assemblies of God provide something for everyone to do. . . . In the worship service all are expected to pray, to testify of that which Jesus Christ has done in their lives, and to sing so that all can hear. . . . All should learn to read so that they can study and read the Bible. There is something for everyone to do."[16] If the ideal be, as C. Conn has said, that "every true Pentecostal believer should be a witness," we must say that they have come close to that goal. Pentecostals witness within their own families or in the places where they work: in the office or in the fields, as taxi-drivers, teachers, or as foremen in construction projects. One of their activities is witnessing to the word of God to small groups in the open, in thoroughfares, or in homes. Theologically there is not much substance in what they say, but the preaching has the flavor of being spontaneous, sincere, and contagious. It is also the way of integrating them into a fraternal community and giving them status within a framework of rights and responsibilities. "The very tasks of street-preaching, giving testimony in worship services, serving and assuming financial commitments prove that the humblest 'brother' is important to the community and responsible for it."[17] At the root of this spirit lies the "second baptism" and the changes it has brought into their lives:

> Christians who have gone through this experience are usually deeply affected by it. A difference is seen in their lives. They now witness with a new enthusiasm. They have something to tell about. They have a testimony of what God did for them, and they want others to know about it. They must help others to get the blessing and to become members of small groups. . . . They have become "participants" in the unfolding of God's redemptive purposes for his church in these latter days.[18]

Thus in many places of Latin America, where the active profession of faith seemed reserved to women, Pentecostal men from every walk of life proclaim on street corners and in *plazas* the good news of the Gospel and exhort their countrymen to conversion. Their example has even impelled groups of Catholic men to do the same.

The structure of Pentecostal congregations is simple when compared to that of the historical churches. Almost overnight and in every field except perhaps in financial matters, their congregations are en trusted to native pastors. "Indigenization" is praised as one of their greatest achievements:

> In all fields occupied by the Assemblies of God, every effort shall be extended to establish autonomous Assemblies of God organizations, composed of co-operating, sovereign assemblies. It is realized that no fixed organizational pattern is possible. Every organization should studiously avoid the practice of proposing a Western type of organization, but should encourage a type readily understood and easily operated by the nationals of the country in question.[19]

To reach this goal, Pentecostals have opened hundreds of Bible schools for the training of ministers and lay-workers. Not all of them are of the same level, although one must gladly note the renewed interest of some of the denominations in raising the standards of training for their future collaborators; at present, however, in most territories such a training is not yet imparted. This writer, who has visited many of the institutions and met with hundreds of native pastors, must confess that, with some exceptions, the situation is simply appalling. They are ignorant of the basic facts of Christian theology, and easily become the laughing stock of the leaders of other churches or lose the esteem of educated people. It is likewise evident that "baptism of the Holy Spirit" is not a substitute for solid learning, nor can native helpers be satisfied with the repetition of a few Scriptural verses, or indulge in accusations against the sins of other churches. A Pentecostalism which intends to make a lasting contribution to the mainstream of Christianity must change its methods of preparing those who carry the main burden in the missions.[20]

These considerations apply to Pentecostal negligence regarding education in general. According to J. T. Nichol, at the beginning of the movement, antipathy to education was grounded on the following motives: (1) that education was harmful to spirituality; (2) that the enormous cost of building, staffing, and maintaining educational facilities would require the diverting of funds from strictly spiritual enterprises such as home and foreign missions; (3) that the words of Jesus in John 16:13 signify that the Holy Spirit personally instructs the believers; therefore it is unnecessary to provide either religious or secular training; finally, (4) that since most of the people who join the Pentecostal churches came from the lower social and economic strata, they had little or no appreciation for education in general and for higher education in particular.[21]

But, according to the same writer, after 1920, "the climate of opinion changed," and after World War II, a "collegiate education atmosphere" has developed in Pentecostalism. He refers to "nearly a score of Bible and liberal arts colleges" established in the United States, citing "as the most auspicious undertaking," the Oral Roberts University at Tulsa, Oklahoma. Unfortunately, that spirit has not yet reached most mission territories. Instances like Chile, where great interest in education has forced Pentecostals to think very seriously about educational problems (even to the extent of planning a university), must remain exceptions. In the public eye, Pentecostal congregations are made up of illiterates, and the churches seem to busy themselves more in convert making than in worrying about education, or else education is geared to purely spiritual aims—Sunday schools and correspondence or vacation Bible courses, and to means that will "develop Christian maturity in believers."[22] In the secular city in which Christianity is involved, such an effort is not enough, and in the opinion of neutral observers, the future of Pentecostalism the world over hinges, to a great extent, on the development of an educational program that will meet the growing needs of its younger generation.

Moral and Social Tenets

Holiness and Pentecostal bodies have also been accused of disregarding the social needs of the people at the very time when the historical churches are so greatly concerned in their missions with bettering socio-economic standards. For religious reasons and in self-defense, Pentecostals and Fundamentalists have shunned any collaboration with the Social Gospel movement and the programs launched by what was the Life and Work branch of the World Council of Churches. This repugnance may spring from the fact that Pentecostals are unable to compete, financially and technically, with those organizations, or from the belief that, in such endeavors, they would be ignoring the central aim of the missions—the preaching of the saving Gospel of Christ. They agree with G. Weber:

> Jesus fed the hungry with food, but he reminded them of their deeper hunger that bread alone could not fill. Thus compassion for those in need is supplemented with the kind of comprehension that is concerned with more than the immediate problems. . . . Christ, not all human schemes put together, is finally sufficient. To Christ, not to their programs to help drug addicts, men must point. It is his healing and love they mediate.[23]

It would nevertheless be unfair to narrow the understanding and practice of social work. Pentecostals do have a social program, founded on Puritan principles and on the firm belief that, by avoiding certain "vices" and fostering certain "virtues" which are part of the Protestant (and more concretely the American) heritage, they contribute to the betterment of individuals and societies. It may even be a more "mystical" way than that attempted by the historical churches, but the aims are the same.[24]

If there is an ugly word in Pentecostal literature, it is "worldliness." Its avoidance, which resembles the *fuga mundi* of the medieval ascetical writers, entails giving up a number of external satisfactions considered unworthy of the Christian. Fundamentally, this escapism derives from a one-sided interpretation given to the idea of "world," in spite of the fact that in Scripture the word has an ambivalent sense —it can mean either "a creation disfigured by sin," or "a created reality loved and redeemed by God."[25] The tendency to consider the "world" as simply evil is not new in Church history. Montanists preached it as an essential condition for Christian life and the Cathars imposed rigorous detachment on their followers. Certain groups of the Left Wing Reformation, such as the Mennonites, the Anabaptists, and Schwenckfeldians, fostered it as a "Christian distinctive." With the English dissenters, such a detachment received the name of Puritanism. Among the Pietists of the eighteenth century, things such as card-playing, dancing, and going to the theater became forbidden because of their "incompatibility" with Christian holiness. Methodism applied these principles to the concrete "vices" of its time. John Wesley, in the Rules written in 1744, explained to his disciples the meaning of the Gospel sentence: "you must abstain from all evil." It contained, among others, the following prohibitions: not to buy or sell anything on Sundays; to abstain from liquor or "water of life" unless prescribed by doctors; not to borrow anything even to save one's life; not to wear any superfluous ornaments: rings, earrings, collars, and similar items; and not to indulge in gambling or the use of tobacco.[26] Pentecostals did not leave their parent churches only for doctrinal reasons but also because of the "worldliness" into which the churches had fallen. The reaction varied from place to place, but it was generally marked by a new severity. The line adopted in order to return to "primitive Christianity" was very simple: to take from the Methodists the list of "forbidden items" and enlarge it to the point where there could be no doubt that they had gone further than their predecessors. At present we cannot speak of a uniform puritanic code for all Pentecostal denominations.[27] Prohibitions considered strictly binding for some groups are irrelevant to others. "Superfluous dress" or "worldly entertainment" mean one thing to the affluent American and quite another to the poorer African. Glancing through the publications one can perhaps list a fairly definite number of prohibitions common to many of their groups. Leisure habits are points at which human activity is regarded as tainted with "worldliness." Movies and television programs may be dismissed as becoming "more sinful and more rotten every day." In the same order come "seductive and sensuous dances." Some have denounced vigorously the "almost total disregard for even a semblance of modesty in female garb," without descending, however, as was common in by-gone days, to particulars regarding the length, the color, or even the buttoning of dresses.[28] Believing that human bodies are created to be temples of God, Pentecostals are opposed to everything that "defiles" them: "tobacco, alcohol, opium, morphine, and all the other drugs that are used to the harm of the body."[29] The Pentecostal Holiness Church adds to these prohibitions to "engage in festivals, ice cream suppers, oyster stews, fairs, bazaars, or any other business in the name of the church for the purpose of financial support."[30] Swearing is condemned for being against the Bible, and gambling as a "fruitless waste of money." In certain groups the Puritan spirit appears in the refusal to enlist in military service or participate in the use of armed force.[31] The Church of God, Cleveland, worries about the hairdress and jewelry of its followers because "in the plan of God, there must be a difference in the way men and women look. The woman's hair is not to look like that of man's, nor the man's look like the woman's."[32] Among the African independent churches, Barrett includes these laws and taboos:

> Elaborate legal constitutions, verbose applications to government, promulgation of apostolic letters, written diplomas and certificates, two holy days each week (Sunday and Wednesday or Friday), sabbatarianism, tithing and fasting, use of unleavened bread, personal authority, prohibition of tobacco, alcohol and pork, vegetarianism, rejection of European medicine, reintroduction of menstrual and other taboos, a marked legalism, severe discipline including death penalty.[33]

Individual Pentecostals in the North American continent are engaged in combatting drug addiction and, as D. R. Wilkerson has described in his book, *The Cross and the Switchblade,* with results far more effective than those achieved by many other medical or psychiatric methods.[34] The most successful social campaign in Latin America has been against alcoholism which affects so disastrously the already ill-fed population. Pentecostals, as a body, have carried on a courageous and systematic campaign to have it wiped out, and inspired their followers with a mystique capable of eradicating that "national disease," too much forgotten by the Catholic Church, and which many thought could not be overcome. The results have not been the same in every republic, but, as a rule, the stern Pentecostal attitude of enforcing abstention from liquor or expelling from the community those members who relapsed, has been highly successful. Their example, crossing church lines, has affected to a greater or lesser degree the other denominations, and called the attention of the public to the danger. Chilean Pentecostals, for example, have become sober and hard-working men who save their salary, do not beat their wives, and send their children to school, in a word, the workmen most sought after by management because they rate among the "best labor force in the country." The Chilean case has been the most publicized, but others could also be adduced.[35]

But Puritanism by itself cannot be identified with the essence of Christianity, and one would like to see Pentecostals imposing the same severity on religious aspects related to individual morality held sacred in the Church for many centuries. Three of them have come specially to the observer's attention.

The first is the ease with which Pentecostal churches, mostly those entrusted to native leaders, permit the retention of ancestral pagan practices. Possibly in the past Western missionaries of the historical churches had been too reserved in this regard, but Pentecostal tolerance has gone beyond permissible boundaries. Ancestor worship was largely tolerated in China, and is becoming one of the features of the independent churches in Africa where Pentecostals not only allow their converts to "communicate" with spirits, but have raised some of them to the ranks of "saints."[36] Nature worship and animistic practices are rampant among many of their communities in Indonesia. A visit to the homes of Pentecostals (or to some of their religious services) in Latin America will prove that much of the ersatz Catholicism they practiced in their mother Church continues to live in their denominations. This tolerant policy helps Pentecostals to swell the statistics of church growth. It remains doubtful if, at least in the case of pagan accretions, it will help to "christianize" the body as a whole.[37]

Divorce has been from the start a touchy issue in Western Pentecostalism on both sides of the Atlantic, and there is no uniform rule that can be applied to all its branches. The United Pentecostal Church believes that when the separation is caused by the adultery of one of the spouses, "the innocent party may be free to remarry, only in the Lord,"[38] although the church, in its desire to "raise a higher standard for the ministry," recommends that "ministers do not remarry."[39] The Assemblies of God, the Pentecostal Church, Inc., the Church of the Foursquare Gospel, and most colored Holiness churches are quite lenient on this matter.[40] The Church of God, Cleveland, has been postponing any theoretical statement, but making concessions in practice. Fornication and adultery would leave the innocent party at liberty to remarry and only the innocent will be eligible for membership in the church. The leaders are waiting for "perfect light" and "perfect understanding"[41] before they make the final decision. Similar concessions are extended to those African tribes where the dismissal of sterile wives is taken for granted. Investigations in Latin America have shown that, in a rather high percentage of cases in Mexico, the Andean republics, and the Caribbean, the possibility of re-marriage has played an important role in the shift from Catholicism to some of the Pentecostal bodies. Reports from certain Brazilian cities confirm that the same policy prevails there.

In the last decades one of the burning issues for the African churches has been that of the permissibility of polygamy for a Christianity that is growing in an environment "quite different" from that of Western society. The defections from historical Christianity caused by this problem have moved certain missionaries and native groups to censor the "loveless, censorious, and legalistic approach" developed by mission groups, an attitude which, in their opinion, "does not reflect the spirit of our Lord Jesus."[42] And since polygamy has been one of the main causes of separatism in African Christendom, the older churches are counseled to consider whether, in spite of the distinct patterns on marriage adopted by the independent bodies, the latter may not still keep a "genuine relationship to Jesus Christ" and, therefore, could not be "recognized as churches with whom possibilities of Christian fellowship must be explored."[43] At this point African Pentecostalism has decided to side with the independent churches. Their policy is described by D. B. Barrett:

> The independent churches have been noted for their leniency towards traditional marriage patterns. Polygamists are accepted for baptism, though further polygamous marriages are forbidden and only the monogamous can hold spiritual office. There are, of course, exceptions to the latter rule. Prophet Harris permitted polygamy, and was always accompanied in his travels along the Ivory Coast by three or four of his white-robed wives. . . . Typical of the majority attitude is that of the African Church of Israel which left in 1948 the Seventh-Day Adventist Mission with the expressed reason to "help polygamists to enter heaven."[44]

The attitude of the Western Pentecostal groups working in Africa remains ambivalent. On principle, most of them are opposed to polygamy, but in practice the cases of admission of polygamists to the ranks of their congregations are too numerous to hide. And the policy will not improve with the assumption by natives of positions of leadership. As a defense, they recur to the Old Testament permissions on the matter as well as to the "special situation" of African Christianity.

Such shortcomings, however, do not detract from the credit Pentecostals deserve for their gallant fight against many of the social and moral evils of the times. Let us also remind ourselves that, in our pragmatic world, and at the hour of truth regarding the "validity" of a church, deeds count almost as much as beliefs. Hence Pentecostalism ranks high among those who look for a religion which "can do something" for the Third World:

> Pentecostals, while far from perfect, have demonstrated that, by the grace of God, they can be counted among those who "live soberly, righteously, and godly in the present world." Around the world they are recognized as honest, respectable people, worthy citizens, who are an influence for good to society. It is a matter of rejoicing to know that the overwhelming majority of Pentecostals practice what they preach, that Pentecostalism is not only a *big* movement, but also a *good* movement.[45]

To what extent can this intensely zealous and fast growing Pentecostalism join forces with the rest of Christendom? The question of the fraternal ties among all those who glory in the name of Christ is vital. And we have to put it to ourselves before we leave our survey of the Pentecostal mission fields. It was in mission lands, a century or so ago, that the ecumenical movement made its start and convinced the sending churches of its utmost urgency. And it is also in mission lands where, after decades of estrangement, we begin to see the first glimpse of a possible understanding between Pentecostalism and the historical churches.[46]

At first sight, Pentecostalism and the ecumenical spirit are almost contradictory terms. Pentecostalism, a product of rejection on the part of the historical churches, and subjected to uninterrupted and not always Christian attacks, has preferred for a long time to live alone and to build up its own spiritual and theological structures. The experience of the West has repeated itself in mission lands whose larger congregations are the result of long drawn-out clashes and disputes with the parent churches. Which side is to be blamed for the split is much harder to decide. As a rule, none of the parties emerges with clean hands. In mission lands the dynamics of separation may be glimpsed from what happened in Africa where the pattern is said to be the following:

1. There was an era in which foreign missionaries brought the Gospel, built churches and opened schools, hospitals, and clinics for the benefit of the population, thus raising hopes of prosperity and happiness.

2. This was followed by disillusionment and bitterness because of the lack of concern of the mission boards for African values and their failure to transfer responsibilities to the natives;

3. Then a period of tension arose between native and foreign leaders, not only on administrative issues, but because the latter were reluctant to incorporate into Christianity certain tribal elements, mainly ancestor cult and the practice of polygamy.

4. The tension was exacerbated by the publication of African translations of the Bible in whose pages the natives discovered a "new vision of Christianity" with emphases on family, land, fertility, ancestor worship, and the permission of polygamy, whereas missionaries, overstepping biblical authority, had been "vocal where the Bible was silent" and while Jesus "had come to fulfill the old order, missions by contrast have come to destroy it."

5. Finally came the hour of mutual separation, the search for a status independent of the ecclesiastical and political authorities, and the rapid growth of the newly-born movement.[47]

Pentecostalism has also suffered seriously from internal disruption.[48] It remains the most fissiparous movement of contemporary Protestantism in Latin America and on the African continent. The Bible and "leading of the Spirit" have often become in the hands of its leaders deadly weapons of division, with the disadvantage that none of their denominations has so far produced a man of stature (as Mormonism, Seventh-day Adventism, and Christian Science have) capable of controlling the centrifugal tendencies within the fold. Some of the denominations, like the Assemblies of God or the Church of the Foursquare Gospel, the Congregacao Crista in Brazil, or the major Chilean congregations, have, thanks to the organizational gifts of the group, become solidly founded corporations. Others remain loosely organized. They continue to grow only because their message spreads like fire among the spiritually hungry populations. But there are also congregations which lead a precarious life or join other churches of kindred theologies and practices. On the whole the jejune Pentecostal ecclesiology continues to be an impediment to those who want to become "founders" of new congregations. Further elements of disruption have been: controversies about organization versus independence; discussions regarding sanctification and the "second work of grace"; the nature and absolute need of glossolalia; the value of revelation, interpretation of dreams and prophecy in the life of the Church; the issue of the "Jesus only baptism"; regulations about food, dress, entertainment, or married life; Free-masonry; reliance on "God only" or recourse to medicine for sickness; and the amount of non-Christian elements that can be incorporated into Christianity:

> It is rather clear that all of this diversity of opinion regarding both matters of faith and order and life and work . . . and the obvious fragmentation of Pentecostals into groups which favored either ardor or order, spontaneity or ritual, legalism or tolerance, and independence or hierarchical control, would preclude the development of unitive Pentecostalism. Not even a common religious experience, the Holy Spirit, would be a sufficiently strong cohesive force, for the taproots of the movement reached back into too many personalities, cultures, and religious heritages. Proliferation, then, would be inevitable.[49]

This situation could be tolerated before the ecumenical era. Pentecostals might be absent from the great missionary conferences of Edinburgh, Jerusalem, or Madras, and no one would notice. They formed only a small and not always respected minority and were just at the beginning of their missionary expansion. Mission leaders spoke disparagingly about the "nuisance" such sects were causing in territories already "occupied" by the historical churches. Because of the poor intellectual standards of their missionaries, Pentecostals could not even be the bearers of Western culture and its "blessings" to the "savages" of Asia and Africa.[50] Now the outlook has radically changed. The historical churches see their mission territories "invaded" by Pentecostals, and they realize that their growth is achieved most of the time at the expense of their own congregations. The idea also is dawning that, after all, Pentecostals might embody elements and characteristics that the older churches have neglected to the detriment of the whole People of God. There are on both sides a few individuals who begin to wonder if, at this time of universal religious indifference, the need of a common Christian witness does not require some kind of *modus vivendi* among those who have been baptized in the same Lord. Bishop Leslie Newbigin, of the Church of South India, goes so far as to state that our unity, which only the Holy Spirit can give, will take place only when "Catholics and Protestants enter into fellowship with Pentecostals."[51] The issue, therefore, boils down to this: Can the historical churches any longer ignore the Pentecostal denominations? Or can the latter remain cut off from the mainstream of Christendom?

It is evident that Western Pentecostalism is losing its isolationist grip. "There is no doubt," Bloch comments, "that the extreme subjectivism within the movement is decreasing. This is seen in the conduct of meetings in various Pentecostal assemblies as well as in the tendency to organize church life."[52] Pentecostalism has entered, often with faltering steps, the hard road towards Christian unity. It may be said that many of the present-day major denominations are already the result of mergers of smaller original bodies.[53] International meetings among Pentecostals were held as early as 1910 at Oslo and in 1920 in Amsterdam. The latter led the way to the foundation of an International European Pentecostal Convention. Another meeting at Stockholm in 1939, attended by delegates from twenty countries, stated that "international conferences have no authority with regard to administration or doctrinal control of the separate Pentecostal churches."[54] American Pentecostalism, less fond of such gatherings, made its first ecumenical move in 1937 when the General Council of the Assemblies of God invited to Memphis representatives from the British, South African, Canadian, and European churches. Another American unitive body, the North American Pentecostal Fellowship, has sponsored forums and seminars for people from various denominations in order to exchange views and prepare common programs of evangelism, religious literature, and work with youth in mission lands. Since 1947, there exists a rather loosely-knit World Conference of Pentecostal Churches. It would have become the movement's international mouthpiece but for the opposition of the Scandinavian denominations. Pentecostals met also in 1949 in Paris "in view of the gravity of the hour and in acknowledgment of the activity of the Spirit of God in drawing together his people in a closer bond of fellowship and spiritual unity." Other Conferences have been held in 1952, 1961 and (the last up to date) in 1967 at Rio de Janeiro.[55]

Faced with the powerful World Council of Churches, or its corresponding National Councils of Churches, Pentecostals have been forced to make a choice. Reconciliation of the two organizations has until now been impossible. Pentecostals have accused the World Council of ecclesiasticism, of admitting to membership "a host of liberals" who were committed to an anti-Christian philosophy, of being "oligarchical" and "super-churchly", of seriously threatening the work of other denominations in the missions, of being "soft" on the Church of

Rome, and above all of perverting or denying basic theological Christian doctrines.[56] In return, Pentecostals were regarded by the World Council as sectarian in spirit, retarded in doctrine, and disruptors of the common effort toward unity. Consequently, only one way was left open to Pentecostals: to join with organizations whose doctrinal positions were "in more accordance with their own." Such was the National Association of Evangelicals, started in 1942, and professing a creed which "all fundamentalist evangelical Christians can enter without difficulty and reservation." Thus they combined a "growing conviction of a need for a correlation of many Christian activities on a soundly evangelical basis and without interference with the internal affairs of constituent bodies."[57] Pentecostals seem satisfied with this cooperation which has helped them to standardize their educational methods, and through its missionary branch, the Evangelical Foreign Mission Organization, to apply to their work the experiences and the political connections of the nation-wide organization.[58] It still remains doubtful whether the influence of the National Association of Evangelicals will help its members to come closer to the universal Church. There seems to be too much that is negative and "anti" in its publications at this time of sincere hopes of brotherhood among the rest of Christianity. But this is beyond the point.[59]

What is the outlook for Pentecostal ecumenism in mission territories? Two decades ago it was discouraging. The native congregations, totally dependent on foreign boards, had little to say on the matter. The policies were issued from headquarters in the West and the "natives" were told to put them into practice. The evolution came with the end of World War II and the emergence of the independent nations. Changes are in the making, although no one seems to know how they will turn out. Here are some of the symptoms. Independence has brought to the native churches a deep-rooted longing to end isolationism. The phenomenon appears particularly in Africa. In the opinion of Sundkler: "It is not unfair to say that any Zulu leader who breaks away from his parent church is immediately ready to become a champion of Church union."[60] The move is made easier because many of the native congregations do not suffer from the "orthodox complex" of the parent churches, or because they have even embodied accretions that have taken different directions. Some have asked for admission into the local National Councils of Churches. The receptivity of the latter has often depended on the strength of the native representation in central committees. The Geredja Bethel Indjil Sapenugh, second largest Indonesian Pentecostal body, is already a full member of the National Council of Churches of Indonesia. In Africa "increasing applications for membership have been made since 1945 to National Christian Councils across the continent,"[61] although very few are being accepted. At times the applications are sent directly to major ecumenical bodies. This has been the case in the Black Continent with the All-African Conference of Churches or the East African United Church, where once again, their petitions seem to have received a cool reception. A third group has made bold to go directly to the World Council of Churches. Some African groups, according to Barrett, are finding that Geneva is in no hurry to comply with their requests. Others have been more successful. Much publicity was given in 1961 to the admission to the ecumenical body of two Chilean denominations: Iglesia Pentecostal de Chile and Misión Evangélica Pentecostal. Leaders like D. Du Plessis went so far as to state that, after nearly half a century of ostracism and misunderstanding, the Pentecostal churches offered their "fellowship in Christ to the whole of his Church, in this hour of history."[62] The reaction was swift. Dr. Du Plessis was "disfellowed" for his ecumenical activities; Th. Zimmermann, General Secretary of the Assemblies of God, gave the "official" opinion of orthodox Pentecostalism regarding the admission of the Chilean denominations:

> We are not personally acquainted with these groups, nor do we know the reasons for joining hands with the World Council of Churches. But, brethren, these are not days in which to compromise! Regarding the efforts of the World Council of Churches and the National Council of Churches who assay to call us "brethren," we are miles apart. Nor can we afford to compromise with them on our more basic, God-given, heaven-blessed position, including the infallibility of God's word, the virgin birth, the atoning death of our Lord and Savior, his resurrection, and his bodily return.[63]

This hostile reception over the years "has bred such a toughness and resistence . . . [among Pentecostals that] they begin to form themselves into independent councils and federations with assistance here and there from liberal elements in the historical churches."[64] Among the new mergers are those of the Assemblies of Zionist and Apostolic Churches. Certain groups from Madagascar and Kenya have joined McIntire's International Council of Churches. In Brazil the Confederacao Pentecostal do Brazil is made up of some thirty Pentecostal denominations. There are similar trends in Mexico. The larger South

American denominations are members of the World Council of Pentecostal Churches.

Proselytism and Church Union

What are the chief difficulties for a better understanding between Pentecostals and historical Christian bodies? Undoubtedly the resentments of the past will not disappear overnight. In the area of doctrine, the extreme conservatism of Pentecostals and, above all, their claims to charismatic gifts, may freeze the contacts for a long time. It may be asked, however, whether the spirit of "comprehensiveness" of a World Council of Churches which harbors members from the Society of Friends, from the Salvation Army, and from extreme liberal denominations, cannot reserve a place for Pentecostals. Some writers have even suggested that the existence of "Pentecostals" within the various historical churches could serve as a bridge for a better understanding of the concepts of Christianity. It must also be remembered that the beliefs and rituals of the more sophisticated Pentecostal groups in Europe and North America (to say nothing of the neo-Pentecostals) do not vastly differ from those of other conservative but "orthodox" bodies.[65]

A great stumbling block, and this applies particularly to relations with Roman Catholicism, lies in the Pentecostal concepts of "evangelism" and "missionary activity." There is in our days an ugly word that embitters our relations—*proselytism.* In its pejorative sense the term has a recent origin. During the Protestant missionary expansion of the last century, the expression was not used, but its dangers became apparent and the missionary societies tried to avoid them by "comity agreements" or by zoning the different areas that were to be assigned to each of the denominations. In Catholic-Protestant relations the concept was non-existent because Catholics endeavored to convert as many Protestants as they could and Protestants did the same with Catholics. But the problem has become acute with the ecumenical movement and the renewed missionary activities of the eschatological and Pentecostal denominations. In the twenties the warnings against "sheep-stealing" came, as we have seen, mostly from the Orthodox Churches which, on more than one occasion, threatened to quit the ecumenical movement unless the "sects" stopped this tactic. The complaints took the tone of strong protest when in 1961 the International

Missionary Council was merged with the World Council of Churches. The latter prepared a report on proselytism which read in part:

> Proselytism is . . . the corruption of witness. Witness is corrupted when cajolery, bribery, undue pressure, or intimidation is used subtly or openly to bring about seeming conversions; when we put the success of our church before the honor of Christ; when we commit the dishonesty of comparing the ideal of our church with the actual achievement of another; when we seek to advance our own cause by bearing false witness against another church; when personal or corporate self-seeking replaces love for every individual soul with whom we are concerned.[66]

The statement concluded with a denunciation of proselytising methods in the mission field as being opposed to the nature of the Gospel:

> During the last years the churches have understood clearly . . . that there is no brotherly love, no true unity between local communities, as long as they have not ceased to proselytize among the members of other churches. More than once has the World Council of Churches drawn attention to the fact that *ecumenism and proselytism are mutually exclusive.*[67]

For perhaps too long the Catholic Church made no statement on the matter. But during Vatican Council II hundreds of bishops from mission territories asked for the Church's clarification on those interferences. As a result the *Declaration on Religious Freedom* contains this important pronouncement:

> Religious bodies also have the right not to be hindered in their public teaching and witness to their faith, whether by the spoken or by the written word. However, in spreading religious faith and introducing religious practices, everyone ought at all times to refrain from any manner of action which might seem to carry a hint of coercion or a kind of persuasion that would be dishonorable or unworthy, especially when dealing with poor or uneducated people. Such a manner of action would have to be considered an abuse of one's right and a violation of the right of others.[68]

The answer from fundamentalist groups (such as the Evangelical Foreign Mission Association to which many Pentecostals belong) is not over-encouraging. It admits that, on certain occasions, their missionaries have "offered to converts, at least by suggestion and implication, money or goods or social advantages in a manner very similar to bribery," or even that certain missions "have offered higher salaries than those paid by other missions if native pastors would leave their mother churches and unite with the new church."[69] But such conduct is "exceptional." It is the liberals who pervert the original meaning of proselytism "because they dislike any radical form of Christian conversion." Fundamentalists hold that: "The purpose of witness is to persuade persons to accept the supreme authority of Christ and to commit themselves to him. In this light any action taken against evangelistic proselytization may in fact be an attack against the very essence of evangelization. Indeed missionary work must include seeking to make converts."[70]

It is a pity that these brethren fail to recognize that many of their missionaries, and still more of their converts, are actually proselytizing and not witnessing. The consensus of all Catholic and Protestant bodies, to which we may add that of neutral observers, leaves no doubt as to where they stand. As far as the Catholic Church is concerned, the sore point with Pentecostals in Latin America lies here. Bishops, priests, and laity are truly worried about the seriousness of the situation. The dreadful shortage of priests which the hemisphere has suffered for generations; the indefatigable missionary work carried by Pentecostals; the allurement of the gift of healing for a population which awaits deliverance from so many evils; the example of sober and hard-working lives given by Pentecostals; often the solid economic help received from foreign agencies; and the unevangelical reasons given for conversion—all these factors contribute to the Pentecostal advance and especially to the loss of many members of the Catholic Church. The bitterness of Pentecostal attacks against the beliefs and practices of Catholicism, and the fact that such an aggression is answered in kind by Catholic groups in a language which does not accord with the basic principles of Christian charity, make mutual understanding very difficult.[71]

Nevertheless, many are convinced that, in the coming decades, the relationship between Pentecostals and other Christians is going to improve. In mission lands isolationism is being replaced by tentative steps to federate among themselves until the time may come when they will be welcomed by other greater ecumenical organizations. Many of their churches in the West are also evolving towards ideals and forms which, while preserving the Pentecostal heritage, might facilitate their acceptance by the mainstream of Christianity. Historical churches also are making an effort to understand what is positive in the Pentecostal message and particularly the role of the Holy Spirit in the life of the Christian. Perhaps this better appreciation will result in brotherly love. This is sure: if our relations improve, the benefits will be mutual. We have many lessons to learn from Pentecostalism. But Pentecostals need also to be closer to the rest of Christendom, not only to enrich themselves, but perhaps even for their survival. The road ahead is steep and rough. In order to cover it, we need to know better and to love more, but especially to remind ourselves that "the holy task of reconciling all Christians in the unity of the one and only Church of Christ trascends human energies and abilities." This realization will help us to place our hope entirely in the prayer of Christ for the Church, in the love of the Father for us, and in the power of the Holy Spirit which the Pentecostal Movement is striving to bring back to the world.

NOTES TO CHAPTER ONE

1. Kelsey, M. T., *Tongue Speaking, An Experiment in Spiritual Experience* (New York, 1964), 15. For a different approach, see L. Cerfaux, *Le chrétien dans la théologie paulinniene* (Brussels, 1962); Gromacki, R. G., *The Modern Tongues Movement* (Philadelphia, 1967); Dollar, G. W., *Church History and the Tongues Movement* (in *Bibliotheca Sacra,* 1963), 316ff.

2. Davies, J. G., *The Early Christian Church* (New York, 1965), 90. However, "we may already observe the beginning of a conflict between tradition (*paradosis*) and succession (*diadoxe*) on the one hand, and the Spirit and *charismata* (1 Clem. Didache) on the other" (R. Seeberg, *Textbook of the History of Doctrines* [Grand Rapids, 1956], 80). See also A. Lemonnyer, *Supplement du Dictionnaire de la Bible* (Paris, 1928), I, col. 1234ff., s.v. *Charismes.*

3. At least this is what Epiphanius (*Panarion,* 84, 4; Migne, J. P., *Patrologicae Cursus,* 41, 1 [Paris, 1858], 862) reports to us about him. In the opinion of Kelsey, *op. cit.,* 34: "there are some current Pentecostal writers who look back to Montanus with some of the same historical reverence a Presbyterian offers to Augustine."

4. Frend, W. H. C., *The Early Church* (New York, 1966), 81. The same historian in *Martyrdom in the Early Church* (New York, 1967), 220, adds: "Though marriage was not forbidden, it was discouraged, sexual continence was preached, and second marriage banned. Behind all these rigors was the aim of preparing Christians to the reception of the Holy Spirit, who, as Tertullian was to point out, could not take up his abode in a body filled with impurities."

5. Eusebius, Pamphili, *Ecclesiastical History* (London, 1870), 284. The impression left by these phenomena varied with individuals. Some thought that the highest stage of revelation had been reached, and the age of the Paraclete had arrived; others, who heard his "spurious utterances, were indignant, and rebuked him as one who was possessed, was under the control of the demon, was led by a deceitful spirit, and was distracting the multitude" (Asterius Urbanus, *Ante-Nicene Fathers* VII [Grand Rapids, 1951], I, 335–36.

6. Baus, K., "From the Apostolic Community to Constantine" (in *Handbook of Church History*), ed. J. Jedin (New York, 1965), 99. It is curious to note that Tertullian himself does not claim to speak in tongues. However, he adduced the practice of glossolalia in the Christian community as a sign that God was with the Christians and not with Marcion. See *Against Marcion* (in *Ante-Nicene Fathers,* III [Grand Rapids, 1951]), 446–47.

7. Seeberg, R., *op. cit.,* 108. The schismatic aspects of Montanism have been well analyzed by S. L. Greenslade, *Schism in the Early Church* (New York, 1954), 108, and the ecclesiological variations in two of his key treatises, *De praescriptione* and *De pudicitia, ibid.,* 110–12.

8. Origen, *Contra Celsum* (in *The Ante-Nicene Fathers,* IV [Grand Rapids, 1950]), sec. 7.8. Ireneus' earlier statement about the existence of glossolalia (*op. cit.*, I, 531) among his contemporaries cannot be dismissed as ambivalent.

9. Duchesne, L., *The Early History of the Church* (London, 1901–22), I, 36.

10. See, Schaff, P., *History of the Christian Church* (Grand Rapids, 1952), 197. The situation, as viewed by H. Leclerq, was as follows: the charisms, remaining precious stimulants to foster the fervor of small congregations, were becoming troublesome and impractical in an organized church. Bishops and doctors were more and more opposed to them because they gave occasion to criticisms and were claimed by individuals whose orthodoxy was in doubt. Thus, by the third century, the gifts, even without disappearing completely, became rare phenomena in the life of the Church (*Dictionnaire d'archéologie chrétienne,* III [Paris, 1914], col. 595).

11. *On Baptism Against the Donatists,* III, xviii, 16–21. The critique against the charisms made by Gregory the Great in his Commentary on the Book of Job was still more sweeping. (See *Supplement du Dictionnaire de la Bible,* I [Paris, 1928], col. 1236).

12. Pearlman,M.,*Knowing the Doctrines of the Bible* (Springfield, Mo., 1937), III, 63.

13. Knox, R., *Enthusiasm: A Chapter in the History of Religion* (Oxford, 1950), 78. See a more recent historical study on the theme by Christine Thouseller, *Catharisme et Valdéisme en Languedoc* (Paris, 1966).

14. Villoslada, G. R., *Historia de la Iglesia Católica* (Madrid, 1963), II, 556–60. See the rather far-fetched conclusions and the supposedly anti-Christian character of the Joachite divisions of history in Norman Cohn's *The Pursuit of the Millenium* (London, 1957), 99–104.

15. For the problem of the Cathars, see F. Niel, *Albigeois et Cathares* (Paris, 1965); E. Fornairon, *Le mystère cathare* (Paris, 1964); J. Malaud, *The Albigensian Crusade* (New York, 1967); R. Nelli, *et al., Les cathares* (Paris, 1940); A. Borst, *Die Katharer* (Stuttgart, 1953).

16. Vicaire, M., *St. Dominic and His Times* (New York, 1964), 49.

17. *Ibid.,* 49–50. Around the middle of the thirteenth century the entire Catharist community comprised about 4,000 "perfect," which possibly represented some hundreds of thousands of followers. They soon became organized under bishops (bisbes) and extended their influence to various regions of France, Northern Italy, Flanders, and England.

18. See R. Nelli, *Le phenomene cathare* (Paris, 1964), 17–65.

19. "The Catharist Christ was altogether different from the Catholic Christ, and there lay the whole difference" (Malaud). He had not

come to atone for man's sins by his sacrifice, but only to *teach* a doctrine of salvation. The Bogomiles assimilated him to the archangel Michael, and never would agree that he was equal to the Father. At times Mary was also compared to an angel. "Thus the Cathars denied both the incarnation and the resurrection of the body, which constitute the basis of Christianity" (Malaud, *op. cit.,* 35).

20. A detailed description of the ceremony may be found in Nelli's *Les cathares,* 148ff.

21. While receiving the *consolamentum,* the candidate read the following prayer: "I pledge to dedicate myself to God and his evangel, never to swear, never to touch a woman, to kill no animals, to eat no meat and to live only on fruit. I pledge furthermore never to travel, never to live or to dine without one of my brethren, and if I should fall into the hands of our enemies or be separated from my brother, to refrain from all food for three days. And, then, I pledge never to betray my faith, no matter with what death I may be threatened" (cited by W. Nigg, *The Heretics* [New York, 1962], 188).

22. Schaff, P., *History of the Christian Church* (Grand Rapids, ed. 1961), V, 480.

23. See G. S. M. Walker, *The Growing Storm, Studies of Church History* (London, 1961), 150–51. We fail to discover glossolalic practices among the Cathars. Obviously divine healing had no place in a system which positively sought the destruction of the human body.

24. Leff, Gordon, *Heresy in the Middle Ages* (New York, 1967) II, 451–52, sees "the fundamental anti-Christian character" of their beliefs in the "denial of the sacraments, the incarnation, Christ's passion and his, or others', bodily resurrection, and Mary's motherhood." These contrasts needed to be pointed out in the presence of those authors who, writing on the Pentecostals, allude without distinctions to their similarities with the Cathars.

25. Williams, G. H., *The Radical Reformation* (Philadelphia, 1962), 83. In the Peasants' War Lutheranism turned its back upon the congregational life of its early days and, becoming territorial, made of the prince a true "chief bishop" of the church. "Luther's Reformation lost its character as a dynamic popular movement. This, and not the actual war itself, was what made that war so tragically and incisively significant in the history of the Reformation" (Franz Guenther, in *The Encyclopedia of the Lutheran Church* [Minneapolis, 1965], III, 1871).

26. Bullinger's accusations were manifold: doctrinally they did not acknowledge the divinity of Christ; morally they were wholly given to "foul and detestable sensuality." From the viewpoint of ecumenism "they divide the church where there is no need," and "stir up sedition and do make every rascal knave a minister of God's word" (Williams, *op. cit.,* 201–03). The author notes that Bullinger's work, translated into English, had great influence in shaping an adverse opinion about Anabaptism.

27. Williams-Melgar, "Spiritual and Anabaptist Writers," in *The Library of Christian Classics* (Philadelphia, 1957), 26.

28. *Ibid.* This is the place to say a word about the "gift of tongues" attributed to certain saints: St. Vincent Ferrer, St. Anthony of Padua, St. Francis Xavier, and adduced by Pentecostals as a further confirmation of their claims. The phenomenon had nothing in common with Pentecostal glossolalia, but was a "miraculous" facility of "speaking foreign languages" which could be easily understood by the audiences.

29. Juillerat, L. H., *History of the Church of God* (Cleveland, Tenn., 1922), 7–8.

30. Williams, G. H., *The Radical Reformation*, 290.

31. Nigg, *op. cit.*, 310–11.

32. Comfort, W. W., *The Quaker Way of Life* (New York, 1941), 65–66. Fox himself used to define it as "that of God which is in your hearts." James Flood has done a fine analysis of the theology of Fox in *A Catholique Critique of the Quaker Doctrine of the Inner Light* (Rome, 1963).

33. Bickley, R., *George Fox and the Early Quakers* (London, 1920), 27. O. Chadwick, *The Reformation* (London, 1964), 242, is not sure of the influence of the mystics upon Quakerism.

34. Truebold, D. E., *The People Called Quakers* (New York, 1966), 85ff.

35. *Ibid.*, 131–32. See also R. H. Thomas, *The Quaker Position on the Sacrament and Worship* (London, 1897). To Fox, sacraments were "shadows," while Christ, through the inner light, came to bring "realities" to men.

36. Williams, G. H., *The Radical Reformation*, 443.

37. Knox, R., *Enthusiasm*, 150. In Colonial New England we find Mrs. Anne Hutchinson, a woman of "ready and wit spirit," admired by some and branded as "that American Jezabel" by others. According to John Winthrop, she had introduced "two dangerous errors," first, that the Holy Spirit dwells in a justified person, who can therefore receive direct revelations from God over and above that given in the Bible, and second, that sanctification is no evidence of God's justification. Only inner assurance can authenticate one's spiritual state before God. She was excommunicated from the Boston church, and after her removal to New York, murdered with her seven children by the Indians. See Smith-Handy *et al.*, *American Christianity* (New York, 1960), I, 115–16.

38. Knox, R., *op. cit.*, 150.

39. See J. H. Nichols, *History of Christianity, 1650-1950* (New York, 1956), 78. The history of these people has been admirably told by R. Jones, *The Quakers in the American Colonies* (New York, 1966). Cotton Mather called them "fanaticks" and stated they held "almost all the fancies and whimsies" of which they were accused in England.

40. Léonard, E., *Histoire Génerale du Protestantisme* (Paris, 1964), III, 16ff.

41. Knox, *op. cit.*, 150. They were also known as the "petits prophètes."

42. Pentecostal historians allude to Shakers as their predecessors. See K. Kendrick, *The Promise Fulfilled* (Springfield, Mo., 1961), 22. It

seems that when their minds were "overloaded with a fiery, strong zeal," they were endowed with the gift of tongues. Two of the best studies on Shakerism in America are E. D. Andrews, *The People Called Shakers: A Search for the Perfect Society* (New York, 1953), and M. F. Felcher, *The Shaker Adventure* (Princeton, 1941).

43. *Journal*, 28/1/1739.

44. Piette, M., *John Wesley in the Evolution of Protestantism* (New York, 1937), 348. Piette adds that, from 1738 on, Wesley's *Journal* abounds in such descriptions.

45. Quoted by Léonard, *op. cit.*, 112, note 3. Wesley, says Léonard, defended in his correspondence the "orthodoxy" of those heavenly manifestations. See also Horton Davies, *Worship and Theology in England* (Princeton, 1961), III, 154.

46. *Op. cit.*, 535. These signs appeared as late as two years before his death.

47. Starkey, L. M., *The Work of the Holy Spirit in Wesleyan Theology* (Nashville, 1962), 75–76. In a meeting with Bishop Butler who complained: "Sir, the pretending of extraordinary revelations and gifts of the Holy Ghost is a horrid thing—a very horrid thing!," Wesley replied: "I pretend to no extraordinary revelations, or gifts of the Holy Ghost: none but what every Christian may receive and ought to expect and pray for" (*Journal*, II, 8/18/1739).

48. About this time appear the Irvingites in England. Edward Irving (1792–1834) was a Presbyterian pastor of London who hoped for the restoration of the charismatic gifts of the early Church. He personally never experienced them, but certain phenomena which broke out in Scotland, mostly glossolalia and "prophesying," convinced him that such a time was at hand. Irving's mantle was inherited by H. Drummond and N. Armstrong who founded the Catholic Apostolic Church which insists on the direct work of the Spirit and the presence of charismatic gifts. See P. E. Shaw, *The Catholic Apostolic Church, Sometimes Called Irvingite, A Historical Study* (New York, 1946).

49. See *The History of American Methodism* (Nashville, 1964). This is a three-volume volume cooperative effort by Methodist scholars. The first two studies, *Early American Contacts* (I, 43–74) by S. C. Henry, and *Methodism in Colonial America*, by M. Potts and A. B. Moss (I, 74–145) are most illuminating.

50. To achieve this purpose was not an easy task. One of its first preachers, Devereux Jarratt, was often abused as an "enthusiast, fanatic visionary, and dissenter." Wesley's "Calm Address to the American Colonies" did not prove convincing to many. Only the patience and diplomacy of Francis Asbury convinced Americans of the "good intentions" of the new preachers.

51. *The History of American Methodism*, I, 232. The rules of American Methodism were laid down in a revised edition of the *Form of Discipline* in which the word "bishop" was dropped in favor of that of "superintendent," the movement was said to be part of the American Church, and even the Church of England was criticized.

52. Cited by W. W. Sweet, *Methodism in American History* (New York, 1954), 76. *The Form of Discipline,* section XXII, strongly defended against "Papists and others" the doctrine of holiness: "Let us strongly and explicitly exhort all believers to go on to perfection. That we may all speak the same thing, we ask once for all. Shall we defend this perfection, or give it up? We all agree to defend it, meaning thereby salvation from all sin, by the love of God and man filling our hearts."

53. Jamison, A. L., "Religions in the Perimeter," in *The Shaping of the American Religion,* ed. J. W. Smith and A. L. Jamison (Series of *Religion in American Life* [Princeton, 1961], I, 192). Regarding American revivals, see C. G. Finney, *Lectures on Revivals* (New York, 1875); W. G. McLoughlin, *Modern Revivalism* (New York, 1959); A. Heimert, *Religion and the American Mind—From the Great Awakening to the Revolution* (Cambridge, 1966); W. W. Sweet, *Revivalism in America* (Nashville, 1944); Mecklin, J. M., *The Story of American Dissent* (New York, 1934), 207–231.

54. Jamison, A. L., *op. cit.,* 203–04.

55. In practice the appeal of revivalism lay as much or more in its violent physical manifestations as in the contents of its theology. As remarked by T. S. Mikayawa: "As long as a person had the jerks, parts of his body would snap back and forth with such rapidity that the long braids of hair cracked like whips. Stories about this particular hysteria circulated widely and thereafter became so popular that safety zones had to be established at some meetings. . . . Many western revivalists regarded the physical phenomena as heavenly visitations, while they resorted to time-tested techniques to induce them in susceptible persons. . . . On the other hand, the better educated Presbyterian and Congregationalist ministers denounced them as vulgar animal displays" *(Protestants and Pioneers* [Chicago, 1964], 237).

56. Jamison, *op. cit.,* 183. More on Jefferson's religion can be found in Smith-Handy's already cited *American Christianity,* I, 513-16, with appropriate quotations. According to these writers, Jefferson's published letters to his bosom companions "leave no doubt that he loathed all forms of Christian orthodoxy" (513).

57. With this conclusion of L. W. Bacon, *A History of American Christianity* (New York, 1907), 237, practically all Holiness and Pentecostal writers concur.

58. Hudson, W. S., *Religion in America* (New York, 1965), 138–39. An excellent treatment of this Second Awakening is given by C. E. Olmstead, *History of Religion in the United States* (Englewood Cliffs, N. J., 1961), 256–62; and by A. Heimert, *op. cit.,* 60–87.

59. McLoughlin, *op. cit.,* 17.

60. *Ibid.,* 18. "He used his lawyer's training to good purpose; he made God, sin, atonement, and repentence as real as houses and lands. He had something of the quick logic and wit of Abraham Lincoln. He treated of sins in the concrete with a clinical knowledge of motives possessed by few evangelicals" (A. L. Drummond, *Story of American Protestantism* [Boston, 1951], 258).

61. See J. H. Nichols, *Romanticism in American Theology: Nevin*

and Schaff at Mercersburg (Chicago, 1961). Drummond credits Finney for being "one of the few evangelists to make any impact on distillers and brewers."

62. Miller, Perry, *Covenant and Revival,* in Smith-Jamison, *op. cit.,* 350.

63. Niebuhr, H. R., *Protestant Movement and Democracy,* in Smith-Jamison, *op. cit.,* 53–54. Among the undesirable products of the Awakening, W. W. Sweet mentions: controversy and division; doctrinal errors; confusion and disorder; a lessening of the sense of sacredness in worship and singing; overemphasis of the emotional and underemphasis of the rational in religious experience (see his *Revivalism in America,* 140ff.). Not all the historians take a similar dim view of the event. "With all its excesses," says Olmstead, "the revival was religiously constructive and left a positive influence for good that would not be effaced from American society for years to come" *(op. cit.,* 263).

64. Latourette, K. S., *A History of the Expansion of Christianity* (New York, 1941), IV, 193. See the complete list of these mergers in H. P. Van Dusen, *One Great Ground of Hope—Christian Missions and Christian Unity* (Philadelphia, 1961), 159ff.; Pearce Beaver, *Ecumenical Beginnings in Protestant World Mission, A History of Comity* (New York, 1962); "Voluntary Movements and the Changing Ecumenical Age," in Rouse-Neill, *A History of the Ecumenical Movement* (Philadelphia, 1967), 309ff.

65. Strangely enough, as remarked by Smith-Handy, "the revivalistic Protestantism of the middle decades of the nineteenth century was strongly anti-Catholic, and the propaganda of the benevolence movement often identified 'Romanism' as a chief enemy of Protestantism, peace, and progress. . . . The burning of several Catholic institutions, the organization of a number of societies to carry the crusade against Catholicism, and the political nativism of the 1850's were directly related to this darker side of the Protestant crusading pattern" *(American Christianity,* II, 19).

NOTES TO CHAPTER TWO

1. There is, to my knowledge, no book that covers this whole period. But extremely useful elements can be found in the following authors: L. Smith, *Revivalism and Social Reform* (Nashville, 1957), and *Called to Holiness—The Story of the Nazarenes* (Kansas, 1963); J. L. Peters, *Christian Perfection in American Methodism* (New York, 1956); H. V. Synam, *The Pentecostal Movement in the United States* (University of Georgia, Ph. D. Thesis, Microfilm, 1967); D. R. Rose, *A Theology of Christian Experience, Interpreting the Historic Wesleyan Message* (Minneapolis, 1965); J. S. Inskip, *Methodism Explained and Defended* (Cincinnati, 1851); H. E. Jessup, *We, the Holiness People* (Chicago, 1948); J. E. Campbell, *The Pentecostal Holiness Church: Its Background and History* (Franklin Springs, Ga., 1951); H. D. Farish, *The Circuit Rider Dismounts—A Social History of Methodism, 1965–1900* (Richmond, Va., 1938); W. W. Cary, *Story of the National Holiness Missionary Society* (Chicago, 1940); M. E. Gaddis, *Christian Perfection in America* (Ph. D. dissertation, University of Chicago, 1929).

2. Wesley, J., *Plain Account of Christian Perfection* (Boston, n.d.), 105. "It was largely this doctrine, in contradistinction to the sterner Calvinism, which gave Methodism its power in the frontier regions of the West" (E. T. Clark, *The Small Sects of America* [Nashville, 1959], 57).

3. Gaddis, M. E., *op. cit.*, 375ff. And yet, two decades after the Civil War, Methodism was still proclaimed "the strongest and most influential Church of the American continent," and the religious force which could do more "to turn back the tide of ruin than any other church" (Farish, *op. cit.*, 1).

4. Smith, L., *Called to Holiness*, 14.

5. Mead, S., *Handbook of Denominations* (New York, 1956), 156–57. See Farish, *op. cit.*, 3, 5, 6.

6. Gaddis, M. E., *op. cit.*, 312. He attributes the revival of perfectionism to Finney and holds that his views were more Wesleyan than those of his contemporaries.

7. Mrs. Palmer thought of santification as "the absolute requirement of the Bible," and as a doctrine "binding upon all, of every name, rather than as a doctrine of a sect." (See D. R. Rose, *op. cit.*, 40.)

8. *General Conference Journal, 1840*, 161. The bishops, after reaffirming the central position of that belief, warned the faithful of the insufficiency of "having that doctrine in our standards [of faith]." See Clark, *op. cit.*, 57.

9. W. McDonald-J. E. Searles, *The Life of Rev. John S. Inskip* (Chicago, 1885), 186.

10. Synam, *op. cit.,* 26. According to an enthusiastic observer, the 1858 revival swept every state of the country, "adding a million converts to the churches, accomplishing untold good, yet being utterly free from the fanaticism which had marred earlier American awakenings" (Rose, *op. cit.,* 44).

11. Smith, L., *op. cit.,* 25–26. The awakening affected "every county in Ulster, Scotland, Wales, and England." The addition of new members to the evangelical churches was also "a million" (Rose, 44). Keswick saw the beginning of controversies among holiness people regarding millenarism, glossolalia, and divine healing. Those discussions were brought back home by Moody, Torrey, Adoniran Gordon, A. B. Simpson, and others.

12. Smith, L., *op. cit.,* 27. The fanatics often preached weird doctrines. For some of them the demons, especially the demon of sickness, were God's servants to chastise his people; the "saints" should not partake of pork and coffee; and those who had been sanctified were already free from "doctors, drugs, and devils." See E. J. Jernigan, *Pioneer Days of the Holiness Movement in the South West* (Kansas, 1919), 150.

13. *Journal of General Conference, 1870,* 164. The situation constituted a novelty in the Methodist Church. Since the days of Wesley, Methodists had been involved in arguments regarding holiness, but the discussions were with other denominations. Now, for the first time, Methodists were engaged with their own brethren over the nature of that characteristic of their church. See Farish, *op. cit.,* 73.

14. Farish, H. D., *op. cit.,* 74–75. Methodism was clearly on the defensive and found it easier to attack its adversaries. "They [the holiness groups] have changed the name of our meetings, substituting Holiness for Methodist. They preach a different doctrine . . . they sing different songs; they patronize and circulate a different literature; they have adopted radically different ways of worship" (cited by Synam, *op. cit.,* 52).

15. Roberts, R., *Christian Perfection and American Methodism,* 139.

16. Quoted by K. B. Kuyper, *The Church in History* (Grand Rapids, 1951), 470–71. Farish believes that the admonition was not without effect in the sense that the Church began to control the evangelists who often infiltrated into their communities: "No preacher," read a new section incorporated in the *Discipline,* "shall enter into the recognized territory of any of our pastoral charges for the purpose of conducting protracted or revival meetings except upon the invitation of the preacher in charge" *(op. cit.,* 75*)*.

17. Synam, *op. cit.,* 57. "Never before in the history of the nation had so many churches been founded in so short a time" (26).

18. See J. L. Trinderud, *The Forming of an American Tradition* (Philadelphia, 1949), 132.

19. Smith, L., *op. cit.,* 97.

20. "We are not out-comers," they said, "but as none of the evan-

gelical bodies seems to desire to push holiness as a second work of grace . . . and as our time here is short . . . we thought the most sensible thing to do was to walk alone with the Triune God" (Smith, *op. cit.*, 67).

21. Morrow, R., in *History of Methodism,* II, 626.

22. Clark, *op. cit.*, 72.

23. Smith-Jamison, *op. cit.*, 55–56. J. E. Campbell admits that the differences which have caused the divisions "have at times been absurdly trivial," while "strange and fatuous teachings have been concocted and made to represent the most extreme vagaries of the human mind" (*op. cit.*, 2).

24. Smith-Jamison, *op. cit.*, 171. "The sect," comments R. Mehl, "is born out of the violence exercised against it by the mother-church" (*Traité de sociologie protestante* [Neuchatel, 1965], 201).

25. See Farish, *op. cit.*, 322–23. On the other hand, Smith-Handy-Loetscher, *American Christianity,* II, 366, conclude that "there is no evidence that church leaders attempted to redefine Christian principles in relation to the new rural conditions in any way parallel to what the formulators of the social gospel were attempting to do in relation to industrial life."

26. Clark, *op. cit.*, 16–17.

27. See Smith-Jamison, 176. The new denominations likewise rejected the traditional ways of mediation accepted by the Reformation churches (Bible and sacraments) because they claimed actually to accomplish that contact with the Spirit, while the churches merely talk about it.

28. Clark, *op. cit.*, 17.

29. Conn, C. W., *Like A Mighty Army,* xx. In the words of R. Mehl: "When the members of a sect derive directly from a church, we must see in their joining of the new denomination a religious protest against the mother-church which they consider sclerotic, incapable of a revival or of a profound reformation" (*op. cit.*, 211).

30. Brumback, *op. cit.*, 3.

31. At the beginning, the rejection was mutual: "The Pentecostals rejected society because they believed it to be corrupt, wicked, hostile, and hopelessly lost, while society rejected the Pentecostals because it believed them to be insanely fanatical, self-righteous, doctrinally in error, and emotionally unstable" (Synam, *op. cit.*, 236).

32. Brumback, *op. cit.*, 4. This is a peculiar Pentecostal interpretation of the sixteenth-century Reformation, or it can, at most, be applied to the Anabaptist branch of the same.

33. Conn, *op. cit.*, 7.

34. Chéry, H. C., *L'offensive des sectes* (Paris, 1960); Seguy, J., *Les sectes protestantes dans la France contemporaine* (Paris, 1956); Colinon, M., *Le phénomène des sectes au XXe siècle* (Paris, 1959); Hutten, K., *Seher Grübler Enthusiasten-Sekten und religiöse Sonder-gemeinschaften der Gegenwart* (Stuttgart, 1966); Sundkler, B. G. M., *Bantu Prophets in South Africa* (London, 1961); Crivelli, C., *Directorio protestante de la América Latina* (Albi, 1933); Damboriena, P., *El protestantismo en la América Latina* (2 vols. Madrid, 1962). Hollenweger's exhaustive manuscript may be consulted in microfilm form at the Li-

brary of the School of Divinity, St. Louis University, St. Louis, Mo.

35. Forney, C. H., *History of the Churches of God* (Harrisburg, 1914); Brown, C. E., *The Church of God, Anderson, Indiana* (in V. Ferm's *The American Church of the Protestant Heritage* (New York, 1953), 435ff. They believe they have to abstain from any church organization as an "indispensable prerequisite for recovering the unity of the Church as it was known in New Testament times." They also deny the "possibility that any group of men can ever succeed in such a colossal undertaking" as the organization of "the one and only Church into which all Christians should come" (Brown, 436).

36. Mayer, F., *The Religious Bodies of America* (St. Louis, 1956), 336. Baptism, whose mode is optional, and the Lord's Supper are practiced as sacraments. The candidate to the church must renounce all worldliness and profess that entire and instantaneous sanctification can be obtained in this life.

37. The membership is reported differently: *World Christian Handbook*, 1968, speaks of 56,506; *Yearbook of American Churches*, 1968, of 32,814. The headquarters of the denomination are in Indianapolis, Ind.

38. Mead, *op. cit.*, 171–172. The main doctrinal tenets of the church are: the inspiration and inerrancy of the Scriptures; repentance, justification, and second blessing; millenarism with the restoration of the Jews; and future judgment. The sacraments include Baptism and the Lord's Supper. Marriage is a "divine institution."

39. Mead, *op. cit.*, 69. "Each family is encouraged to raise just so large a family of children as God will be pleased to give them, tithing is practiced, and love for friend and enemy is emphasized. Days of fasting and prayer are observed, the sick and the needy are assisted, and camp meetings are strongly supported." In spite of all efforts, its membership stands at 450 in 25 churches.

40. Gründler, *op. cit.*, I, 0461ff. See also Hütten, *op. cit.*, 443ff.

41. *Yearbook of American Churches, 1968*, 36; Mead, *op. cit.*, 91. The denomination prescribes for its followers a "third sacrament," the washing of the feet of the saints which has to be held during the evening services together with the Lord's Supper. It has 36,000 members, and directs a co-educational college and a seminary in Findlay, Pa.

42. Simpson, A. B., *Wholly Sanctified* (Harrisburg, 1925). See Mead, *op. cit.*, 64, and Gründler, *op. cit.*, I, 272. "It is not a sectarian body, but allows liberty in the matter of church government, and is in fraternal union with evangelical Christians of all denominations, accepting missionaries from the various churches, provided they are in sympathy with the evangelical standards of the Alliance" *(Religious Bodies of the USA* [Washington, D. C., 1941], II, 1,365).

43. For the Pentecostal version of the incident see Brumback, *op. cit.*, 91–92. That of the Alliance may be seen in one of its official publications, *Wingspread* (Harrisburg, 1943) 133ff.

44. See K. Algermissen, *Christian Sects* (New York, 1962), 121–23; Hütten, *op. cit.*, 736–38; Clark, 124–27; C. S. Braden, *They Also Believe* (New York, 1949); and W. R. Martin, *The Rise of Cults* (Grand Rapids,

1960), 84–103. All these authors study the phenomenon critically and from the Christian viewpoint. For more novelistic and literary accounts, see J. Hoshor, *God in a Rolls-Royce* (New York, 1936), and R. W. Parker, *Incredible Messiah* (New York, 1938). "The theological aspects of the Peace Mission," comments A. L. Jamison, "are too confused to permit orderly analysis, he [Father Divine] has somewhere drunk at the fountain of New Thought; the Bible still figures prominently in the cult ideology, but the binding revelations are contained in the torrential pronouncements of Father himself—the new Bible is to be read in the verbatim transcripts of his every public address, published in the *New Day*, a periodical" (*Religions in the Perimeter*, 228).

NOTES TO CHAPTER THREE

1. Conn, C. W., *Like A Mighty Army Moves the Church of God, 1886-1955* (Cleveland, Tenn., 1955), XIX. Nils Bloch-Hoell, *The Pentecostal Movement—Its Origin, Development and Character* (Copenhagen, 1964), 12, comes closer to the truth when he considers Pentecostalism as "having its roots in the Holiness Movement." As a short bibliographical note on the Pentecostal movement, besides the authors mentioned in the previous chapters, the following are recommended: Ewart, F., *The Phenomenon of Pentecost* (St. Louis, 1947); Du Plessis, D., *A Brief History of American Pentecostalism* (manuscript); Kendrick, K., *The Promise Fulfilled, A History of the Modern Pentecostal Movement* (Springfield, 1961); Simmons, E. L., *History of the Church of God* (Cleveland, Tenn., 1938); Harrison, J. I., *A History of the Assemblies of God* (Thesis, Berkeley, 1954); Gee, D., *Winds of Flame* (London, 1967); Lemmons, F. W., *Our Pentecostal Heritage* (Cleveland, Tenn., 1963); Moore, E. L., *Handbook of Pentecostal Denominations in the United States* (Thesis, Pasadena, Calif., 1954); Goss, E., *The Winds of God, The Story of the Early Pentecostal Days* (New York, 1958); Harper, M., *The Twentieth Century Pentecostal Revival* (New York, 1965).

2. Kendrick, *op. cit.,* 33. Clark traces this rather gloomy picture of Pentecostals as a religious group: "They constitute the left-wing of perfectionism. They flourish mainly among the ignorant and nervously unstable sections of the population, and differ from the common variety of Holiness groups in the extreme degree of emotionalism. Primitive traits and the experience of frontier revivalism make their last stand among these groups" (*op. cit.,* 85).

3. Kendrick, *op. cit.,* 35.

4. Conn, *op. cit.,* 23 and 32. Spurling was a Baptist minister. His counterpart in N. Carolina was A. J. Tomlinson whose *Journal of Happenings,* in five volumes, was once eagerly read by his followers.

5. The Pentecostal understanding that phenomenon can be seen in C. Brumback's book, *What Meaneth This?* (Springfield, 1947), 8. The answer of conservative theologians is found in A. Hoekema, *What About Tongue-Speaking?* (Grand Rapids, 1966), 51–53.

6. Winehouse, I., *The Assemblies of God* (New York, 1959), 14. The exegesis of Jamieson-Fausset appears in *The Critical and Explanatory Commentary* (Grand Rapids, 1950), II, 439.

7. Olmstead, C. *(History of Religion in the United States),* 455–56, calls Torrey "an oddity in the world of revivalism." He had been trained in historical criticism at Yale and Leipzig, and was an ordained Congregational minister. He became superintendent of the Moody

Institute in Chicago, and was in 1910 one of the editors of *The Fundamentals,* the vade-mecum of conservatism.

8. Quoted by Kendrick, *op. cit.,* 50–1. "I want you, students," he said, "to study out diligently what is the Bible evidence of the baptism of the Holy Ghost, that we might go before the world with something that is indisputable because it tallies with the Word" (cited by Brumback, *Suddenly . . . from Heaven,* 22).

9. Parham, Sarah E., *The Life of Charles F. Parham, Founder of the Apostolic Faith Movement* (Joplin, Mo., 1930), 38.

10. Kendrick, *op. cit.,* 53. "Most Pentecostal writers acknowledge Parham's place as the formulator of the Pentecostal doctrine, but none call him the *father* of the movement. Because of latter questions about his personal ethics, his place in Pentecostal history has been de-emphasized. Many refer to the Pentecostal movement as 'a movement without a man' " (Synam, *op. cit.,* 119).

11. See F. Bartleman, *What Really Happened at Azusa Street?* (Northridge, 1964). "The importance of the Azusa Street revival was that it acted as a catalytic agent that congealed tongue-speaking into a fully developed doctrine. For years the phenomena had been recognized, but not singled out as a necessary 'evidence' of the baptism of the Holy Spirit. It was Parham's insistence that tongues were necessary as the biblical evidence of the Holy Ghost baptism that caused division between the Holiness ranks" (Synam, *op. cit.,* 149).

12. Frodsham, S. H., *With Signs Following—The Story of the Pentecostal Revival in the Twentieth Century* (Springfield, 1946), 35–36. At times the kind of glossolalia practiced at Azusa seemed peculiar. There was a Brother Lee, a converted Catholic, and a Sister Anna Hall, who spoke Russian "as the Spirit gave utterance" (35). Also "two of the saints quite a distance apart saw the Spirit fall" upon Brother Seymour (37).

13. Brumback, *op. cit.,* 12.

14. As a consequence, says Brumback, "God had now become so real, so near, that great faith was aroused, and the children of the Lord began to believe in a restoration of the gifts as a whole."

15. Kendrick, *op. cit.,* 59. For more details see Frodsham, *op. cit.,* 41ff. The narratives reveal the blind faith given to the events by the author.

16. Conn, *op. cit.,* 55.

17. Kendrick, *op. cit.,* 62. Thus Pentecostalism succeeded in "doing what the Holiness movement could not do in that it offered the believer a repeatable and unmistakable motor expression which, in effect, guaranteed its possession by the Spirit" (J. Lapsey-J. Simpson, "Speaking in Tongues," *The Princeton Seminary Bulletin,* February, 1965, 6–7).

18. See her own memories, *This is That. Personal Experiences* (3d. ed. Los Angeles, 1923).

19. But, at that time, the irradiating center for the Eastern seaboard was the Bible Institute founded by A. B. Simpson at Nyack on

the Hudson. Meanwhile, a periodical, *The Pentecostal Testimony*, was issuing as many as 70,000 copies for distribution.

20. Jamison, *op. cit.*, 184. Regarding the Fundamentalist crisis, see N. F. Furniss, *The Fundamentalist Controversy* (New Haven, 1954), and L. Casper, *The Fundamentalist Movement* (The Hague, 1963).

21. Kendrick, *op. cit.*, 70.

22. *Ibid.*, 83. Brumback, *op. cit.*, 164ff. gives the names of some of the "founding fathers" at the convention: E. N. Bell, "the bighearted chairman," Howard A. Goss, "the ardent promoter," J. W. Welch, "the steadying influence," J. Roswell Flower, "the perennial secretary," M. M. Pinson, "the fiery keynoter," T. K. Leonard, "a foundation stone," Arch P. Collins, "the saintly peacemaker," and D. C. O. Opperman, "the pioneer educator."

23. See Winehouse, *op. cit.*, 35. Here Pentecostals affirm that "it was clear" their believers "did not desire to start a church." The convention was being called upon to recognize that the Church had already been established by Christ, and that all true believers are members of that Church" (Brumback, *op. cit.*, 175).

24. To say with Du Plessis that Pentecostal churches have no founder or that the founder is only the Holy Spirit seems to be a rhetorical figure. See *The Spirit Bade Me Go* (n.p. 1961), 9.

25. To the obvious objection that Pentecostals, after rejecting "over-organization" in the mother-churches, have ended up by adopting a stronger ecclesiastical organization, Brumback replies that the brethren, far from contemplating a "pyramiding hierarchy," simply believed that "each assembly should feel a responsibility towards the movement as a whole" (*op. cit.*, 160–61).

26. *Pentecostal Testimony*, May 1938, 11.

27. Cited by Brumback, *op. cit.*, 282–83. The antagonism of Fundamentalists is largely directed against the charismatic gifts claimed by Pentecostals; they agree on a number of other theological issues.

28. Gee, D., *The Pentecostal Movement* (ed. 1949, London), 18.

29. Pentecostalism had given rise in 14 years to at least 25 separate denominations. Methodism, to achieve a similar separatism, had needed a full century. See Synam, *op. cit.*, 207.

30. Conn, *Like a Mighty Army*, 130–31.

31. "It is well to bear in mind," says historian W. W. Sweet, "that Baptists, Methodists, Disciples, and Quakers were once trouble-makers for the respectable churches, the Congregationalists, the Presbyterians, and the Episcopalians. And only a little further back in time, the Episcopalians, the Congregationalists, and the Presbyterians were, in their turn, trouble-makers. As someone has suggested it, it is the *cranks* which turn the world" *(Revivalism in America)*, 177.

32. Barratt's biography, conversion, and activities have been fully covered by Bloch-Hoell, *op. cit.*, 65ff. On pages 239–40 the author presents a bibliographical list of Barratt's writings.

33. Bloch-Hoell, *op. cit.*, 70. For a "warmer" description of the events, see Frodsham, *op. cit.*, 71ff.

34. *Ibid.,* 74ff. "The majority of the [Norwegian] are not Spirit-baptized and have never spoken in tongues."

35. Frodsham, *op. cit.,* 77ff. Only the Baptists have a larger total community, 150,000. But their full communicants are only 35,540 to the 91,000 of Pentecostals.

36. The official title of the communion is Apostolic Church Assembly. See *World Christian Handbook,* 1968, 205. The Mission Covenant Church (Danske Missionsförbund) seems to belong to the Holiness family. See Gründler, *op. cit.,* I, 391. It carries mission work in Tanganyika, Aden, India, and Formosa.

37. Bloch-Hoell, *op. cit.,* 83–5. See *World Christian Handbook,* 1968, 189. The small Finnish Free Mission (Fria Missionsforbundet) has a total community of 2,000, and practices faith-healing.

38. Hutten, K., *Seher Grübler Enthusiasten,* 516ff. The information provided by the 1968 edition of the *World Christian Handbook* is extremely deficient.

39. See K. Algermissen, *Christian Sects* (New York, 1962), 109–111.

40. The Assemblies of God have 6,450 followers, and the Church of God, Cleveland, 3,049.

41. According to the *World Christian Handbook,* in Switzerland the Assemblies of God have 150 members, the Apostolic Church 1,500, and the Bund Frier Evangelischer Gemeinder in der Schweiz, 315.

42. Nichol, J., *Pentecostalism* (New York, 1966), 196.

43. The totals given for Spain are: Assemblies of God, 766, and Church of God, Cleveland, 304. It is obvious that such low estimates do not correspond to the real situation. In spite of legal strictures, the activities of the Pentecostal groups are growing in different parts of the peninsula.

44. See *World Christian Handbook,* 1968, 190–191. The Assemblies of God make up ninety per cent of the Pentecostal community. Writers usually do not include in the list the many "healing sects," indigenous or imported, such as Antonianism, or the movement started by Georges Roux, and called The Christ of Montfavet. In many respects they seem like pale imitations of Mary Baker Eddy's Christian Science.

45. See W. Kolarz, *Religion in the Soviet Union* (New York, 1961), 355. In the *Handbook* of 1968 the corresponding totals are: Rumania, 50,000; Bulgaria, 5,000; Hungary, 6,700; Czechoslovakia, no details; Poland, 3,859. For Russia, the compilers note, without further details, the presence of the Assemblies of God, the Church of God, Cleveland, and a vague group called Pentecostals. As a commentary they add: "The Church of God, with headquarters at Queen's Village, New York, claims some *millions* of followers in both the USSR and China" (207).

46. Nichol, *op. cit.,* 198.

47. Wilson, Bryan R., *Sects and Society* (Berkeley, 1961), 15. See also E. Jeffreys, *Stephen Jeffreys—the Beloved Evangelist* (London, 1946); *Constitutions of the Elim Foursquare Gospel Alliance* (London, 1952).

48. The 1968 statistics are higher: 308 places of worship, 271 or-

dained ministers, 44,800 members of total community and 20,000 communicants. There is also another denomination by the name of Elim Pentecostal Church with 2,000 followers.

49. Again the latest estimates are different: Assemblies of God, 65,972 members; Church of God, Cleveland, 5,491; Pentecostal Holiness Church, 1,500. See *World Christian Handbook*, 1968, 194—95. On several occasions the Elim Alliance has tried to merge with the Assemblies of God. The reason adduced by the former for the refusal was: "the blessing of God which has rested so conspicuously upon their chosen methods," which "might be jeopardized if they became merged with a body working on a different governmental basis" (Nichol, *op. cit.*, 185).

50. Clark, *op. cit.*, 98; Kendrick, *op. cit.*, 4; Bloch-Hoell, *op. cit.*, 58–59. Moore's listing, which is the most up-to-date of all, is found in his manuscript thesis: *Pentecostal Denominations in the United States.* Each entry carries, besides a historical sketch, a short account of its doctrines.

51. The description does not apply to neo-Pentecostals. Here the writer is tempted to dwell on cultic practices such as the handling of snakes or drinking poisonous beverages. Reports of their existence come from the mountainous and backward regions of Kentucky, Virginia, and Tennessee. In spite of a few similarities, they do not belong to the Pentecostal fold, and the movement has sternly refused to include them in its ranks. The practices have in themselves little that is Christian. See E. T. Clark, *op. cit.*, 98–99, and more extensively Nichol, *op. cit.*, 151–57.

52. Mayer, *op. cit.*, 383; Clark, *op. cit.*, 122; Mead, *Handbook of American Churches* (1965), 169.

53. At the beginning, says Kendrick, "many individuals followed their inclinations, and as a consequence local groups were sometimes in a state of confusion—every person an authority unto himself" (*op. cit.*, 73). The best available bibliography is still that of Kendrick, Winehouse, Brumback, and D. Gee.

54. Kendrick, *The Promise Fulfilled*, 82.

55. *Word and Witness*, March 20, 1914.

56. There was long debate regarding the adopted name. Against the tradition of twenty centuries, and for Scriptural and philological reasons derived from the Greek, German, and Scotch languages, they rejected the name *Church* and adopted instead that of the *Assemblies of God* which, "in addition to being scriptural, expresses the very heart of the Pentecostal Movement, the emphasis upon the assembling of believers together in His name" (Brumback, *op. cit.*, 182).

57. The new totals for the North American constituency in 1968 were: 8,443 places of worship, 10,519 ordained pastors, 572,123 members of total community. It is much harder to compile their totals in mission lands. Some of them will be adduced in our chapter on missions.

58. Sources: Campbell, J. E., *The Pentecostal Holiness Church*

(Franklin Springs, 1951); *Discipline of the Pentecostal Holiness Church* (Franklin Springs, 1949); King, H., and Blanche, L., *Yet Speaketh, Memoirs of the Late Bishop Joseph L. King* (Franklin Springs, 1949); Kendrick, *op. cit.*, 177ff.

59. The headquarters of the denomination publishes a flow of material regarding the origins, developments, and doctrinal positions of the church. Here are some, all published in Los Angeles: A. S. McPherson, *The Story of My Life* (1923); *In the Service of the King*, (1927); *This Is That* (1923); *The Holy Spirit* (1931); *The Iron Furnace* (1931); *The Crimson Road* (1932).

60. Clark, *op. cit.*, 115. For one of the most controversial incidents in her life, see L. Thomas, *The Vanishing Evangelist (The Aimée Semple McPherson Kidnaping Affair)* (New York, 1959).

61. McPherson, *The Foursquare Gospel* (Los Angeles, 1946), 22. "In all this she professed to be under the direct guidance of God" (Clark).

62. *Declaration of Faith of the International Church of the Foursquare Gospel* (Los Angeles, 1965). During her lifetime Aimée S. McPherson admitted that to her followers she remained "the Lord's anointed, sent to herald his second coming," while at the opposite extreme were "the scoffers" who saw in her "nothing but a clever mountebank, devoid of genuine intelligence or sincerity." In our days opinion is divided almost in the same way.

63. C. W. Conn, *Like A Mighty Army*, 180–81. In spite of many signs to the contrary, Conn is persuaded that his church "had kept itself in unity and love, had kept itself with the cause of Christ, had kept itself free from rancor and malice—it had kept itself in truth, as well as in name, the Church of God."

64. Homer Tomlinson's character, in many ways, well matches those of Aimée McPherson and Father Divine. He accused his brother Milton (and his Church of God) of idolatry of their famous shrine of Cherokee County, N.C., and of abusing "orders" since, being only a deacon, he had ordained himself a bishop. On more solemn occasions, Brother Homer and his wife, robed as king and queen, enter the temple, spread ashes at the entrance, and invite people to repent as did Nineveh in order to avoid utter destruction. See *Minutes of the 58 Annual General Assembly—The Church of God* (Cape Girardeau, Mo., 1963), 8. His political arm is called "The Theocratic Party," and his program contains, among other interesting items: 1) a new criminal code by which criminals will be forgiven 490 times (Matt. 6:14; 18:21–22); 2) a new civil law in which the covetous would lose all their possessions; and 3) tithing as a substitute for the present system of taxation.

65. "Beauty," says one of its pamphlets, "is in salvation and not in ornaments and jewelry." The church is called at times the "Flag Church" because of the "All Nations Flag" which they display.

66. Conn, *op. cit.*, 284ff.

67. See its *General Constitutions and By-Laws* (Kansas, 1947). Its attitude towards divorced people is more lenient than that of most other Pentecostal churches. They can even be readmitted into the

ministry. The reason given is the welfare of the children. The doctrinal and organizational aspects of the church are well described by Kendrick, *op. cit.*, 149ff., and Mead, *op. cit.*, 168.

68. *Op. cit.*, 117.

69. *Ibid.*, 118. Mead, *op.cit.*, 168.

70. Vouga, O., *Our Gospel Message* (St. Louis, n.d.), 29. See also F. J. Ewart, *The Phenomenon of Pentecost, A History of the Latter Rain* (St. Louis, 1947).

71. Burr, M. H., *The Hair Question* (St. Louis, n.d.), 1–16.

72. For unknown reasons, the Church of God in Christ, which in Clark's estimate had a membership of 35,000, has jumped by 1968 to 425,000. It has 4,500 places of worship and 6,000 ordained clergy. It is a Negro church with headquarters in Lexington, Mississippi, and sends missionaries to Africa, the Caribbean, and various Asiatic countries. Here are a few other names taken from Moore's *Handbook of Pentecostal Denominations in the United States*: The Jesus Church, The Full Standard Salvation Church, The Associated Brotherhood of Christians, The Apostolic Church, The Pentecostal Assemblies of the World, The Church of God (Mountain Assembly), World Church, United Fundamentalist Church, United Full Gospel Fellowship of America, The Independent Assemblies of God, The Christian Church of America, The California Evangelistic Association, The Church of God of the Apostolic Church, Faith Tabernacle, The United Apostolic Faith Church, The World-Wide Fellowship Association, and The Pentecostal Church of New Antioch.

73. Bibliography: Kelsey, M. T., *Tongue Speaking*; Du Plessis, D., *The Spirit Bade Me Go*; Sherrill, J.L., *They Speak With Tongues*; Wilkerson, D., *The Cross and the Switchblade*; Bergsma, S., *Speaking with Tongues: Some Psychological and Physiological Implications of Modern Glossolalia*; Metz, D., *Speaking in Tongues*; Gromacki, R. G., *The Modern Tongues Movement*; Hoekema, A., *What about Tongue-Speaking?*

NOTES TO CHAPTER FOUR

1. Algermissen, K., *Konfessionskunde* (Ital. tr. *La Chiesa e le chiese* [Brescia, 1961]), 927–28. In the same vein Bloch-Hoell admits the difficulty of characterizing Pentecostal theology "because of its subjectivism and the resulting lack of unity in its doctrines, liturgy, and, to a certain extent, organization" (*op. cit.*, 174).

2. Conn, *Pillars of Pentecost* (Cleveland, Tenn., 1956), 23. Basic for our study are the Statements, Constitutions, and Declarations of Faith of the main denominations.

3. Du Plessis, D., *The Spirit Bade Me Go*, 8. The *Manual of the United Pentecostal Church* expresses the same idea: "As regards salvation by justification, we are Lutherans. In baptismal matters we are Baptists. As regards sanctification, we are Methodists. In aggressive evangelism, we are the Salvation Army. But, as regards Baptism in the Holy Spirit, we are Pentecostals inasmuch as we preach that it is possible to be baptized in or filled by the Holy Ghost just as on the day of Pentecost."

4. Campbell, *op. cit.*, 172–73. He is convinced that "historians of the future will be forced to allocate to these somewhat despised groups just recompense for their noteworthy contribution in preserving the orthodox, evangelical faith."

5. *Ibid.*, 172. Do they belong by right to the Reformation family? The answer may be delayed till the end of this and the two following chapters. Pentecostals, however, do not doubt about it, and gladly adduce a French Dominican who has defined Pentecostalism as "a reform of the Reformation, a movement which intends to take up the work of the great Reformers by purifying the Church and providing the Christian communities with a new life, that of the day of Pentecost" (Chéry, C., *L'Offensive des sectes,* Paris, 1960).

6. Conn, *op. cit.*, 26. For this author the five basic doctrines which form the bedrock of Pentecostalism are: the inerrancy and infallibility of the Bible; the virgin birth and complete divinity of Christ; the literal resurrection of the body; the atoning sacrifice of Christ for the sins of the world; and his coming in bodily form to the earth.

7. Campbell, *op. cit.*, 104.

8. Jamison, *op. cit.*, 197.

9. *Ibid.*, 179. On the other hand, this simplistic approach gives to their belief a firmness which is lacking in members of many other denominations. "The fact," writes a French sociologist, "that the word of Scripture is the word of God without human intermediaries of any kind, that each sign and each letter has been written by God's hand,

gives them the same guarantee of direct contact with him as inspiration. If the book came from heaven, it becomes a kind of God's fragment put at our disposal by him" (R. Mehl, *Traité de sociologie du protestantisme,* 215).

10. Winehouse, I., *The Assemblies of God,* 82–83. Pentecostals have been accused of stressing too much the emotional aspect of religion. Winehouse answers: "God has made man with the emotional parts of his nature very real and even proper. Emotion finds expression in politics, in sports, in love. Why not in faith? . . . I don't think this is wholesome or fair according to nature. If we are genuinely involved and interested and our hearts are sincerely stirred by that in which we are participating, then emotional expression will appear. . . . If I have the real heart of true religion, then from the heart come the real feelings of men" *(op. cit.,* 82).

11. There is not much of a bibliography to be quoted. But the following works written by Pentecostals will be used: Williams, E. S., *Systematic Theology* (Springfield, Mo., 1953), 3 vols.; Riggs, R. M., *We Believe* (Springfield, Mo., 1954); *id., The Spirit Himself* (Springfield, Mo., 1949); Pearlman, M., *Knowing the Doctrines of the Bible* (Springfield, Mo., 1937); Paulk, E. P., *Your Pentecostal Neighbor* (Cleveland, Tenn., 1958); Nelson, P. C., *Bible Doctrines* (Springfield, Mo., 1958); Lemons, F. W., *Our Pentecostal Heritage* (Cleveland, Tenn., 1963); McPherson, A. S., *The Foursquare Gospel* (Los Angeles, 1946); Gee, D., *Pentecost* (Springfield, Mo., 1932). Mayer, Hutten, Kendrick, Campbell, Conn, Brumback, Clark, and Frodsham contain much useful material.

12. The objection was raised against the United Pentecostal Church and its "oneness" doctrine regarding the Trinitarian mystery.

13. Brumback, *op. cit.,* 202.

14. Conn, *op. cit.,* 23; Wilson, B., *Sects and Society,* 16; Bloch-Hoell, 110. Among the other American Pentecostal denominations, the Trinitarian profession is clear in the following: Pentecostal Church of New Antioch, Inc.; Open Bible Standard Churches; International Foursquare Gospel; Congregational Holiness Church; Church of the Living God; Church of God Prophecy; Pentecostal Church of God in America; Christian Church of North America; Elim Missionary Assemblies; National David Spiritual Temple of Christian Church Union; Church of God in Christ; International Pentecostal Assemblies; Pentecostal Church of Christ, and others. On the contrary, the Jesus Church, the Apostolic Overcoming Holy Church of God, the Apostolic Church, and the Church of the Lord Jesus Christ of the Apostolic Faith. In others the statements are not clear.

15. Williams, *op. cit.,* I, 92ff..

16. *Ibid.,* 107–108. A. B. Simpson, founder of the Christian and Missionary Alliance, was convinced that trichotomy was "a division recognized in the Scriptures" *(Wholly Sanctified,* 25).

17. Wood, W. W., *Cultures and Personalities, Aspects of the Holiness Religion* (Le Hague, 1965), 17.

18. *Ibid.,* 17. However, Pentecostal demonology is much weaker

than that of the Jehovah's Witnesses where the basic doctrines of the denominations center around the struggle between Jehovah and Armageddon. See Mayer, *op. cit.,* 461ff.

19. Williams, *op. cit.,* 133. Certain Pentecostals make a distinction between demonic *possession* and demonic *influence.* Unbelievers (i. e., non-Pentecostals) are exposed to the first, while the "saints" will be subjected only to the latter. Regarding African demon-possession see H. W. Turner, *African Independent Church* (Oxford, 1967), 2 vols., and F. B. Welbourn, *The Importance of Ghosts* (in *African Independent Church Movements,* edited by W. E. V. Hayward [Edinburgh, 1963], 15ff.).

20. Williams, *op. cit.,* 100. Angels do not seem to have much to do with man's ways and troubles: "The good angels worship and serve God, but the bad angels worship and serve Satan" (Riggs, *Christian Doctrines,* 17).

21. Pearlman *(op. cit.,* I, 85) says "we cannot be dogmatic about the guardian angels"; however, "the promises of angelic help are sufficiently numerous and plain to prove a source of encouragement to every Christian."

22. Pearlman, *op. cit.,* 133; Bloch-Hoell, *op. cit.,* 113. Pentecostals love to use the Methodist expression of "inborn sin."

23. Williams devotes eleven pages to original sin and its consequences, in contrast to the thirty-four dealing with demonology.

24. Riggs, *op. cit.,* 18; Mayer, *op. cit.,* 320.

25. "The Pentecostal concept of justification is," according to Bloch-Hoell, "very different from that of genuine Lutheranism" *(op. cit.,* 121). Is this accusation borne by facts? As we shall see in the next chapter, justification by faith remains for Pentecostals an "imperfect stage" which must be completed by sanctification. It is also true that, in a number of Statements of Faith, this article is not mentioned among those which are most important. On the other hand the doctrine is not absent from a number of other declarations. Moreover, some authors (for instance, Pearlman II, 93ff.), use a vocabulary borrowed to the letter from Lutheran theology.

26. Williams, *op. cit.,* II, 199; Pearlman, *op. cit.,* II, 51ff.

27. *Constitutions of the Assemblies of God, 1959; Pentecostal Church of God of America, General Constitutions and By-Laws* (Chicago, 1953); *Manual of the United Pentecostal Church* (St., Louis, 1955). The documents insist mainly on the conditions of membership to be part of the community (second baptism, belief in charisms, rejections of secret societies, etc.), rather than on the nature of the Church.

28. Pearlman, *op. cit.,* II, 79. "The Church is the body of Christ, He being the head, its earthly constituents are made of men and women born of the Spirit, possessing eternal life. To it is delegated the various gifts and offices of the Holy Spirit" *(Pentecostal Church of God in America).*

29. Nelson, *op. cit.,* 105.

30. *Op. cit.,* 30.

31. *Traité de sociologie du protestantisme,* 215. In his opinion, "it is in the measure in which the [Protestant] Reformation was a movement of rupture, of return to the sources, and an effort to find the dynamism and simplicity of the primitive Church that we can establish a link between the sects and the Reformation churches" (203).

32. See the excellent article *Pietism* by Martin Schmidt in *The Encyclopedia of the Lutheran Church* (Minneapolis, 1965), III, 188–89.

33. Schmidt, *op. cit.* On the other hand these denominations "stress the role of charism over function, spontaneity over organization, prophetism over priesthood, inspiration over doctrine" (Mehl, *op. cit.,* 203).

34. Nelson, *op. cit.,* 105. See K. Hutten, *op. cit.,* 493ff.; Wilson, *op. cit.,* 67; Bloch-Hoell, *op. cit.,* 151–52. Genetically this is a repetition of the Covenant doctrine of Puritanism. See M. M. Knappen, *Tudor Puritanism* (London, 1965), 339ff., and Perry Miller, *The New England Mind: The Seventeenth Century* (Boston, 1954).

35. *Op. cit.,* II, 98.

36. *Ibid.,* 96. Many other Pentecostals insist in the visibility of the Church.

37. *Ibid.,* 103. Thus the very nature of Pentecostal ecclesiology requires that its congregations remain *small.*

38. Williams, *op. cit.,* 22–23. Pentecostals have not developed systematically their theology of Church unity.

39. *Op. cit.,* 116–7. "It is clear that the Lord Jesus Christ purposed that there should be a society of his followers to give mankind his gospel and to represent him to the world" (Pearlman).

40. Williams, *op. cit.,* 130–4.

41. See Winehouse, *op. cit.,* 227. Pentecostals "see plainly that there is no warrant in the New Testament for the merging of the churches into an ecclesiastical authority governed by a hierarchy" (Pearlman, *op. cit.,* III, 97). And yet, in some of their denominations, like the Church of God, Cleveland, the General Assembly is the body "in which is vested the full power and authority to dictate and promulgate and to govern the local churches"—a government which they themselves call "theocratic in form as interpreted by its officials."

42. "In this well-organized religious corporation everything necessary to produce tangible results was provided. If anyone was by-passed by the Foursquare technique, it was definitely not for want of departmentalization" (Bach, *They Have Also Found a Faith,* 75). Regarding Brazilian Pentecostals, see W. C. Reed, *New Patterns of Growth in Brazil* (Grand Rapids, 1965), 135.

43. Wilson, *op. cit.,* 66.

44. *Constitutions and By-Laws of the Assemblies of God.*

45. This is more true in mission lands where neophytes must be impressed with the rigorous standards of Pentecostalism, in contrast with the "laxness" of the historical churches in the place.

46. *Varieties of Protestantism* (Philadelphia, 1960), 132ff. Thus the Lord's Supper, "which is simply a formal ritual," becomes "of little or

no value" except that, "as we kneel together around the table, we may be made to feel our kinship with one another with a new poignancy." Similarly Baptism "must not be regarded as having any saving efficacy, lest man should place confidence in a merely external act . . . when the only baptism which really matters is the baptism of the Holy Spirit."

47. *Op. cit.*, 204, 214.

48. Conn, *op. cit.*, 95. This same lack of interest is noticed in the meager space (six pages in three volumes) devoted by E. S. Williams to sacraments. Is this a *logical* consequence of the sacramental principles laid down by the Reformation, and a growth of the opposition to the *ex opere operato* of Catholicism? See H. T. Kerr, *The Christian Sacraments* (Philadelphia, 1954), 50–53.

49. Bloch-Hoell rightly remarks that Pentecostal churches "in their declarations of faith, inasmuch as they refer to Baptism, give merely negative and polemical statements on the effects of Baptism" (*op. cit.*, 165).

50. See *The Encyclopedia of Southern Baptists* (Nashville, 1960), I, 106.

51. Paulk, *op. cit.*, 160. The same ideas are repeated by the Elim Church, the Church of God, Cleveland, the Pentecostal Church of God in America, the Open Bible Standard Church, the International Church of the Foursquare Gospel, and others. The Fire Baptized Church denies completely the power of the water in order to insist in the Baptism of Fire. The Pentecostal Holiness Church accepts only the baptism in the Holy Spirit "as the early Church received and taught it" (*Pentecostal Holiness Advocate*, 1953, 4).

52. Williams, *op. cit.*, III, 49.

53. The important thing is not the rite but the disposition of the individual. In the words of Conn: "Repentance is an *inward* act of faith cleansing [the soul] from sin and separating from the world. Baptism is an *outward sign of obedience*, signifying spiritual death unto life. Baptism without repentance is impotent" (*op. cit.*, 76).

54. Williams, *op. cit.*, 153.

55. *Ibid.*, 273. "None of the dear little ones who are, of course, not responsible for their coming into existence, can perish if they die before they are old enough to decide for themselves. In this sense it can be said that there do not exist any heathen children" (Barratt, quoted by Bloch-Hoell, *op. cit.*, 114).

56. Paulk, *op. cit.*, 163.

57. See the instructions—doctrinal as well as liturgical—regarding the ceremony that are given by R. Riggs, *The Spirit Filled Pastor's Guide* (Springfield, 1948), 223–24.

58. Williams, *op. cit.*, III, 153.

59. The Pentecostal Holiness Church *allows* the children to be baptized or dedicated, while the Full Salvation Union believes that babies dying without baptism will remain small in heaven. Practically all Latin American Pentecostal groups practice water baptism.

60. In my list of American denominations this seems the practice of most of those who admit water-baptism. In both missions and in Latin America baptism by immersion and in the open is a feature

which distinguishes Pentecostals from the rather "secret" ceremonies carried on without solemnity in the back of the local church. Doubtless that gives them also much publicity.

61. Nelson, *op. cit.,* 58.

62. According to Pearlman, "when the Church forsook the simplicity of the New Testament and became influenced by pagan ideas, it attached an un-scriptural importance to water baptism.... It was then administered to the sick and dying. Since immersion was out of the question in such cases, baptism was administered by sprinkling. Later because of the convenience of the methol, it was made general" *(op. cit.,* III, 88).

63. *Op. cit.,* 151–52.

64. The list of "oneness" churches, some American and some indigenous, compiled by Hollenwager, is very large. Most of them are spread throughout Africa, but both Latin America and Asia (mostly Japan) have their share.

65. "The Trinitarian formula," says Pearlman, "is a description of an experience; those who are baptized in the name of the Triune God are thereby testifying that they have been plunged into spiritual communion with the Trinity" *(op. cit.,* III, 89).

66. Nelson, *op. cit.,* 61.

67. Riggs, *op. cit.,* 200–01. The candidate is baptized "upon his public confession of faith" and "his determination to leave all and follow him." The Jesus Church uses this formula: "In obedience to the command of Jesus, and upon the confession of your faith, and with the authority which is invested in me, I now baptize you in Jesus." (See Moore, *Handbook of Pentecostal Denominations in the United States).*

68. Some of the denominations clearly state the purely symbolic character of the Eucharist. Many others simply omit the mention of the Eucharist in their statements of faith. There is one denomination, the World Church, which seems to admit some kind of real presence. With these waverings in the home churches, clear eucharistic ideas in their off-shoots in mission lands cannot be expected.

69. Riggs, *We Believe,* 32.

70. "This holy ordinance *symbolizes* the broken body.... It *represents* our union with him.... It is a *memorial* of his death" (Nelson, *op. cit.,* 64).

71. Pearlman, *op. cit.,* 91. Hence Bloch-Hoell's conclusion: "it would be contradictory to the basic Pentecostal interpretation of Christianity to believe that the Holy Communion should be a real sacrament, conveying forgiveness of sins and saving grace" *(op. cit.,* 170).

72. This is done in locally printed pamphlets, at times with "testimonies" of ex-priests who have joined Pentecostal ranks. Their converts are also at the forefront of those who try to interrupt the eucharistic processions.

73. Pearlman, *op. cit.,* 94–99.

74. These considerations synthetize my observations of Pentecostal communion practices in various parts of the world. In a very dry way Riggs shows to the pastors of the Assemblies of God the mechanics of

a communion service. We are told there that "this is a ceremony which is solemn and sacred and, by the presence of the Holy Spirit throughout, should be expected to yield rich spiritual blessing" (*The Spirit-Filled Pastor's Guide,* 219–20).

75. *Op. cit.,* 279. According to Conn, "the practice had been once common among the revivalists of the nation. . . . From its inception this tender token of subservience and brotherhood has been part of Pentecostal worship" *(Like An Army,* 65).

76. Brumback, *op. cit.,* 279. R. G. Spurling prescribed it once a year for the members of the Church of God, Cleveland.

77. A survey of religious bodies in the United States published in 1941 alludes to 42 denominations, many of them belonging to the holiness and pentecostal families, which practiced foot-washing. The totals have certainly grown in the following decades.

78. See H. W. Turner, *History of an African Independent Church —The Church of the Lord (Aladura)* (Oxford, 1967, II).

79. *Op. cit.,* 166. For the Apostolic Faith it "is just as necessary that we should obey this command as the command to observe the Lord's Supper" (quoted by Bloch-Hoell, *op. cit.,* 171).

80. Pearlman, *op. cit.,* I, 142; II, 79.

81. Pearlman, *op. cit.,* 106–07.

82. Slay, *op. cit.,* 130–31.

83. It was proposed by Daniel Whitby, an English theologian of the seventeenth century. None of the denominations in my list profess explicitly this type of millenarism which has been proposed by certain eschatological groups.

84. Nelson, *op. cit.,* 136–37. Antemillennialism is rejected as "a Romish invention."

85. Pearlman, *op. cit.,* II, 133ff.

The whole problem, from the Pentecostal viewpoint, is well developed by F. M. Boyd, *Introduction to Prophecy* (Springfield, Mo., 1948), 119–28. In his opinion, the events of World Wars I and II, and the resurgence of the Middle-East independent nations, prove that the stage is prepared for the appearance of the anti-Christ.

86. Boyd, *op. cit.,* 110ff.

87. Riggs, *We Believe,* II, 40—41.

88. Boyd, *op. cit.,* 128ff.

89. Let us note, however, that, departing from the common Christian tradition, this judgment of the "wicked dead" will take place "a thousand years after the judgment of nations" (Boyd, *op. cit.,* 134).

NOTES TO CHAPTER FIVE

1. Brumback, *Suddenly . . . from Heaven,* 116. The impression has not altogether disappeared in our day, and Pentecostal writers, after dismissing as irrelevant what bishops, synods, church conventions, psychologists "and fellow-travellers," linguists, and theologians have said about their peculiarities, conclude that such attempts "to interpret the charismatic manifestations of the Holy Spirit without a charismatic experience is as fatuous as the application of the Christian ethic apart from a regenerate dynamic" (H. M. Ervin, *These Are Not Drunken As Ye Suppose* (Plainfield, N. J., 1968), 3.

2. These features belong to practically all Pentecostal denominations and can be found in their Constitutions or Declarations of Faith. A few make a specific mention of prophecy, or of the possession of all nine gifts of the Holy Spirit. The Church of God, Prophecy, includes among its gifts the casting out of devils and even the handling of serpents. In African Pentecostalism the interpretation of dreams is given a prominent place.

3. Gee, D., *Spiritual Gifts in the Work of the Ministry Today* (Springfield, 1963), 12. See also Paulk, *op. cit.,* 61ff.; Wilson, *op. cit.,* 39–41; Nichol, *op. cit.,* 3–4.

4. Mayer, F., *The Religious Bodies of America,* 315.

5. See L. Dewar, *The Holy Spirit and Modern Thought* (London, 1959), IX.

6. Mackay, J. L., *Ecumenics, The Science of the Church Universal* (Englewood, 1964), 198. It is interesting to note the importance given to the work of the Holy Spirit (but without insistence on his charismatic gifts) by one of the pioneers of missionary adaptation in modern times, the Anglican Roland Allen. See his "Pentecost and the World," in David M. Paton, ed., *The Ministry of the Spirit, Selected Writings of Roland Allen* (Grand Rapids, 1962), 1—63.

7. Cited by J. L. Sherrill, *They Speak with Other Tongues,* 69. D. Gee sees a special intervention of the Spirit in the fact that Pentecostalism, after surviving its weaknesses and excesses, "stands today as a spiritual force that is compelling the attention of the historical churches" *(op. cit.,* 2).

8. This is one instance where Pentecostals can with some justice fault the other denominations for the marginal role they ascribe to the Holy Spirit in the life of the Church. "In most churches," writes Molland, "sermons about the Holy Spirit are reserved for once a year, on Whit Sunday, and then they are notoriously vague" *(Christendom,* [London, 1962], 239).

9. In this matter Pentecostals have not been satisfied with a "mere intellectual assent to some article in the creed." Their own personal reception of the Holy Spirit "was an intensely vivid experience; they knew when he came, where he came, and how he came. . . . The challenge was to experience, not to doctrine" (D. Gee, *Concerning Spiritual Gifts* [Springfield, 1938], 4).

10. Cited by Dewar, *op. cit.,* VIII.

11. Dewar, *op. cit.,* VII. Nevertheless, as noted by Algermissen, we cannot forget that Pentecostals have excessively stressed the role of the sole infallible action of the Spirit upon the readers of the Bible, and made of their movement "the most fractioned group among the churches of the Reformation" *(Konfessionskunde,* 1961 [Ital. tr. Rome, 1962], 943).

12. Lindstrom, H., *Wesley and Sanctification* (London, n.d.), 86. See also L. M. Starkey's illuminating chapter, "Sanctifying Work of the Holy Spirit" in his book, *The Work of the Holy Spirit—A Study of Wesleyan Theology* (New York, 1962), 114ff.

13. One of the classic texts of the founder of Methodism reads: "The New Birth is a part of sanctification, not the whole. It is the gate to it, the entrance into it. When we are born again, then our santification, our inward and outward life begins. And thenceforward we are gradually to grow up in him who is our head. . . . A child is born of a woman in a moment, or at least in a very short time. Afterward he gradually and slowly grows till he attains to the stature of man. In like manner, a child is born of God in a short time, if not in a moment. But it is by slow degrees that he afterwards grows to the full stature of Christ. The same relation, therefore, that there is between our natural birth and our growth, there is also between our new birth and sanctification" *(Wesley's Works,* ed. 1820), V, 74.

14. Wesley believed that Christian perfection implies being so crucified with Christ that the believer can do no wrong since all his actions are motivated by love. If he did not use the words "sinless perfection," he did not oppose the expression. Again it is not clear whether, in his thought, sin had been completely eradicated or only suppressed in a "sanctified" person (see Mayer, *op. cit.,* 293–94).

15. Hall, H. F., "The Search of Perfection," in Anderson, *Methodism* (New York, 1947), 144. Charles Wesley wrote about "the redeeming power which saves us to the uttermost, till we can sin no more," and his brother John made some extreme statements in the same vein. (See *Wesley's Works,* V, 560–61.)

16. See his *Lectures on Systematic Theology* (Oberlin, 1878), 317–18.

17. "In the early stages of the Awakening the revival was greeted by its partisans as a divine shower seemingly beyond human comprehension. Much of the effort in the first delirious months went into formulating the signs or symptoms of authentic conversion, this being still conceived as a seizure from above. . . . [On the other hand] critics argued that the 'religious stir' was evidence only of the ease with which

demagogues can induce a flight from sanity" (Heimert, A., *Religion and the American Mind, From the Great Awakening to the Revolution,* 38–39).

18. Simpson, A. B., *Wholly Sanctified* (Harrisburg, 1925), 101.

19. Kendrick, C., *The Promise Fulfilled,* 39.

20. In Moore's *Handbook of Pentecostal Denominations in the United States,* there is not a single exception to the rule.

21. *Cultures and Personalities, Aspects of the Holiness Religion,* 99. This experience from the backward sections of America applies, almost to the letter, to mission countries.

22. This is called the "Wesleyan concept of sanctification." It teaches that sanctification is definitely "a second work of grace." "In the experience of regeneration," says the Church of God, Tomlinson, "we are forgiven the sins we have committed. In the experience of sanctification, the stain of the sin of Adam, and the nature thereof, are taken out of us."

23. This type of sanctification is at times called "the finished work of Christ," and its followers are said to belong to the "Baptistic branch of Pentecostalism" in the sense that they eliminate the "second experience" of the perfectionists, which they think is out of place. The concept is more appealing to modern neo-Pentecostalists. See Kendrick, *op. cit.,* 145, and Moore, *op. cit.,* 115.

24. How far this regeneration is the result of fiducial faith is dubious. Some of their statements come close to those of Lutheranism. See Bloch-Hoell, 123. Others look more like the Catholic idea of contrition. In any event, justification must be "experienced" to a degree which far exceeds that of the Reformers.

25. Pearlman, *op. cit.,* II, 119–20.

26. *The Apostolic Faith Pamphlets,* n. 5.

27. Will, E. S., cited by Nelson, *op. cit.,* 99.

28. Mayer, *op. cit.,* 313. Hills carried his parallel to the point of saying that "the sanctified [person] partakes of Christ's nature and, in a measure, of the qualities which Christ has. Even as Christ himself received a mighty baptism in the Spirit which marked a great change in his ministry, so the baptism in the Spirit today anoints a person with power and confers upon him the full complement of the gifts of the Spirit" (Hills, *op. cit.,* 79).

29. Pearlman, *op. cit.,* 121.

30. Scolfield, C. I., *The New Scolfield Reference Bible* (New York, ed. 1967), 1286–87.

31. Lockyer, H., *All The Doctrines of the Bible* (Springfield, 1964), 206.

32. Williams, *op. cit.,* II, 142.

33. Quoted by Bloch-Hoell, *op. cit.,* 139.

34. P. S. Sanders, in an unpublished thesis, *An Appraisal of John Wesley's Sacramentalism in the Evolution of Early American Methodism* (Union Theological Seminary, New York, 1954), distinguishes two stages in Wesley's thought on baptism: one common to that of Angli-

canism, and another in which, leaving the old path, he stressed the symbolic character of the elements, and separated baptism and regeneration as if the latter had not much to do with the former (314–18). See also Lindstrom, *op. cit.,* 108.

35. *Op. cit.,* 139.

36. Conn, *Like A Mighty Army,* 136.

37. Among the Western Pentecostal denominations studied by Moore and Hollenweger there is hardly one which departs from the rule. The trait appears also clearly in the Latin American and African Pentecostal churches.

38. Its nature is described as something of a far higher order than the New Birth. The latter "has to do with the sinner and is the one way to God's family," while baptism with the Holy Spirit "has to do only with those who are already children of God." "It is the enduement of power upon the yielding, confiding disciple, as beautifully portrayed in that loving, happy, worshipful company in the Upper Room, as well as in Samaria and elsewhere" (see W. W. Wood, *op. cit.,* 99).

39. Hoekema, A., *Speaking with Tongues,* 81. The whole issue will be further analyzed in the next chapter.

40. "Speaking in Tongues" (in *Princeton Seminary Bulletin,* February, 1965), 9–10.

41. The revivals of A. J. Tomlinson at the end of the last century "were attended by groaning, dancing, weeping, trances, and other demonstrations" (Conn, *Like a Mighty Army,* 98).

42. According to R. Riggs, there are in the Pentecostal services "demonstrations and manifestations which are in contrast to the staid, still atmosphere of many modern churches." Among them he mentions: lifting of holy hands in prayer, clapping hands by way of applause to the Lord (never to the preacher), dancing in the Spirit, loud shouting of God's praises, and prostration in the presence of the Lord. *(op. cit.,* 183ff).

43. *Op. cit.,* 94. A much coarser experience at the House of Prayer is described on pages 122–24. On the contrary, the worship in many churches of the Assemblies of God (to take one example) runs much more according to the patterns of other historical conservative congregations. The difference from the other churches is that in Pentecostalism "the operation [guidance] of the Holy Spirit takes precedence over any ritual, and that the 'real presence' of Christ is expected throughout the service." (See Masserano, F. L., *A Study of Worship Forms in the Assemblies of God Denomination,* Thesis, Princeton, 1966, 71ff.)

44. Sherrill, *op. cit.,* 113–14. The author adds two interesting details: 1) the breakfast meeting lasted four hours, and 2) "As I watched her, a phenomenon occurred. It was very hot in the room, perhaps 85 degrees. Yet, while grandmother danced, I distinctily saw, against the dark velvet curtains of the room, soft billows of visible breath coming from her mouth as if she were standing in the cold" (116–18).

45. Nelson calls it "the great mountain-peak promise which towers above all the rest of the Father's promises following the promise of

the Messiah" *(op. cit.,* 72). Hence, concludes Riggs, "when any soul has been saved [by regeneration], he should at once be urged to seek the baptism of the Holy Spirit" *(Personal Worker's Course,* 84–85).

46. Brumback, *op. cit.,* 138; Paulk, 61ff.

47. Brumback, *op. cit.,* 341.

48. Riggs, *We Believe,* 39.

49. Algermissen, K., *Christian Sects,* 113. D. Webster is closer to reality when he says that, "unless one is being very deliberately detached and coldly critical, it is extraordinarily easy to get caught up in the thrill of the Pentecostal worship" *(op. cit.,* 13).

50. *Op. cit.,* 79.

51. Frodsham, *op. cit.,* 278.

52. Wood, *op. cit.,* 24.

53. Miyakawa, T. S., *Protestants and Pioneers* (Chicago, 1964), 164–65. Brumback, speaking of the first decades of Pentecostal history, mentions "divinely called men who were guilty of grave misconduct," although in his book *What Meaneth This?,* 107–08, he tries also to find an explanation for the abuses. See also his *Suddenly . . . from Heaven,* 112–14.

54. Cf. my study, *Etapas y desarrollo de las misiones protestantes en China* (Ph. D. Thesis, Gregorian University, 1952), 215ff.

55. Personal correspondence with missionaries from the former Belgian Congo, Southern Rhodesia, and South Africa.

56. Vergara, I., *El Protestantismo en Chile,* 165. I have heard the same complaints from several Latin American bishops and have had occasion to check personally one of the reports with the father of the girl who had been involved in the case. The reason given by the native pastor was that the reception of the Holy Spirit had made them immune to any transgression.

57. Gee, D., *Spiritual Gifts in the Work of the Ministry Today.* See also Brown, C. E., *The Meaning of Santification* (Anderson, Ind., 1945).

58. In this Pentecostalism believes to be following "God's way" as on the Day of Pentecost. "The gifts," comments D. Gee, "would appear to have been especially reserved by God to mark the Church Dispensation of Grace. This adds greatly to the significance of this phenomenon on the Day of Pentecost, when the present dispensation was ushered in. God was doing 'a new thing,' and it was accompanied by a new sign and a new manifestation of the Eternal Spirit" (*Concerning Spiritual Gifts,* 63).

59. Gee, D., *op. cit.,* 14ff. "The ultimate and full purpose of spiritual gifts is . . . to bring men face to face with the reality of the Invisible God. To make the Church realize that the Holy Spirit is ever present, and that all true ministry springs from Him who is her only source of life and power; and to make the unbeliever equally conscious that God cannot be forgotten, and that sin dare not be trifled with" (19).

60. How are we to distinguish whether the gifts are from God, from the devil or from our own hypnotic powers?—All three possibilities have been admitted by Pentecostals. Usually their version is that

"the enemy of the souls" who "hates this revival" is "seeking to destroy it in every way, to belittle it, and to bring it injury," challenging the supernatural origins of the gifts. (See Frodsham, *op. cit.*, 278). However, there are a few among their commentators who confess that at this point they are in a blind alley. "We have no ground to distinguish between the gifts," says David Gee. "The present challenge of Spiritism, and all the other forms of super-natural power at work to-day which are *not* from God, make us all the more ready to believe that the God who answered Jannes and Jambres of old by a still greater exhibition of *His* power will meet this challenge in the same way today" (*op. cit.*, 41).

NOTES TO CHAPTER SIX

1. Slay, J. L., *This We Believe* (Cleveland, Tenn., 1963), 91. H. Carter has called glossolalia "the greatest stumbling block in the movement. . . . If only this obstacle could be overcome, many orthodox sections of the Christian Church would be pleased to have greater fellowship with Pentecostal believers" (*Pentecostal Evangel* [May, 1946], 8). Pentecostals also admit that ecstatic utterances "may be of the devil as well as of God, and that one may not be readily distinguished from the other" (H. R. Wilson, *Sects and Society,* 20).

2. Wilson, *op. cit.,* 21. A synthesis of the Catholic Apostolic Church may be found in F. L. Mayer, *The Religious Bodies of America,* 430–32. Some of the abuses which have taken place in tongue speaking have been studied by D. Gee, *Spiritual Gifts in the Work of the Ministry Today,* 89–90.

3. Wilson, *op. cit.,* 21.

4. Kelsey, *op. cit.,* 68. For the special sources used in this chapter see: Horton, W. H., *The Gifts of the Spirit* (London, 1945); Brumback, K., *What Meaneth This?* (Springfield, 1947); Cutten, G. B., *Speaking with Tongues* (New Haven, 1927); Dalton, R., *Tongues, Like as Fire* (Springfield, 1947); Ervin, H. M., *These Are Not Drunken as You Suppose* (Plainfield, N. J., 1968); Grant, H., *How To Receive the Holy Spirit* (Dallas, n.d.); Martin, I., *Glossolalia in the Apostolic Church* (Berea, Ky., 1960); Frodsham, S., *With Signs Following* (Springfield, 1941); Roberts, O., *The Baptism of the Spirit with Signs Following* (Tulsa, 1964); Metz, D., *Speaking in Tongues: An Analysis* (Kansas City, 1964); Sherrill, J. L., *They Speak with Other Tongues* (New York, 1964); Kelsey, M. T., *Tongue Speaking* (New York, 1964); Stagg, F., Hinson, E., Oates, W., *Glossolalia, Tongue Speaking in Biblical, Historical, and Psychological Perspective* (Nashville, 1967); Hutten, K., *Seher, Grübler, Enthusiasten* (Stuttgart, 1966); Hoekema, A., *What About Tongue-Speaking?* (Grand Rapids, 1966); Gromacki, R. G., *The Modern Tongues Movement* (Philadelphia, 1967); Vivier, L. M. E., *Glossolalia* (unpublished thesis [Johannesburg, 1960]); Lapsey, J., Simpson, J., "Speaking in Tongues," *The Princeton Seminary Bulletin* (Febr., 1965), 1–18.

5. Wilson, *op. cit.,* 21–22. Pentecostalism has added a contribution of its own: a theory and a theological basis about glossolalia. Regarding the way and the extent to which this phenomenon has affected the historical churches, the FGBMFI has been publishing a series of pamphlets under the editorship of J. Jensen: *Baptists and The Baptism of the Holy Spirit; Episcopalians and the Baptism of the Holy Spirit; Presbyterians and the Baptism of the Holy Spirit,* etc. In spite of their onesidedness, they are worth reading.

6. *The Alliance Witness* (May 1, 1963), 19. The damage to the Alliance was severe because whole congregations with their property went over to the Pentecostals.

7. Mead, F. S., *Handbook of Denominations* (New York, 1956), 78–79. At present the Church of the Nazarene is a middle-of-the-road church, neither ritualistic nor completely informal; one church historian has called it "the right wing of the Holiness movement."

8. *Minutes of the Assemblies of God,* 1918, cited by Brumback, *Suddenly . . . from Heaven,* 223.

9. Gee, D., *Concerning Spiritual Gifts,* 83. Glossolalia "was the reason for our separate existence and even the point of divergence with other evangelical groups. . . . It was that belief that marked a person as a Pentecostal" (Brumback).

10. Gee calls glossolalia "a cardinal doctrine of almost all Pentecostal denominations" *(op. cit.,* 88). The neo-Pentecostal attitude has been summed up by Hoekema, *op. cit.,* 44–48: all groups admit its importance as evidence of Spirit-baptism; most of them do not wish to encourage it at the regular Sunday services, but prefer to exercise it in smaller prayer groups.

11. Slay, *op.cit.,* 91. The stand of the Scandinavian groups may be seen in Bloch-Hoell, *op. cit.,* 141.

12. Concrete instances will be adduced elsewhere. Of glossolalia as an instrument of evangelization, Gee thinks it "thrills participants with the hope that more and other restored gifts of the Spirit will follow. The hope must be wisely directed in the truth and not allowed to drift into fanaticism" *(Concerning Spiritual Gifts,* 88).

13. *World Pentecostal Conference, 1948.* Among the American Pentecostal denominations, besides those already quoted, glossolalia is officially accepted and practiced by no less than nineteen.

14. Kittel, G. (ed.), *Theological Dictionary of the New Testament* (Grand Rapids, 1964) I, 722–726. See also X. Ducross, art. "Charismes," in *Dictionnaire de Spiritualité* (Paris, 1940), cols. 503–507, and the well-known treatise of Dom Marechaux, *Les charismes du Saint Esprit* (Paris, 1921).

15. Kittel, *op. cit.,* 726. See F. Prat, *The Theology of Saint Paul* (New York, 1952), I, 129ff.

16. Jung defined the phenomenon as a "semi-somnambulistic state, the automatism giving evidence of the activity of the sub-conscious self, and independent of the consciousness" (see Vivier, *op. cit.,* 132). The scientifically-tested information we possess about glossolalia in non-Christian religions is very incomplete.

17. I realize that, by relying on one author, I run the risk of being challenged by others who have different ideas about the nature of glossolalia. But in discussing a movement that has no theological unity, one is bound to have recourse to some well-known and respected writer. W. H. Horton is at present General Overseer of the Church of God, Cleveland, Tenn.

18. Horton, *op. cit.,* 150. Other definitions: "a supernatural mani-

festation of the Spirit of God using man's vocal organs to speak in different kinds of languages, whether earthly or heavenly" (Grant, *op.* cit., 37). "When the Holy Spirit comes in his fullness to abide in the believer, he takes possession of the spirit, soul, and body, which are then completely subjected to his will, and he uses the tongue in a supernatural way" (Nelson, *op. cit.,* 88).

19. Brumback, *What Meaneth This?,* 291–98; 327–28; 299–317. For the primitive Church the most important seems to have been "the supernatural ability to pray to or praise God in a strange language with an enthusiasm bordering on exaltation" (Prat, *op. cit.,* I, 130).

20. There are Pentecostal authorities who claim that their glossolalia is the speaking of actual human languages, although these are unknown to the speaker (Brumback, *op. cit.,* 113, 245, 263, 295). Gee equates the phenomenon with the speaking of genuine foreign languages *(Concerning Spiritual Gifts,* 57, 61, 62, 96). On the contrary, W. J. Samarin, a professor of linguistics at the Hartford Seminary Foundation, defines glossolalia: "A meaningless but phonogetically structured human utterance believed by the speaker to be a real language but bearing no systematic resemblance to any actual language, living or dead" ("The Linguisticality of Glossolalia," in *The Hartford Quarterly,* 196, 61).

21. This division, first proposed by Cutten, has been adopted by many others. It is useful more as a logical tool than applicable to the real situation in many of the younger Pentecostal congregations. The allusion to "old Basque," whatever that may be, is found in Lapsey-Simpson *(art. cit.,* 5).

22. Bloch-Hoell, *op. cit.,* 143. Among those who have spoken "the automatic language" (close to the inspired or prophetical) he mentions the Camisards and the spiritualist mediums.

23. Webster, *op. cit.,* 23. This was already the impression of Cutten, *op. cit.,* 175, and has been confirmed by W. E. Wilmers (see *Christianity Today,* 8 Nov. 1964). Bloch-Hoell is therefore right when he concludes that "even with the greatest of good-will, it seems impossible to find [in those utterings] a real language" (*op. cit.,* 145). Lapsey-Simpson, on the other hand, mention the existence of a glossolalia of "speech-like sound . . . and of an almost art-like quality" (*art. cit.,* 4).

24. *Op. cit.,* 23. "When a Christian receives the baptism with the Holy Spirit . . . the Holy Spirit confirms it with a supernatural ability to speak in a language unknown to the speaker" *(Trinity,* a neo-Pentecostal magazine, Eastertide, 1963, 34).

25. *Op.cit.,* 75.

26. Du Plessis, *The Spirit Bade Me Go,* 80.

27. Conn, *Pillars of Pentecost,* 57. This parallel between glossolalia and the biblical word of God sounds almost blasphemous to many Christians. It is not so to Pentecostals. Ervin has identified it as "an intuitive knowledge of the divine counsels supernaturally revealed and spontaneously uttered for the 'edification and exhortation and consolation' of the assembled worshipers" (*op. cit.,* 123).

28. *Op. cit.,* 14–15. It is perhaps the presence of so many "miraculous" elements that make it a difficult phenomenon to understand. "Of all these spiritual manifestations, tongues is the most frequently misunderstood and misrepresented" (Ervin, *op. cit.,* 124).

29. *Concerning Spiritual Gifts,* 57. An effort to vindicate the Pentecostal interpretation is the already quoted volume of H. M. Ervin, assistant Dean and Professor of Old Testament, the Graduate School of Theology, Oral Roberts University, Tulsa. There are, however, Pentecostal writers who advise their colleagues "to spend little time to convince others of the reality of this experience by means of arguments.... Those with a closed mind [on this matter] are not candidates for the Holy Ghost experience at any price" (Paulk, *op. cit.,* 103).

30. Pearlman, *op.cit.,* III, 47. Writers of neo-Pentecostal leanings find "direct references" to glossolalia in the New Testament, and "eight other descriptions in which it could well be that glossolalia is meant." There are many more Biblical references to healing, dreams, visions, or to things belonging to the demonic and angelic realm, but what is said about glossolalia in the sacred pages "is certainly central to the apostolic narrative" (Kelsey, *op. cit.,* 17, 31). For a different evaluation, see Hoekema, *op. cit.,*49ff.; Stagg, *op.cit.,* 20ff.

31. Pearlman, *op. cit.,* 67. Exegetically the passages in Acts are not without difficulties. See Stagg, *op. cit.,* 25ff.; *Encyclopedic Dictionary of the Bible* (Eng. adapt. New York, 1963), 2471–73.

32. Riggs, *op. cit.,* 28.

33. Non-Pentecostals are less sure about such an interpretation. From these texts, says Hoekema, one is justified in concluding that "believers need to be filled with the Spirit again and again," but it is much more difficult to infer that "after one has been converted, one needs to be baptized with the Spirit as a kind of second blessing" *(op. cit.,* 66). Gromacki *(op. cit.,* 89–90) argues forcefully in the same negative sense. Ervin *(op. cit.,* 62ff.; 89ff) insists on the meaning of Acts 4:31, and identifies it, as far as its content goes, with the experience of the day of Pentecost. Others are less sanguine about it: "The only correct interpretation of this passage is that the disciples prayed that God might give them boldness to carry on a public ministry in the face of threats and persecutions by the Jewish leaders. The phenomenon of speaking in tongues is not found here" (Gromacki, *op. cit.,* 87). To which Ervin retorts: "It is a reflection of an *a priori* bias against tongues *per se* to insist that the Pentecostal pattern of the baptism of the Holy Spirit was interrupted short of tongues simply because they [tongues] are not mentioned explicitly in this place" *(op. cit.,* 92).

34. In this "only clear instance in which the New Testament speaks of a baptism with the Holy Spirit as occurring subsequent to Pentecost" (Hoekema), the conclusions of Pentecostals and non-Pentecostals are at great variance. "That tongues are the evidence of the baptism . . . with the Holy Spirit is unmistakably clear in this place" (Ervin, *op. cit.,* 101). "There is no indication of a language barrier on either occasion (at Cornelius' home or at Ephesus, Acts, 19:6), and this

would seem to rule out the need for a miracle of language as Luke indicates at Pentecost" (Stagg, *op. cit.*, 35). Hoekema is less apodictic and argues that Cornelius' was an extraordinary case which "by no means proves that every believer should receive this gift" (73).

35. Ervin (*op. cit.*, 101–04), cannot doubt that "In Ephesus the normal pattern of the baptism in the Holy Spirit was repeated.... When [the Ephesians] received the Spirit of the living God in charismatic fullness, they manifested his overflowing presence by speaking with other tongues." Here the arguments of the opposite party are weak.

36. Slay, *op. cit.*, 90. The argument does not lack popular appeal, and Kelsey (*op. cit.*, 31) recurs to it.

37. *Op. cit.*, 33.

38. Hoekema, *op. cit.*, 95.

39. Prat, *op. cit.*, I, 130.

40. Cerfaux, L., *Le chrétien dans la théologie paulinniene* (Paris, 1963), 229.

41. Ervin, *op. cit.*, 157ff.

42. Gromacki, *op. cit.*

43. Stagg, *op. cit.*, 42ff.; Hoekema, *op. cit.*, 81ff.

44. Hoekema, *op. cit.*, 142.

45. The relationship between the gift of tongues and personal holiness has been well brought up by Gee, *Concerning Spiritual Gifts*, 71.

46. One has to be circumspect with the arguments drawn from history. On the one hand, Church historians might agree "that there is no scientific or convincing evidence for any continuity in the gift of tongues" (Webster). But, on the other, neither Scripture nor history show convincingly that a phenomenon which certainly took place in the early Church cannot repeat itself in our time. The compelling argument must come from other, external sources. Here, it would seem, the historical churches are fighting a lost battle.

47. Barratt, founder of Scandinavian Pentecostalism, felt that "the power" took his jawbone and his tongue, and "expelled the languages clearly and instinctively." "Once I felt a pain in my throat, then I believe it was Welsh that I spoke. . . . Another time there were nasal sounds, probably French, Italian" (Bloch-Hoell, *op. cit.*, 143–44). At the beginning of the movement, people used to shout in tongues for days and nights "until the foundation of the house gave in" (Kendrick, *op. cit.*, 65). Others were even able to show how "cloven tongues like as of fire came down into the corner of the room." A glossolalist experienced that "the Spirit of God struck him like a bolt of lightning." Then "the power of God surged through my body, and I again began to speak in tongues" (Goss, R., *The Winds of God*, 1958, 56).

48. Sherrill, *op. cit.*, 122–23. Another interesting personal experience is recounted in M. Bach (*op. cit.*, 50–51).

49. Williams, *Systematic Theology*, III, 49.

50. Brumback adduces examples of such blunders: a person who spoke "Chinese" went to China as a missionary only to find that real

Mandarin was something different and harder to learn than tongues; partners who were advised whom to pick for marriage discovered after years "that the supposedly divine directive was spurious" *(What Meaneth,* 112). Similar weird instances still take place in mission territories, mostly among uneducated native leaders.

51. Anderson, R., *Spiritual Manifestations and the Gift of Tongues* (New York, n.d.), 31.

52. Kuyper, A., the well-known Dutch conservative theologian, quoted by Stolee (*op. cit.,* 65). Stolee has been accused of bias against Pentecostalism.

53. Dean Farrer, quoted by Williams, *op. cit.,* 66.

54. Bergsma, S., "Speaking with Tongues," *Torch and Trumpet,* Nov.–Dec. 1964. "The theologian will immediately grant that if this charism were essential at any moment in God's economy, the Spirit would supply it. But in its manifestation among Pentecostals it is an extreme form of 'enthusiasm,' the theory that an intuitive and experimental knowledge supersedes the written word" (Mayer, *op. cit.,* 329).

55. Cutten, G. B., *Speaking with Tongues,* 169ff.

56. Clark, *Small Sects of America,* 97. "Psychologically," says Bloch-Hoell, "the most reasonable explanation of true xenolalia is *cryptomnesia* or *hypermnesia.* When the emotional religious concentration passes into ecstasy with motoric speech, memories emerge from the 'store' of the subconscious mind when the ecstasy occurred. Cryptomnesia seems to explain a number of Pentecostal records of xenolalia" (*op. cit.,* 144).

57. *Art. cit.,* 7. This fear of demons is still very common in mission territories and in Latin America.

58. *Art. cit.,* 11.

59. *Art. cit.* W. O. Oates, from Southern Baptist Theological Seminary, Louisville, Ky., finds striking similarities between the Pentecostal glossolalia and "a childlike form of language." Thus, following the findings of Piaget, our author thinks that, "by analogy, speaking in tongues is not solely an autistic, ego-centric expression of child-like language, but also an attempt at socialization." Moreover, as with the child, "exhibitionism tends to be a hall-mark of the glossolalic who is suffering from a psychic reaction." Exhibitionism, in turn, is "another symptom of regressive behavior" or "a childish megalomania." (Stagg-Hinson-Oates, *Glossolalia,* 92–96).

60. *Op.* cit., 8. Kelsey has been classed among the "sympathetic students and observers of glossolalia."

61. *Ibid.,* 222. If his theory were correct Pentecostalism should have flourished among the Eastern churches.

62. *Ibid.,* 188ff. Kelsey also quotes approvingly a Swiss psychiatrist, Theodore Flournoy, "*the* authority on tongue-speaking in the psychological world." Unfortunately for our case, Flournoy's studies were published at the beginning of the century when Pentecostalism was an almost unknown phenomenon even in America.

63. *Ibid.,* 204–05.

64. A copy of Vivier's dissertation is extant at the Oral Roberts University, Tulsa, Oklahoma. Vivier thinks that glossolalics "can be considered as a group of people who, psychologically speaking, have had a poor beginning in life. This has been reflected by their difficulty in adjustment to the home situation in infancy and later adulthood. It can therefore be said that they have been torn by insecurity, conflict, tension, and emotional difficulties . . . [and] have turned from the culturally accepted, traditional, orthodox, and formalized, to something that held out for them the unorthodox, the supernatural, to an environment of sensitiveness for emotional feeling and a group of people bound within the same purpose and clinging to each other for support.... They prayed for, and expected from God the power to free themselves from themselves. To be baptised by the Spirit would solve their difficulties . . . "(432–33).

65. Most psychiatrists—Vivier and Lapsey-Simpson among others—have found that Pentecostals show a higher percentage of emotionally-perturbed and unstable characters.

66. *Ibid.*, 209. Andrew D. Lester, after a firsthand visitation to neo-Pentecostalist groups, draws the conclusion: "The terrible isolation and loneliness of successful people in the middle-class churches has broken out in other forms and manners in this generation. The hyperdependence upon alcohol, the high incidence of psychomatic disorders, the absence of a clear-cut family structure, and the conventionalization of the church life all provide a fertile soil for the sudden chaotic breakthrough represented in glossolalia" (Oates, *op. cit.*, 97).

67. *Ibid.*, 211–12.

68. *Ibid.*, 213. As pointed out in note 20 above, glossolalia has also been studied from the linguistic angle by W. J. Samarin, although his conclusions are of only a relative importance to our point. "Glossolalia," he says, "is a form of pseudo-language that is available to every normal person.... It is always meaningless in the linguistic sense, that is, there are no consistent correlations between units of speech and experience. ... If a glossa is meaningless, this does not mean it is gibberish.... In glossolalia the speaker is subconsciously motivated to produce a new language.... Strictly speaking, glossolalia cannot be learned.... But in another sense there is learning; there must be, because the acquisition of glossolalia is generally associated with becoming a member of a social group with its own patterns of behavior and value" (From two papers of W. J. Samarin: *The Linguisticality of Glossolalia* [*The Hartford Quarterly,* 196, 49ff.] and *Glossolalia as Learned Behavior,* presented at the Conference of the Society for the Scientific Study of Religion, Montreal, October, 1968).

69. Gee, *Concerning Spiritual Gifts,* 61–62. For Pearlman, interpretation "is a purely spiritual operation," and comes from the Holy Spirit as something "inspirational, ecstatic, and spontaneous." "Tongues plus interpretation are equal to prophecy" *(op. cit.,* III, 60–61).

70. Williams, *op. cit.,* III, 75.

71. The order in which the gifts are granted is, first "stammering lips; then interpretation of tongues; then prophecy."

72. Williams, *op cit.,* 75.

73. Brumback, *What Meaneth This,* 308.

74. Cited by Cutten, *op.cit.,* 181. In our own days Howard M. Ervin mentions some of the languages spoken by himself while in trance and identified by his listeners: Russian, Spanish, Portuguese, Biblical Greek, Italian, Japanese, "a dialect spoken by the Indian colonial troops of the British empire," and Kurdish. "Needless to say," he comments, "all of these languages are unknown to the writer, and consequently were spoken 'as the Spirit himself gave utterance' " (Ervin, *op. cit.,* 127–28).

75. In Pentecostalism there is no "office" of interpreter as in the early Church. "Reason and prudence, however, command that, generally speaking, the gift of interpretation should be restricted to 'proved' individuals, and especially in larger and more responsible gatherings" (Gee, *op. cit.,* 61).

76. Sherrill, *op. cit.,* 95.

77. Gee, *op. cit.,* 94.

78. *Op. cit.,* 306.

79. Conn, *Pillars of Pentecost,* 104. "The commonplace assumption that biblical glossolalia is the result of pathological emotional states simply ignores the fact that they are a supernatural manifestation of the Holy Spirit. To ascribe them to the abnormal workings of a damaged psyche is to impugn the veracity of the biblical records, to say nothing of the integrity of multiplied thousands of tongue-speaking Christians whose emotional health is equal, if not superior, to that of their critics. Perhaps even worse than that, it is closer to blasphemy than to heresy to thus project the neuroses of a neurotic age into the deity" (H. Ervin, *op.cit.,* 124).

80. *Op. cit.,* 222. The reality of this peace of soul is magnificently reflected in the answers to the questionnaire sent by Vivier to Pentecostals in South Africa *(op. cit.,* 416–20).

81. *Op. cit.,* 223.

82. *Ibid.,* 231. This is very true of original Pentecostalism in mission lands, and I am afraid the feature is reappearing among many neo-Pentecostals.

83. *Ibid.,* 219. Such is the impression given, for instance, by Brazilian Pentecostals. See W. R. Reed, *New Patterns of Church Growth in Brazil,* 139.

84. This may occur rather frequently among the so-called nonliturgical Protestant denominations. I find it less likely in Lutheranism, among Episcopalians, or in the Roman Catholic Church.

85. *Op. cit.,* 231.

NOTES TO CHAPTER SEVEN

1. Kendrick, K., *The Promise Fulfilled,* 59. The first chapters of S. H. Frodsham, *With Signs Following,* and of Brumback, *Suddenly . . . from Heaven,* are full of narratives of this type from various parts of the country.

2. *1966 Minutes of the 51st General Assembly of the Church of God, Cleveland, Tenn.,* 12–13. Pearlman, *op. cit.,* III, 75, calls divine healing "a sign-gift specially valuable to the evangelist for attracting the people's attention to the Gospel." For D. Gee healings and miracles "may reverently be called God's method of divine advertising for the preaching of the Gospel" *(Concerning Spiritual Gifts,* 72).

3. Gee, D., *Concerning Spiritual Gifts,* 37.

4. Brumback, *Suddenly . . . from Heaven,* 9–10. Wesley in his *Journal* records no less than 240 cases of divine healing in his ministry. On the contrary, the "gift" was not enjoyed by any of the great Protestant missionaries of early days. Carey, Adoniram Judson, Moffat never advocated this method (the case of Murray was an exception) which is also not mentioned in treatises of their missiologists from Hoornbeek to Warneck. The accent was on medical missions as the "divine instrument" to heal bodies and lead people to the acceptance of Christ.

5. Simpson, A. B., *The Gospel of Healing* (Harrisburg, 1925), 8.

6. *Ibid.,* 162–63. It seems that, in one way or another, most founders and foundresses of Pentecostal—and often also of Holiness—denominations received "the gift" of healing.

7. Nelson, *op. cit.,* 121.

8. *Op. cit.,* 113.

9. More quotations from Pentecostal writers in F. Mayer, *op. cit.,* 321–323.

10. Sundkler, *Bantu Prophets* (London, 1961), 220. See in *Pentecostal Evangel,* January, 1957, an interesting survey on healing.

11. Debrunner, H. W., *A Church Between Colonial Powers—A Study of the Church in Togo* (London, 1965), 279.

12. Mitchell, R. C., "Christian Healing," in E. W. Hayward, ed., *African Independent Church Movements* (London, 1963), 47.

13. *International Review of Missions, 1963,* 168. Gee, *op. cit.,* 88. In the following chapter devoted to missions we will deal with healing as practised in Latin American Pentecostalism.

14. "The Pentecostal attitude is that healing is provided in the atonement, and the emphasis is on Christ 'by whose stripes we have been healed' " (Conn, *Like a Mighty Army,* 77). See also Mayer, *op. cit.,* 321.

15. Scherzer, C., *The Church and Healing* (New York, 1950); Ikin, G., *New Concept of Healing, Medical, Psychological, Religious* (New York, 1956); Edwards, H., *The Power of Spiritual Healing* (London, 1963); Buskirk, J. D., *Religion, Healing, and Health* (New York, 1952); Purcell, A., *The Church's Ministry of Healing* (New York, 1959); Weatherhead, L., *Psychology, Religion and Healing* (London, 1962); World Council of Churches, *The Healing Church* (Geneva, 1965).

16. Simpson, A. B., *The Gospel of Healing,* 31; Gee, D., *Spiritual Gifts,* 66–67.

17. *Personal Worker's Course, Assemblies of God,* 66–67.

18. Let us recall Luther's profoundly Christian theology of the cross: "He who does not know Christ does not know God hidden in suffering. Therefore he prefers works to suffering, glory to the cross, strength to weakness, wisdom to folly, and, in general, good to evil. These are the people whom the apostle calls 'enemies of the cross of Christ' [Phil 3:18], for they hate the cross and suffering and love works, and the glory of works; . . . God can be found only in suffering and the cross" *(Luther's Works, Career of the Reformer* [Philadelphia, 1957], 31, 53). See also Gleason, R., *Christ and the Christian* (New York, 1962), 62, 66, 67.

19. *Personal Worker's Course,* 67; Slay, *op. cit.,* 94–96. The same simplistic approach is evident in one of Oral Roberts's pamphlets, *Your Healing Problems and How to Solve Them* (Tulsa, 1966), 41–44.

20. Nelson, *op. cit.,* 124. It is at this point that Pentecostals come closer to Christian Science and other esoteric healing groups.

21. Here Mayer's assessment is correct: "Faith healing ignores the true nature of sin and thus vitiates the true nature of Christ's redemptive work. The demonic power which Satan exercises over man is not so much a physical ailment as rather eternal separation from God. Therefore Christ bore our infirmities and our sickness not primarily to free us from our physical ailments but to conquer Satan" *(op. cit.,* 322).

22. Gee, D., *Concerning Spiritual Gifts,* 75. Gee even goes on to say that "there are times when our request for miracles can savor of presumption rather than of faith."

23. Slay, *op. cit.,* 94.

24. Simpson, *op. cit.,* 60, 61, 64.

25. The quotations are from A. B. Simpson's *The Foursquare Gospel.* The whole third chapter is devoted to *Christ our Healer.* See also Hutten, *op. cit., Lehre und Praxis der Heilungsbewegung,* 565ff.

26. Simpson, *op. cit.,* 54.

27. Gee, *Concerning Spiritual Gifts,* 73. With a stubbornness which is offensive to the other churches, Pentecostals insist in separating divine healing from the magnificent work of curing bodies and souls that missions have carried on the world over. "It is absolutely hopeless to make any legitimate connection between the gift of healing and medical missions. . . . The New Testament gifts of healing had no connection with medical science, but were supernatural and attributed directly to the Spirit of God" (Gee, *Concerning Spiritual Gifts,* 39).

28. Clebsch, W. A., and Jaekle, C. R., *Pastoral Care in Historical Perspective* (New York, 1967), contain a good introduction, with appropriate examples, of what Christendom has thought of suffering and the ways devised to confront it (11–67). The testimonies of the early Church (87ff.) are very enlightening.

29. Horton, *op. cit.,* 112. A. B. Simpson was also quite emphatic on the matter: "God has nowhere prescribed medical means, and we have no right to infer that drugs are ordinarily his means.... And if miraculous healing is God's way of healing, then the other methods must be man's ways, and there must be some risk in deliberately repudiating the former for the latter" (*op. cit.,* 67, 70).

30. Dougall, J. W., *Christians in the African Revolution* (Edinburgh, 1963), 63. The reason adduced is that, in spite of the grateful acceptance of Western medicine, "the cure of the real root of the illness is awaited from prayer, the laying on of hands, and the anointing" (Debrunner, *op. cit.,* 280). "In modern Western thought, sickness is generally regarded as caused by either physical or psychological causes. In traditional African thought . . . these are joined by a third all-pervasive aspect of causation, the supernatural. This is the realm of spirits and divinities, of evil and witchcraft, of God himself" (Mitchell, *art. cit.,* 48).

31. Wilson, *op. cit.,* 95–96.

32. Conn, *Pillars of Faith,* 115. In the lists at my disposal, it is extremely hard to make out which denominations that admit divine healing altogether reject medical help. In missions, and with the African exceptions already noted, the trend is clearly to use both healing and medical care.

33. Partly on account of these Pentecostal activities, the historical churches have begun to look more seriously at the role of faith healing among their own communities. See the Report of the Anglican Archbishop's Commission on the Church's Ministry of Healing (1958); the United Presbyterian Report on The Relation of Christian Faith to Health (1960); the United Lutheran Church Statement on Anointing and Healing (1962); the two (1962 and 1967) Consultations at Tübingen on the Healing Church; the Coonoor Conference on the Healing Ministry of the Church, 1967, of the Lutheran Church, Missouri Synod. Several articles on the topic have appeared in the *International Review of Missions.*

34. I am willing to endorse R. Miller's observation that, "The majority of all faith healing practitioners are honest and basically sincere." See *Modern Divine Healing* (New York, 1952), 150.

35. Sundkler, B., "Chief and Prophet in Zululand and Swaziland," in the book published by the Third International African Seminar, *African Systems of Thought* (Salisbury, 1960), 280.

36. See W. R. Reed, *New Patterns of Church Growth in Brazil,* 114ff. The healers of Chile, Mexico, and Central America (as well as those from Asiatic countries) are not, as a rule, even of national stature.

37. Edwards, H., *The Power of the Spiritual Healing,* 43–44.

38. See N. McNeill, *"As of a Rushing Wind," An Assessment of the American Pentecostal Movement* (unpublished thesis), 84–85. Osborn has written *The Purpose of Pentecost* (Tulsa, n.d.) with an account of his travels. One example of his approach: "I was challenged by a Mohammedan to prove that Jesus Christ was the Son of God and that he had risen from the dead. No *miracles* were happening in my ministry. I preached, and there was no *evidence.* But in 1947 God showed me the power of his works. . . . Since then I have had the privilege of leading thousands of Islams to Jesus Christ in a single meeting because the Holy Ghost working in me gave evidence to what I preached by miracles" *(op. cit.,* 14). Other missionaries have not yet found such a short-cut to the followers of Mohammet!

39. Hutten, *op. cit.,* 560ff. For the German share of faith-healers, see the same work, 570–83, and K. Algermissen, *Christian Sects,* 108–11. The Scandinavian situation is treated by Bloch-Hoell, *op. cit.,* 67–71. France, besides Pentecostalism, has other healing sects *(sectes guérisseuses).* See M. Colinon, *op. cit.,* 69–106.

40. The story of Dorothy Kevin, her mystical experiences, healing powers, and organizational abilities have been told by D. M. Arnold, *Called by Christ to Heal* (New York, 1966).

41. Edwards, *op. cit.,* 32. The Federation of National Healers ran into trouble and was condemned by the British Medical Association in its Annual Conference of 1960. Parliament was petitioned that healers should not be allowed to visit hospitals, but the Federation won, and healers are said to pay regular visits to more than 1,500 hospitals in the country.

42. Together with his autobiography, *My Own Story* (New York, 1960), the best source of information are the issues of his periodical *Abundant Life* which closely follow his movements. For Roberts' TV shows which have been so popular and, reportedly, brought health of body and soul to many thousands, see H. B. Jacobs, "Oral Roberts: High Priest of Faith Healing," in *Harper's Magazine,* 1962, 40.

43. R. Nelson, *Modern Divine Healing* (New York, 1950), 121–22.

44. Scherzer, *op. cit.,* 215; Ikin, *op. cit.,* 236–37.

45. Miller, *op. cit.,* 123. According to an unsympathetic observer, this happens with patients suffering from physical injuries: "No healer will come near any really crippled or disabled person if he can avoid it. . . . They are avoided like the plague. When pressed for an explanation, the healers profess to be able to discern those who have faith, which is never found among those really sick, it seems. If one of them, by mischance, gets into the line, the healer will say: 'Get up here on the platform with me and wait until the line is over and then I'll give you special attention. . . . Needless to say, these promises are never kept. The 'wearied' healer always slips away as furtively and hastily as possible" *(Presbyterian Outlook,* 1955, 5ff.).

46. The books of Simpson and McPherson bear the same title, *The Foursquare Gospel.* These injunctions, given with the hypnotic magnetism of the healers, prove simply overwhelming to patients waiting for the "miracle."

47. Miller, *op. cit.,* 131.

48. J. H. Gerstner, *The Theology of the Major Sects* (Grand Rapids, 1960), 110.
49. *Abundant Life,* May 1965, 5–12.
50. Roberts, O., *If You Need Healing,* 91–92.
51. Gee, D., *Spiritual Gifts,* 72, 75.
52. The "startling differences between the bona fide miracles of the Bible and the current [Pentecostal] miracles" are the following:

Biblical healings	*Modern divine healing*
Always successful	Usually unsuccessful
No-known relapses	Many admitted relapses
Immediate-or almost	Usually not-mainly gradual
Raising of the dead	Not extended to the dead
All kinds of diseases	Usually functional diseases
Usually played down by Jesus	Much played up by healers
Credentials of divine revelation	No credentials of divine revelation
No psychological build-up	Conspicuous psychological build-up

(Gerstner, *op. cit.,* 117).

53. Mayer, *op. cit.,* 332. Why do people believe in faith cures? Miller answers: 1) Sick people are abnormally credulous; 2) Sincere, although erroneous, acceptance of faith-healing as part of the Bible; 3) Exhibition of great faith and hope for the hopeless; 4) An insatiable curiosity for the wondrous; 5) Rebellion against medical orders which seem to them unbearable *(op. cit.,* 207–208).
54. Oral Robert's reference in Gerstner, *op. cit.,* 110. Ikin *(op. cit.,* 248), insists on the need of being extremely cautious on this matter. Debrunner, after referring to the un-Biblical fashion in which T. L. Osborn spreads one-sided propaganda for his healings, which depend on mass-suggestion, adds: "It is therefore not surprising that many of those ostensibly cured by Osborn are now in a worse condition than before, because he conveyed to them for the moment by suggestion the feeling of health, but only in a very few cases did he really heal them" *(op. cit.,* 281).
55. Crespi, George, *La guérison par la foi* (Paris, 1952), 51–53. He calls it also "le pouvoir sédatif des guérisseurs."
56. Gerstner, *op. cit.,* 105.
57. Crespi's attitude *(op. cit.,* 33) seems reasonable: "Unless we are ready to deny systematically all the miracles reported by Church history . . . we must understand them in this sense: God, in his freedom, chooses the servants he wants and confers on them certain *apostolic prerogatives.* . . . But, far from constituting the general rule, such gifts constitute a miraculous exception."
58. *Dogmatic Constitution on the Church,* II, 15.
59. Two quotations will explain my still doubtful position on the matter. The first is from the already named French Protestant theolo-

gian, G. Crespi: "Almost all healers make use of the divine name, and proclaim their power to be from God. But in the exact measure in which that name and that power are directed (canalisée) towards aims fixed by man himself, the Christian will have to refuse to him an approval which might easily become a complicity" *(op. cit.,* 50). The second comes from the Rev. Bertram Woods, Chairman of the Central Committee of the Churches Fellowship for Psychical Study: "Some healers (especially those who have become famous for their cures), have undoubtedly a very special gift. What the precise nature of this gift is, is still a matter of debate" (cited by Edwards, *op. cit.,* 164).

NOTES TO CHAPTER EIGHT

1. Glover, R. H., and Kane, J. H. *The Progress of World-Wide Missions* (New York, 1960), 40. Protestant leaders at that time tended to say: "Missions are neither obligatory, nor desirable, and our lack of them cannot be held against us as blindness or unfaithfulness" (Stephen Neill, *A History of Christian Missions* [Baltimore, 1964], 222). The reasons adduced by H. W. Gensichen, *Missionsgeschichte der neuren Zeit*, 1961, 5ff. remain unconvincing. In my book, *Fe Católica e Iglesias y Sectas de la Reforma* (Madrid, 1962), I have devoted a long chapter (pp. 1036–1099) to the origins, motivations, methods, and achievements of Protestant Missions. For their historical survey K. S. Latourette's works: *A History of the Expansion of Christianity* (7 vols., New York, 1937–45), and *Christianity in a Revolutionary Age* (New York, 1958–1962), are indispensable.

2. Latourette, *The World Christian Mission Today* (New York, 1954), 105.

3. Sundkler, B., *The World of Mission* (Grand Rapids, 1965), 51–52. This position was carried to extremes by Hocking in another book, *Living Religions and a World Faith* (New York, 1940). The reaction to those theological conceptions which were "as different as could be from those of the earlier missionaries," ranged from that of the Barthian inspired work of H. Kraemer, *The Christian Message in the Non-Christian World* (London, 1938), to that of the fundamentalists who saw in Hocking the symbol of the "evil of liberalism" they had been denouncing for years.

4. Murch, J. D., *Cooperation without Compromise, A History of the National Association of Evangelicals* (Grand Rapids, 1956), devotes a whole chapter to the matter. "The largest per capita giving in Protestantism for foreign missions is in strictly evangelical denominations. ... The largest number of new foreign missionaries have been sent out by evangelical boards. In fact, if it were not for these boards there would be a tragic loss of zeal and accomplishment in the total picture of Protestant Christian missions" (97).

5. Frodsham, *op. cit.*, 50–51; see also N. Perkin and J. Garlock, *Our World Witness* (Springfield, 1963), 22.

6. See B. L. Goddard, ed., *The Encyclopedia of Modern Christian Missions* (London, 1967), 43.

7. "We accept without reserve world evangelization as the supreme purpose in the will of God for the Pentecostal Revival. ... When the Lord gave his final charge to the apostles ... he coupled with it the promise of the gift of the Holy Ghost for power to fulfill a commission

which extended to the 'uttermost part of the earth.' . . . The continuance in spiritual prosperity of the Pentecostal Revival depends upon continual consecration to the worldwide missions. If our spiritual gifts cannot flourish in the wide arena of universal witness there is something wrong. Their use in evangelism is a healthy test for their validity and our use of them" (Gee, *Spiritual Gifts,* 95–96).

8. Brumback, *op. cit.,* 339–40. "In this century, with all its missionary activity, the dynamic character of the Pentecostal movement has made it, comparatively, the Christian denomination with the greatest number of missionaries in foreign fields" (Bloch-Hoell, *op. cit.,* 89).

9. Kendrick, *op. cit.,* 96ff.

10. Brumback, *op. cit.,* 345. Among the other well-organized Pentecostal mission boards are those of the Church of God, Cleveland, Tenn., the Pentecostal Holiness Church, and the International Church of the Foursquare Gospel.

11. Reed, *New Patterns of Church Growth in Brazil,* 117.

12. Statistics provided by the *World Christian Handbook,* 1968, ed. W. Coxill, K. Grubb, and K. Knapp (London, 1968). In the remaining Middle-East nations the Assemblies work in Iran (1,868 followers), and Lebanon (90 members); and the Church of God has in Lebanon 400 members. Neither Yemen nor Kuwait has any Pentecostals.

13. See my thesis *Etapas y desarrollo de las misiones protestantes en China* (Gregorian University, Rome, 1952). The healing sessions attracted "immense crowds" and were followed by "thousands of people" who asked to be baptized. About the *Jesus Family* see the rather optimistic report of the *International Review of Missions,* January 1950, 168ff. In 1948 the Assemblies of God, the dominant Pentecostal body, had 88 missionaries, 148 assemblies, six Bible schools and a total community of 7,500.

14. Judging from Hollenweger's lists *(Handbuch der Pfingstbewegung)* there are in India twelve Holiness denominations and no less than thirty-seven Pentecostal bodies. Not all of them are mentioned in Coxill's *Handbook,* and those which are show a membership of a thousand or less. The total Protestant community of India is put at 5,303,206.

15. The *World Christian Handbook,* 1968, lists 101 Protestant denominations working on Japanese soil. Meanwhile Hollenweger names 21 Holiness and 29 Pentecostal denominations. In that case almost half of the Protestant missionary force is in the hands of the latter two groupings. Both sources list a Spirit of Jesus Church *(Iesum no Mitama Kyokai Kyodan)* with an estimate of 280,074 followers (all of whom are rated as full communicants). Hollenweger lists it among the "unclassified" denominations, which means he is not completely sure of its Pentecostal connections.

16. *Ibid.,* 177. Manalo's Church is officially called *Iglesia ni Cristo.* The Pentecostal thrust is lighter than that of the Seventh Day Adventists who have 234,000 followers. The lists do not mention the International Church of the Foursquare Gospel. Its missionaries have been in

the islands for forty years, and their work has reached "monumental proportions" *(Foursquare World Advance,* Jan. 1967). Nevertheless, their total membership remains at 6,432.

17. The groupings, with the corresponding statistics, are taken from J. T. Nichol, *Pentecostalism,* 176–77, who apparently draws heavily from a letter written from Australia by an Indonesian Pentecostal student. The names given to the denominations do not correspond with those appearing in the *World Christian Handbook.*

18. An article, abbreviated from the Dutch and appearing under the title of "The Pentecostal Movement in Indonesia" *(Pentecost,* June–August 1964), speaks of "three sundry (Pentecostal) denominations": 1) the biggest of all, called "The Pentecostal Church in Indonesia," linked with the Bethel Temple Church; 2) the "Pentecostal Movement in Indonesia," connected with the German Assemblies of God; and 3) the "Pentecostal Mission," a splinter group of the Bethel Church. The article adds that "there are many other groups, most of them local assemblies having the name of *Pentekosta."* Actually this name is attached to several of the thirty-six Pentecostal denominations reported by Hollenweger *(op. cit.,* 1189–1212), but it is not mentioned by Coxill.

19. This is due to the fact that Indonesian Islam itself allows the persistence of such spurious elements in its beliefs and cult. Indonesian Protestantism has a membership of 4,371,237.

20. *Op. cit.,* 209.

21. *Ibid.,* 211–219.

22. "Chief and Prophet in Zululand and Swaziland," in *The African Systems of Thought,* 286. In 1905 there were said to be only three sectarian bodies with some 25,000 members. In 1925 they had become 130, while the census of 1946 spoke of 1,300 denominations with 1,089,479 followers. The estimates of 1960 speak of 2,000 religious bodies.

23. Gerdener, G. B. A., *Recent Developments in the South African Mission Field* (London, 1961), 188. "The multiplication of Bantu sects in South Africa, with a total of more than one million members, may be ominous. Springing from the soil, they can be interpreted as a foretaste of what an *indigenous* Christianity would be, divorced from the steadying influence of missionaries from the older churches. They are a mixture of paganism and Christianity, and morally and intellectually their leadership and membership leave much to be desired" (Latourette, *The Christian World Mission in Our Day,* 104.)

24. Barrett, David B., *Schism and Renewal in Africa, An Analysis of Six Thousand Contemporary Religious Movements* (Nairobi, 1968).

25. Grimley, J. B., and Robinson, E., *Church Growth in Central and Southern Nigeria* (London, 1961), 314.

26. Barratt, *op. laud.,* 140. See also Dom G. Guariglia, "Le grandes charactéristiques des sectes modernes" in *XXXIe. Semaine de Missiologie* (Louvain, 1961), 26.

27. Grimley and Robinson, *op. cit.,* 314. See also Barratt on the importance of biblical translations into African languages as a cause for the discrepancies with the older churches (*op. cit.,* 268–9).

28. Such was the case of polygamy and ancestor worship in the field of morals. There is no doubt that most sects, free from hierarchical structures, binding confessions of faith, and even fixed rituals, may think that they open a broader and more direct way to God.

29. Three of the instances most frequently adduced are healing, miracles, and prayer. In all these cases western Christianity (mostly that of Protestant tradition) has direct recourse to the Almighty, and this in an over-respectful, almost formalistic way. To the African the world is peopled by spirits whom we also need to placate to heal us, to save and protect us in our everyday needs. See B. Sundkler, *What is at Stake?*, in Hayward, *op. cit.*, 31. "Failure in this area separates religion from the here and now life of the people and brings disillusionment with a Christianity based on and aimed at meeting needs in Western social patterns" (Grimley and Robinson, *op. cit.*, 315).

30. Dom Guariglia, *art. cit.*, 23. The reaction of some church leaders has been radical: "We must," a Bantu from South Africa is reported to have said, "sooner or later so reform church dogmas as to bring Christianity away from European cultural ideologies, down to within reach of Bantu cultural life" (quoted by Gerdener, *op. cit.*, 194).

31. This applies to all mission countries and to Latin America. A failure to understand it leads some writers to misinterpret the worldwide (and not purely North American) nature of the Pentecostal movement.

32. H. W. Turner, of the University of Leicester, and an eminent Africanist, has drawn up a very complete—but also complicated—classification of African independent bodies. See his paper *A Typology for African Religious Movements* (1965). Very often the two elements go together, but they can also be separate. Dom Guariglia defines a *prophet:* "Some native who, as a rule, has received his religious education in Protestant missions" (*op. cit.*, 23). Barrett gives this definition of prophetic movement: "A religious awakening founded and led by the charismatic figure of a prophet or prophetess, who speaks from within a consciousness of being set apart for some divine purpose, adopts a critical stance towards the established order, proclaims a new religious idea or allegiance, and in the process attracts a considerable following" *(op. cit.*, 47).

33. The term was coined by Sundkler and has been gladly accepted by Africans. The independence may be purely spiritual or appear also in anti-white, pan-African trends. It seeks to find the promise and actual beginning of the African Church in the Scriptures, especially in Psalm 68:31 and Acts 8:26–39. "The kingdom of Ethiopia, with its ancient Christian Church, has become the symbol for the wider independent Christian Church which it is hoped will yet arise throughout the African continent" (Turner, *op. cit.*, 23).

34. The term *Zionistic* seems to derive from some of the Churches of Zion existing among American Holiness and Pentecostal groups doing mission work in Africa. To designate the same trend West Africans introduced the word *Aladura* ("one who prays") which is often

used as being more indigenous and penetrating to the center of the life of these churches which all stress prayer.

35. *Bantu Prophets in South Africa* (ed. 1961), 54. For Eberdant its features are: the believer's baptism by immersion, healing through prayer, revelatory messages through prophets and tongues which have to be interpreted; sabbatarianism; African traditional elements in worship; concern to find land and establish a holy city; seasonal festivals incorporating traditional African occasions; prohibitions of alcohol, tobacco, medicines, and certain other things; polygamy *(Messianismes en Afrique du Sud* [*Archives de Sociologie des Religions,* 1957], 31–36). Debrunner arrives at the same conclusion. The features of his grouping are: prophecies; tongues; much emotion in the religious services; interest in baptism; development of their own rites; sometimes stressing second baptism; toleration of polygamy; and strong emphasis on faith healing *(Witchcraft in Ghana* [Kumasi, 1959], 151).

36. As a sub-group of the Aladura churches may be classed the *Messianic* movements, or groups "centred around a dominant personality who claims for himself special powers involving a form of identification with Christ" *(Statement on African Independent Church Movements,* in Howard, *op. cit.,* 71).

37. F. B. Welbourn, "The African Israel Church Nineveh," in Welbourn and Ogot, *A Place to Feel at Home* (London, 1966), 73ff. The founder's thought about dreams: "I am convinced that the only way in which God speaks to his children is through dreams. . . . Nothing important happens in this world which is not revealed [in dreams] to God's prophets" (78).

38. *Op. cit.,* 31. See also Turner, *art. cit.,* 30.

39. J. Gründler, *Lexikon der Christlichen Kirchen und Sekten* (Vienna, 1961), II, Appendix, 9ff.

40. Barrett, *op. cit.,* 18; 148–49; 19. Healing churches became prominent after independence, 1957. There are at least two hundred of them and they are winning followers even from the Roman Catholic Church.

41. Grimley and Robinson, *op. cit.,* 311.

42. See P. Decapmaeker, *Le Kimbanguisme (XXXIe Semaine de Missiologie,* Louvain, 1961), 52–67; Barrett, *op. cit.,* 72. We cannot even attempt to give in a footnote the whole list of African Pentecostal (or Pentecostal-like) denominations collected by Hollenweger *(op. cit.,* 200ff). Their distribution is as follows: Dahomey has one; Ghana twenty; Kenya six; Congo an uncertain number; Mozambique four. The names given for Nigeria are not clearly classified as Pentecostal, although many of them belong to the Aladura grouping. South Africa has a good share (twelve) of churches of native origin, as well as a long list (438 in my counting) of unclassified or autonomous denominations, more than half of them belonging to the Aladura family.

43. See J. W. Dougall, "African Separatist Churches" *(Intern. Miss. Review,* 1956, July).

44. The information of the *World Christian Handbook* is

confirmed by Hollenweger's manuscript. To the list we must add the Spanish African colonies, Cabo Verde and Tchad. The case of Brazzaville in the Congo is hard to believe.

45. In this group the strange case is Madagascar where the thrust of the historical churches has been very deep (over a million members), and even the Adventists show far higher gains than the Pentecostals.

46. These totals are made up by denominations of foreign origin, mainly the Apostolic Church, the Churches of Christ, the Pilgrim Church, and the Assemblies of God. The numerous Aladura and Seraphim churches of the land are not even mentioned.

47. The two main bodies are the Pentecostal Assemblies of God (by far the strongest), and the Church of God, East Africa.

48. See *World Christian Handbook*, 82–83; 85; 93; 60–61.

49. American and Canadian Pentecostals work in Liberia; in Burundi the missionaries of the Svenska Fria Missionen whose statistics often tend to be exaggerated.

50. Subsequent to the Congo independence (1960), Barrett estimates that "hundreds of new separatist bodies have been formed, making a total of some 500 distinct groups. Unlike the situation in almost all other African territories, a large number of these groups and their membership originated in the Roman Catholic Church" (*op. cit.*, 26). I am unable to check the accuracy of the statement or to decide on how many of the splinter groups belong to the Pentecostal fold.

51. But, again, nobody seems to know the real numerical strength of the Aladura churches. Barrett speaks of 3,000 secessions from 1872 to 1965 *(op. cit.*, 22–23).

52. Barratt, *op. cit.*, 273; 169.

53. D'Epinay, L., in *The Ecumenical Review*, Jan. 1968, 16. Stereotyped expressions like these are very dear to certain writers.

54. Two main attempts have been made in the last years to assess the situation in the whole hemisphere: C. W. Taylor and W. T. Coggins, *Protestant Missions in Latin America* (Washington, D.C., 1961); first volume, statistics, second volume, maps; and P. Damboriena, *El protestantismo en América Latina* (2 vols., Madrid, 1962).

55. See M. Cassaretto, *El Movimiento Protestante en México* (México City, 1956); C. Crivelli, *Directorio Protestante de la América Latina* (Roma, 1933), 290ff.

56. To Mexican observers Pentecostalism gives the impression of ubiquity: "Its progress among us is such that there is hardly a village in the whole republic without one or several chapels run by Pentecostals, 'Alleluyas,' Holiness churches, or Assemblies of God" (P. Rivera, *Protestantismo Mexicano, Su desarrollo y estado actual* [Mexico, 1961], 55).

57. Here, in the lack of clergy to take care of the Catholic population, lies the main cause for the advance of Pentecostalism, not only in Mexico but also in the whole hemisphere.

58. Hollenweger's list of Pentecostal denominations in Mexico is much larger than that of the *World Christian Handbook*—sixteen

bodies, to which we have to add nine Holiness churches. From the available literature one gets the impression that the Puritanic practices of Mexican Pentecostals are not as strict as those of other Latin American countries.

59. Mr. Ingram, of the Church of God, Cleveland, wrote a letter to the President of Guatemala in 1934 expressing his wish to start work there. "The president graciously replied with a registered letter, extending a warm 'personal invitation to come and tell his people about the . . . Church of God' " (Conn, *Like a Mighty Army,* 223).

60. *Foursquare World Advance,* Jan. 1967, 28. The Bethel Bands and an Iglesia Apostólica de la Fe en Cristo Jesús are working there. See Taylor-Coggins, *op. cit.,* 235.

61. *World Christian Handbook,* 108–109. Hollenweger speaks of the existence of 80,000 Protestants in the country. Taylor-Coggins spoke in 1961 of only 43,078.

62. The slow progress in Costa Rica is symptomatic, and could be attributed either to the higher educational and economic level of the population, or to the indifferent religious attitude of its leading classes.

63. I think the vicinity of the Canal Zone has had little or no influence over this penetration. The answer must be sought in the extreme poverty of the "morenos," and in projects like that of San Miguelito parish.

64. Conn, *op. cit.,* 225.

65. The survey does not take into account those native movements of a Voodoo-Holiness type which, to a certain extent, play the role of Pentecostalism.

66. See *World Christian Handbook:* 119 (Puerto Rico); 107–108 (Dominican Republic); 106–107 (Cuba). See also Taylor-Coggins, *op. cit.,* 107.

67. *World Christian Handbook:* Jamaica (112–13); Barbados (101); Bahamas (100); British Honduras (102). It must be noted, though, that the majority of the population in the territory belongs to some Protestant denomination.

68. Unfortunately the figures, mostly those of the Iglesia Pentecostal Unida, are challenged, and even dismissed by observers on the spot as well as by official authorities. The strongly anti-Catholic attitude of the group and the poor quality of its native leaders does not help to reveal the facts in their true light. In 1961 Taylor-Coggins did not even know of the existence of that Pentecostal body.

69. At least this is the impression I have got while visiting the two countries several times, speaking to the clergy involved in pastoral work, and attending some of their conventions and public healing sessions. In this sense Taylor-Coggins is of little help.

70. In 1967 the International Church of the Foursquare Gospel had 2 missionaries, 48 churches, 15 national pastors, and only 100 converts in Bolivia. See also *World Christian Handbook,* 132. The totals are close to 7,000. In Cochabamba there is also a *Misión de Cristo Redentor* (not listed by Coxill or Taylor-Coggins), founded by a Spanish ex-

priest, José M. Ruiz, whose preaching strongly resembles that of the Holiness and Pentecostal denominations. Hollenweger lists also as working in Peru the Church of God, Cleveland; the Church of God, Prophecy; the Church of the Foursquare Gospel; a Peru-Mission; the Svenska Fria Missionen; one Iglesia Evangélica de Cristo; the Iglesias Pentecostales Autónomas; and a few groups of Chilean Pentecostals.

71. *World Christian Handbook,* 130–31. The most active group seems to be the Canadian Pentecostals, followed by the Svenska Fria Missionen.

72. We find it hard to conceive of their work as "growing rapidly" with "Argentinian Indians" among whom, apparently, "over twenty churches" out of the nineteen listed are located.

73. For Uruguay see *World Christian Handbook,* 143; for Paraguay see Damboriena, *op. cit.,* II, 134ff. This second part of my study contains information, statistics, and charts about each one of the Latin American nations. On many occasions I could no more trust the government totals than those provided by the denominations or by the particular agencies consulted. Hence the contradictions between the various sources.

74. Vergara, I., *El Protestantismo en Chile* (Santiago, 1962); Muñoz Ramírez, H., *Sociología Religiosa de Chile* (Santiago, 1957); Chacón, A., *The Pentecostal Movement in Chile* (Student World, 1964), 84ff.; Wilson, D., *A Mission to the People: The Pentecostal Movement in Chile* (n.d.); Willems, E., *Followers of the New Faith, Culture Change and the Rise of Protestantism in Brazil and Chile* (Vanderbilt University, 1967).

75. Vergara, *op. cit.,* 112–16; Hoover, *op. cit.,* 2–30.

76. Vergara, *op. cit.,* 143–44. In the following description I am relying largely on Vergara's book. It has the advantage of having been written by an expert who knows his country and has checked facts and names on the spot.

77. *Op. cit.,* 146–47. It is one of the smallest Pentecostal bodies in the country.

78. *Op. cit.,* 160ff. The group is very mission-minded and has extended its work into the neighboring republics. In its preaching it stresses the millenary kingdom in the crudest form.

79. No mention of it or of its membership is made in the 1968 *World Christian Handbook.* Its headquarters are at Curicó and its influence is far greater in the southern regions of the country. In 1960 it had 136 places of worship.

80. Vergara, 163–65. The rumors about the morality of some of the members of the last grouping are not always reassuring.

81. One notices that, in several instances, the founders of these churches, before joining Pentecostalism, had studied for the priesthood in Catholic seminaries. Such was the case with the founder of this denomination.

82. Vergara, *op. cit.,* 167–68.

83. Detached from the Methodist Pentecostal Church whose pastors were accused of accepting salaries when they were supposed to support themselves. The dozen Chilean Pentecostal churches we have named are only part of the spectrum. Vergara speaks of "several more"

detached from other Pentecostal bodies. Their number rises in Hollenweger to thirty-six, which is the second highest in Latin America.

84. *World Christian Handbook,* 135.

85. Hollengewer *(op. cit.,* 954) puts the totals of Pentecostal and Holiness denominations in Chile (1964) at 1,029,549. Willems seems to reject the estimates made by various sources and to conclude that our information is "unavailable or vague" *(op. cit.,* 67).

86. D'Epinay, *art. cit.,* 20.

87. I do not see the movement as "a protest against the Catholic Church and its ally, the ruling classes." There are more than a dozen Latin American republics where the clergy has been more powerful and domineering than in Chile and in which Pentecostalism has had few gains. As far as democracy goes, Seventh Day Adventism has little to learn from Pentecostalism. And yet its followers in Chile are only 14,862. The roots of the phenomenon are to be searched for elsewhere.

88. The Pentecostal movement in Brazil can be studied in the following sources: Reed, *New Patterns of Church Growth in Brazil;* E. Léonard, *L'illuminisme dans un protestantisme de constitution récente* (Paris, 1953); A. Rossi, *Diretório Protestante no Brasil* (Campinas, 1938) together with a series of articles published between 1952–1954 in *Revista Eclesiastica Brasileira;* E. Tognini, *Batismo no Espirito Santo* (Sao Paulo, 1960); E. Conde, *História das Assambleias de Deus do Brasil* (Rio, 1960); E. Willems, *Followers of the New Faith* (Vanderbilt Univ., 1967).

89. Reed, *op. cit.,* 122; Willems, *op. cit.,* 218. The dispensaries and orphanages cannot be many since the whole denomination reports having only nine dispensaries and "sponsoring" thirteen orphanages in the whole world (Goddard, *Mission Encyclopedia,* 1967, 44).

90. Rossi, *O Pentecostalismo no Brasil (Revista Ecclesiastica Brasileira,* 1952), 767ff.; Reed, 126; *World Christian Handbook,* 1968, 133.

91. Rossi, *art. cit.;* Reed, *op. cit.,* 121–22.

92. It is certainly the latter, although they have also received help from Americans of Scandinavian origin. See Goddard, *op. cit.,* 627. They were organized as Assemblies in the 1920's. In 1926 they sent twenty of their men to Brazil. None of them received a salary or was assured of pecuniary aid. The number of their missionaries in the world is now close to five hundred.

93. The totals of the *World Christian Handbook* are still higher: 1,700,000 members, and 1,400,000 communicants. The responsibility is already in the hands of Brazilians. These Pentecostals have stressed from the beginning the independence of local congregations. The few Swedish missionaries still in Brazil devote themselves to Bible training and counseling native leaders. They have a publishing house and broadcasting stations.

94. The founder left to his followers a narrative of his work in Brazil as well as what might be called the statements of faith and the rules of ritual for his church. See Luigi Francescone, *Resumo de uma Ramificacao da Obra de Deus, Pelo Spirito Santo, No Século Atual* (Sao Paulo, 1958). An excellent view of the whole movement is Reed's chap-

ter: "An Italian People Movement in Brazil," *op. cit.,* 19–44.

95. "After all," they say, "the Holy Spirit will fill our mouths with the right words at the right time. There is no need to prepare, study or learn. Doing too much human preparation, the other churches have erred in the past" (Reed, 40).

96. Of the total community no less than half a million is rated among the "communicants." This is a far cry for the 264,020 assigned by Willems for 1962 (*op. cit.,* 65).

97. Reed, *op. cit.,* 153–54. The movement is ignored by Taylor-Coggins and the *World Christian Handbook, 1968.*

98. At least this is often the conclusion of those who watch Melo's exhibitionism and certain features of the movement. His program seems to be: "Rome has brought to the world idolatry, Russia the terrors of communism, the U.S.A. the demon of capitalism; we Brazilians, nation of the poor, shall bring to the world the Gospel" (Meyer, H., *Die Pfingstbewegung in Brasilien,* 1968).

99. They seem actively engaged in politics.

100. Reed, *op. cit.,* 161–62. Those *cruzadas* are an imitation of the American tent evangelism. "Out of these tent meetings have come many separate independent *cruzadas.* These have planted many churches which have been organized into new denominations, some of whose pastors have come out of the traditional Pentecostal churches" *(ibid.,* 164). It is evident that these fissiparous tendencies cannot be explained by the simplistic method of recurring to "caudillism" and "rebellion against" authority (Willems, 113, 120). Those traits, even supposing they are exclusive of Latin America, are present also in the Catholic Church and do not lead to the same results. There must be a deeper religious reason than that.

101. Hollengewer *(op. cit.,* 883–902) puts the number of Pentecostal denominations for Brazil at thirty-six.Most likely the actual numbers are higher. As in Chile a good percentage of them is native.

102. I accept as valid the total of 3,278,000 members of the Pentecostal community for Brazil. If that is the correct number, the totals for 1969 would be closer to four million. Reed believes that Brazil is "in the midst of the greatest revival the world has ever seen—and it is only the beginning." His guess is also that, at the present rate of increase, by the year 2004 the country will have no less than 34,000,000 Pentecostals of total community *(op. cit.,* 179).

NOTES TO CHAPTER NINE

1. There is very little bibliography on Pentecostal missionary methods and still less on Pentecostal ecumenical ideas and achievements. Most treatises dealing with Church union overlook these "marginal" Christian groupings. John A. Mackay, *Ecumenics, The Science of the Church Universal,* is one of the rare exceptions. Of late, a series of studies and articles begin to show a concern for the issue. They will be mentioned as the occasion arrives.

2. Brumback, *Suddenly . . . from Heaven,* 138. Through the second baptism, "Christ became 'born' in people, who in turn became 'incarnate' in the most concrete sense in the lives of their fellow Chileans. These people, witnessing to what God can do when the Gospel of Christ and the reality of the Holy Spirit are exalted, are a living witness to what that eminent Anglican, Roland Allen, called the 'spontaneous expansion of the Church' " (Mackay, *op. cit.,* 178).

3. Conn, *Pillars of Fire,* 21. In the early days one of the questions put to the prospective missionary was whether he had an "experimental knowledge of salvation and the baptism of the Holy Spirit with speaking in tongues" (Perkin-Garlock, *Our World Witness,* 30).

4. *Minutes of the 51 General Assembly of the Church of God, Cleveland,* 19. In the same breath Horton reminds his listeners to beware of the Church of Rome. "The old, ecclesiastical clutches of Catholicism are an ever-present threat not only to our national liberty, but also to our spiritual liberty as well. Do not be fooled by the Catholic Church's alleged concessions. If the Church makes any concessions at all, it will be to woo and win back into its tainted and besmeared fold the lukewarm, unsuspecting, and gullible Protestants that (as it well knows) have ceased to protest long, long ago." (19) This was written just after the closing of Vatican Council II, and is reproduced here in all charity to show that ecumenism is not yet a fact in some sectors of Pentecostalism.

5. *Ibid.,* 20–21.

6. This was very true at the beginning of the movement when their missionaries "were unprepared for the language problems and culture difficulties they would face" Perkin-Parlock, *op. cit.,* 28; Conn, *Like A Mighty Army,* 112–14. One of the purposes of the Oral Roberts University, Tulsa, is precisely to raise the educational and theological standards of their candidates for mission work.

7. Pentecostal interest for the conversion of countries where paganism is a dominant and militant force has been very limited. Even in Africa their growth is largely at the expense of other Christian churches.

8. Protestant denominations have adopted this policy mostly in Africa, Roman Catholics in Latin America. The expression "unevangelical tactics" reveals the intensity of the protest on the part of historical Christianity.

9. Brumback, *op. cit.*, 138.

10. Brumback, *op. cit.*, 139.

11. *Ibid.* Of course, it is a gratuitous presupposition to state that the other Christian missions have forgotten the role of the Holy Spirit in the evangelization of the world. See, for Catholic missiology, Ohm, *Faites des disciples de toutes les nations* (French tr., Paris, 1965, 210ff.) with the appropriate bibliography. The case of Protestant missions has been validly stated by H. Lindsell, *Missionary Principles and Practice* (Westwood, N.J., 1955), 315–331.

12. Brumback, *op. cit.*, 140.

13. Willems, E., *Followers of the New Faith*, 122ff. "Repeating the affirmation, 'God loves you,' their visiting friend would open up to his incredulous, but soon enraptured hearers, the story of the love of God for men. The Evangel was understood and accepted. The moment the people believed that their abject lives had a significance for the deity, they responded in simple, evangelical faith" (Mackay, 110).

14. Barrett, *Schism and Revival in Africa*, 167. "To a man in the midst of a world hunger, sickness, and death, Pentecostalism proclaims a saving God who saves—or more concretely, who heals. In these ways, Pentecostalism gives the Chilean masses the human dignity which society denies them" (Ch. L. D'Epinay, "The Pentecostal 'Conquista' in Chile," *Ecumenical Review*, 1968, 23).

15. Barratt, *op. cit.*, 168–69. Whether these two features extend also beyond the pale of Pentecostalism is another question. I am afraid the verdict of missionaries will often be negative. In Europe and in the United States the case is different.

16. Reed, *New Patterns of Church Growth in Brazil*, 132; I. Vergara, *El protestantismo en Chile*, 325.

17. D'Epinay, *art. cit.*, 23; Willems, *op. cit.*, 145ff. Merle J. Davies stresses the importance of Pentecostal folk music in Brazil: "These hundreds of underprivileged people found a release for their lives in the various channels of emotional expression provided by the [religious] service. Through music the pastor has won the following of one hundred of his people . . . and through instruments and song they not only express themselves in the service of the Lord but provide an atmosphere and an artistic program through which a great company of the city's poor are lifted and inspired" (*How the Church Grows in Brazil*, New York, 1943, 83).

18. Reed, *op. cit.*, 139. "The most important effect of the communication of the Spirit is the *change in life.* . . . For this reason Pentecostals insist, perhaps more than other denominations, in the moralizing aspect of Christianity" (*op. cit.*, 125). In Africa, even keeping in mind what we have said of *philadelphia* and *philanthropia*, the moral changes of the converted seem less apparent.

19. Kendrick, *op. cit.*, 99; Perkin-Garlock, *op. cit.*, 63. Pentecostals have made their own the famous Nevius Plan for missions whose char-

acteristics are: an indigenous church is self-propagating, self-supporting, and self-governing. From the missiological viewpoint, this policy can be put into practice more easily among purely evangelistic missionary societies than among those which have diversified their activities into multiple fields and require native experts in all of them.

20. Perkin-Garlock, *op. cit.,* 68ff. This has given the indigenous churches a freedom of movement which the older denominations cannot afford, mostly in the administrative and cultural fields. In Africa, for instance, instead of inheriting huge church buildings which are half-empty on Sundays, "they hold their services in small rooms which always appear packed to bursting. Their communities therefore resemble the familiar patterns of present-day African society far more than the larger Europeanized mission churches" (Barratt, 172).

21. It is a happy omen that the Assemblies of God have more than 73 Bible schools outside the United States. But one questions the claim of Perkin and Garlock that "a Bible school is not merely for the purpose of producing learned men . . . it is for the purpose of causing more people to hear the Word" (*op. cit.,* 69). Willems (*op. cit.,* 117–18) speaks of one of the most successful Chilean Pentecostal pastors who told him that at the beginning of his career he had a "revelation" that "ordered him to burn all books in his possession." "Much knowlege," he added, "extinguishes the Spirit."

22. Nichol, *op. cit.,* 231.

23. Yet, the world-wide achievements of the well-organized Assemblies of God remain modest: 184 elementary schools, 1 high school in Upper Volta, 1 technical school in India, and 13 schools for children of missionaries (Goddard, *Mission Encyclopedia,* 1967, 43). In Chile, which has one of the highest literacy percentages in Latin America, "very few of the Pentecostalists' children pass their [elementary] school-leaving examination" (D'Epinay, *art. cit.,* 27). In Brazil "any kind of learning beyond mere literacy—the *crente* must of course read the Bible—is frowned upon, and educated members who show intellectual interests or ambitions are watched with considerable suspicion" (Willems, 117).

24. Weber, G., *The Congregation in Mission* (New York, 1964), 154–55. Pentecostals would say with the fundamentalists that they are more afraid of "shutting our hearts to those whose need is heavy on the heart of Christ," than of making "rice Christians." The thought of the historical churches is much more nuanced. See Newbigin in *International Review of Missions,* Oct. 1965, 422.

25. Mehl, R., *op. cit.,* 217. "The Gospel," he writes, "has maintained the ambivalent character of the world, the sect has given to it a univocal sense."

26. Piette, M., *Jean Wesley,* 264.

27. In pamphlets issued for general reading, the International Church of the Foursquare Gospel does not show animosity to worldliness. What is said under the headings of "Daily Christian Life," "The Spirit-Filled Life," and "Moderation" could be endorsed by the historical churches.

28. *Minutes of the Church of God* (1966), 19–20; Bloch-Hoell, 116–

17. D. Gee, in his book *Pentecost,* has an interesting chapter, "The Fruits of the Spirit," 75ff., but does not come down to particulars. Latin American Pentecostals, who lack a Methodist tradition, do not seem to worry as much about dances, spectacles, hairdying or lipsticks as their North American brethren do. In Africa restrictions and probibitions refer to local celebrations.

29. Paulk, *op. cit.,* 192.

30. *Discipline of the Pentecostal Holiness Church,* 46ff. The issue of membership in secret societies agitated numerous churches for a time and led to further denominational divisions. Some of them, like the Congregational Holiness Church, excluded labor unions from such "societies."

31. The problem of war and military service affects only Anglo-American and a few European denominations.

32. "Modesty" in women's dress and ornament has too long obsessed some of their churches. The Church of the Living God decrees: "The female members of the Church are not to cut the hair to make it short, or to patronize the beauty shops for the purpose of permanent waves or other hair styling that would be unbecoming to women professing holiness" (*Discipline and Articles of Faith*). The Church of the Lord Jesus Christ of the Apostolic Faith condemns "women wearing men's apparel."

33. Barratt, *op. cit.,* 266–67.

34. New York, 1963, and *Twelve Angels from Hell* (New Jersey, 1965). The narratives, however, are not too convincing. For other local projects, see K. McDonnell, "The Ideology of Pentecostal Conversion," *Ecumenical Studies,* Winter 1967, 118–19. However these social activities cannot match, for instance, those of the Seventh Day Adventists. For a good summary of the latter see R. Mitchell, *Faith In Action* (New York, 1958).

35. Damboriena, P., *El protestantismo en Chile,* (Mensaje, 1957), 146–54; Willems, *op. cit.,* 176ff. Since I know the Colombian situation, at first hand, I would be more cautious in accepting certain claims about social changes effected by Pentecostal converts in that republic.

36. Barratt, *op. cit.,* 120–21. Conversations with scholars of the Congo situation, like V. Van Bulk, and personal correspondence with missionaries in Indonesia confirm these statements. On the contrary, it seems that Brazilian Pentecostalism, far from being contaminated by widespread spiritualism, is becoming a force against it.

37. Pentecostal pastors have often complained of the difficulty of "eradicating" those Roman "superstitions." A visit to many of their out-of-the-way homes becomes in this respect convincing. In public the use of mantillas, the making of the sign of the cross, or the wearing of scapulars point in the same direction. As a group the Brazilian Pentecostals of Italian origin retain much of this "ersatz" Catholicism.

38. *Constitutions of the United Pentecostal Church.*

39. *Ibid.*

40. Brumback, *op. cit.,* 109ff.

41. Conn, *Like A Mighty Army,* 83–84.

42. See T. A. Adejunmobi, *Polygamy,* in Hayward, ed., *African*

Independent Church Movements, 53ff.; also, *ibid., Statement on African Independent Church Movements,* 76–77. Adejunmobi states that Christianity, which has succeeded in eradicating slavery, trial by ordeal, human sacrifices, and other evil practices, has been unable to deal effectively with polygamy.

43. *Art. cit.,* 57.

44. Barratt, *op. cit.,* 118, 149, 172; passim. "Both the Church of Christ in Africa, and the African Church Nineveh (at least the second is clearly Pentecostal) admit polygamous members under certain circumstances. Some other independent churches claim that monogamy is the western, polygamy the African form of marriage. . . . The mission churches have largely failed to persuade their baptized members to adopt monogamy" (Welbourn-Ogot, *A Place to Feel at Home,* 145). "Many ministers today, if they were starting *de novo,* would have the Church grant full communicant status to first-generation Christians who were polygamous" (T. A. Beetham, *Christianity and the New Africa,* New York, 1967, 43). The Church of Christ in Africa allows polygamists to receive Holy Communion. "They reason that Christ gave Holy Communion to Judas who was possessed by the devil, in order to give him a chance to repent. . . . After all, all kinds of sinners receive Holy Communion: liars, those who practice color bar, adulterers, etc. Why should adultery be the only sin (if it is a sin) to be condemned?" (Welbourn-Ogot, 70–71).

45. Brumback, *op. cit.,* 129.

46. "Unity," said Bishop Azariah of Dornakal, India, "may be theoretically desirable in Europe and America, but it is vital to the life of the Church in the mission field. The divisions of Christendom may be a source of weakness in Christian countries, but in non-Christian lands they are a sin and a scandal" (quoted by Sundkler, *The World of Mission,* 272).

47. Barratt, *op. cit.,* 265ff.

48. Kendrick, *op. cit.,* 203.

49. Nichol, *Pentecostalism,* 115.

50. One looks in vain for contemporary ecumenical or missionary documents that express Christian concern for Pentecostals and other "fringe" Christian organizations. It is true that contemporary Pentecostals tend to be "exclusive and very critical of all who did not agree with them," and have thus developed a "holier than thou complex" (Kendrick, *op. cit.,* 217). But is the blame only on their side?

51. Newbigin, *The Household of God* (London, 1958), 110. See Kilian McDonnell, "Holy Spirit and Pentecostalism," *Commonweal,* 8 Nov. 1968, 198ff.

52. *Op. cit.,* "*Is the distinctive character of the Pentecostal Movement the same in 1961 as it was sixty years ago?*" (176–77). See also Marcus Bach, *Spiritual Breakthroughs for our Times,* 53–54.

53. Kendrick, *op. cit.,* 203ff.

54. *Ibid.,* 204. D. Gee, an exceptional witness to these developments, has described them in his latest book, *Wind and Flame* (London, 1967).

55. Gee, *op.cit.,* 239ff. The second conference took place in 1952

(London), the third at Stockholm (1955), the third at Toronto in 1958. These were followed by those of Jerusalem (1961), and Helsinski (1964). Regarding the Rio Conference (July 18–23, 1967), I have been able to see only anecdotic reports that speak about the "priest ridden country for 400 years." Certainly something more important than that detail must have been discussed at that gathering.

56. Kendrick, *op. cit.,* 204–05. Those relations (which extend also to the Orthodox churches) "threaten to weaken, if not eventually destroy, the distinctive testimony of Protestantism."

57. Kendrick, *op. cit.,* 59. These contacts were taking place long before the International Missionary Council decided to join the World Council of Churches, although when that event took place, "the Pentecostals felt that they had to withdraw" from the world organization (Gee, *op. cit.,* 233).

58. Murch, *Co-operation without Compromise,* 70.

59. "Conservative evangelicals seem increasingly willing to have fellowship with us, and we are very happy to reciprocate in Christ. This does not mean that the other denominations have been converted to our particular doctrine, neither does it mean that we are prepared to compromise . . . But Pentecostal leaders can now express ninety-five percent agreement with their fellow evangelists, and with that large measure of hearty agreement there is ample room for fruitful fellowship in the things of God" (D. Gee, *All with One Accord,* Springfield, 1961, 32).

60. Sundkler, *Bantu Prophets,* 50. "There is no doubt, however," adds Barrett, "that most independent bodies today have a deep desire for ecumenical fellowship with other types of Christian church" *(op. cit.,* 200).

61. Barratt, *ibid.*

62. "The World Council of Churches and Pentecostalism in *Ecumenical Review* (1964, 8ff.). John Mackay called that union "moving . . . symbolic . . . and epoch-making" *(op. cit.,* 16). D. Gee, who apparently had been invited to New Delhi but, under pressure, did not attend, explained to the BBC the reasons why the Chilean Pentecostal detente was not liked by many in the movement. The latter wanted to retain their theological conservatism and disagreed with the "confessed" objective of the WCC of achieving a visible united church on earth, and with the apparent drift of the WWC to Rome *(Wind and Flame,* 309).

63. Quoted by Nichol, *op. cit.,* 220. See also F. M. Boyd, *Ecumenicity—False and True,* in the official organ *Pentecostal Evangel* (Oct. 7, 1962), 4–5.

64. Barratt, *op. cit.,* 203. Some twenty independent Pentecostal denominations agreed in 1964 to a Union of Independent Pentecostal Churches with 200,000 members.

65. In an unsigned article in the *Ecumenical Review,* 1967, 461, entitled "The Pentecostal Movement in Europe," we read: "The member churches of the WCC should see that there is both the possibility

and necessity for continuing conversation with the representatives of the Pentecostal movement. In this connection it should be remembered that not inconsiderable resources are available with the member churches of men and women who have received spiritual gifts with which many are unfamiliar and who can aid in achieving mutual understanding."

66. *Evanston to New Delhi, Third Assembly World Council of Churches, 1961,* Appendix VIII. The whole document is worth reading. Similar ideas were expressed in the Conferences of Montreal and Mexico City.

67. *Op. cit.,* b. 244. In my opinion the issue did not receive enough attention at the Uppsala Conference of 1968.

68. Abbott, W. M., ed., *The Documents of Vatican II* (New York, 1966), 682. Latin American bishops had strongly favored the insertion of this paragraph which had not been thought necessary in the first drafts of the document.

69. Lindsell, ed., *The Church's Worldwide Mission* (Waco, Texas, 1966), 113–14. "Sectarianism belongs to the essence of the movement" (Willems). One of their own famous leaders, Lewi Pethrus, says: "The Pentecostal revival is not a fanatic revival but fanaticism follows it like a shadow" and at present there seems to be "an epidemic of fanaticism" (Noel Brooks, *Pentecost and Fanaticism,* London). According to E. Castro, one of the reasons for shunning ecumenism with the Church of Rome is the question: "If we are now so brotherly with the Catholics and if they can no longer be considered as a mission field, then, whom shall we evangelize and why"? *(Lutheran World,* n. 4., 1968, *Ecumenical Relationships in Latin America,* 274).

70. Lindsell, *op. cit.,* 122.

71. At this point it would be necessary to have recent information from the mission field on how these mutual contacts are evolving. In its initial stages Pentecostalism in mission areas showed little interest in contacts. Only after attaining some stability and strength did it timidly approach the historical churches in certain fields. The latter, both Catholic and Protestant, even without dropping some of their former objections, have taken an initial step: they are on the way of being convinced that the stalemate cannot continue and something must be done to improve things. See E. Castro, *art. cit.,* 274ff. "I can discern," says D. Du Plessis, "a deep spiritual stir in the hearts of all ranks, but particularly do I find a sincere recognition of the work of the Holy Spirit among the top echelons of Pentecostalism" (cited by D. Gee, *op. cit.,* 283).

SELECTED BIBLIOGRAPHY

GENERAL READING ON PENTECOSTALISM

BLOCH-HOELL, N. *The Pentecostal Movement: Its Origin, Development and Character.* Copenhagen, 1964.

BRUMBACK, C. *Suddenly from Heaven: A History of the Assemblies of God.* Springfield, Mo., 1961.

CLARK, E. *The Small Sects in America.* Rev. ed. Nashville, Tenn., 1959.

GEE, D. *Winds of Flame.* London, 1967.

KELSEY, N. *Tongue-Speaking: An Experiment in Spiritual Experience.* New York, 1964.

KENDRICK, K. *The Promise Fulfilled: A History of the Modern Pentecostal Movement.* Springfield, Mo., 1961.

MAYER, F. *The Religious Bodies of America.* St. Louis, Mo., 1961.

NICHOL, J. *Pentecostalism.* New York, 1966.

HISTORICAL BACKGROUND

DAVIES, J. *The Early Christian Church.* New York, 1965.

FINNEY, C. *Lectures on Revivals.* New York, 1875.

HEIMERT, A. *Religion and the American Mind: From the Great Awakening to the Revolution.* Cambridge, Eng., 1966.

JAMISON, A. "Religions in the Perimeter." *The Shaping of the American Religion.* Edited by J. Smith and A. Jamison. Princeton, N.J., 1961.

KNOX, R. *Enthusiasm: A Chapter in the History of Religion.* Oxford, Eng., 1951.

MCLOUGHLIN, S. *Modern Revivalism.* New York, 1959.

MALAUD, J. *The Albigenses Crusade.* New York, 1967.

PIETTE, M. *John Wesley in the Evolution of Protestantism.* New York, 1937.

SEEBERG, R. *Text-Book of the History of Doctrines.* Grand Rapids, Mich., 1956.

WILLIAMS, G. *The Radical Reformation.* Philadelphia, 1962.

THE HOLINESS MOVEMENT

BROWN, C. "The Church of God, Anderson, Indiana." *The American Church of the Protestant Heritage.* Edited by V. Ferm'. New York, 1953.

FARISH, D. *The Circuit Rider Dismounts: A Social History of Methodism.* Richmond, Va., 1938.

GADDIS, M. *Christian Perfection in America.* Ph.D. dissertation, University of Chicago, 1929.

JESSUP, H. *We, the Holiness People.* Chicago, 1948.

MEAD, S. *Handbook of Denominations in the United States.* New York, 1965.

ROSE, D. *A Theology of Christian Experience: Interpreting the Historical Wesleyan Message.* Minneapolis, Minn., 1965.

SIMPSON, A. *Wholly Sanctified.* Harrisburg, Pa., 1925.

SMITH, T. L. *Called unto Holiness.* Kansas City, Mo., 1962.

SWEET, W. *Revivalism in America.* New York, 1944.

PENTECOSTAL CHURCHES

CAMPBELL, J. *The Pentecostal Holiness Church.* Franklin Springs, Ga., 1951.

CHERY, R. *L'Offensive des sectes en France.* Paris, 1960.

CONN, C. W. *Like a Mighty Army Moves the Church of God.* Cleveland, Tenn., 1955.

EWART, F. *The Phenomenon of Pentecost.* St. Louis, Mo., 1947.

HARPER, M. *The Twentieth Century Pentecostal Revival.* New York, 1965.

HARRISON, J. *A History of the Assemblies of God.* Thesis. Berkeley, Calif., 1954.

HUTTEN, K. *Seher, Grübler, Enthusiasten.* Stuttgart, 1967.

MOORE, E. *Handbook of Protestant Denominations in the United States.* Thesis. Pasadena, Calif., 1954.

SHAW, P. *The Catholic Apostolic Church.* New York, 1946.

WILSON, R. *Sects and Society.* Berkeley, Calif., 1961.

PENTECOSTAL THEOLOGY (GENERAL)

ALGERMISSEN, K. *Christian Sects.* New York, 1963.

CONN, C. W. *Pillars of Pentecost.* Cleveland, Tenn., 1956.

FRODSHAM, S. *With Signs Following.* Springfield, Mo., 1941.

LEMMONS, F. *Our Pentecostal Heritage.* Cleveland, Tenn., 1958.

PEARLMAN, F. *Knowing the Doctrines of the Bible.* 3 vols. Springfield, Mo., 1937.

RIGGS, R. *We Believe.* Springfield, Mo., 1954.

SLAY, J. *This We Believe.* Cleveland, Tenn., 1963.

VARIOUS DENOMINATIONS. *Constitutions* and *Statements of Faith.*

WILLIAMS, E. *Systematic Theology.* 3 vols. Springfield, Mo., 1953.

WINEHOUSE, I. *The Assemblies of God.* New York, 1959.

PENTECOSTAL THEOLOGY (SPECIAL)

GEE, D. *Spiritual Gifts in the Ministry.* Springfield, Mo., 1963.

LINDSTROM, H. *Wesley and Sanctification.* London, n.d.

MCPHERSON, A. S. *The Foursquare Gospel.* Los Angeles, 1946.

MASSERANO, F. *A Study of Worship Forms in the Assemblies of God Denomination.* Thesis. Princeton, N.J., 1966.

PAULK, E. *Your Pentecostal Neighbor.* Cleveland, Tenn., 1958.

RIGGS, R. *The Pastor's Manual.* Springfield, Mo., 1956.

TORREY, R. *The Baptism of the Holy Spirit.* New York, 1897.

VOUGA, O. *Our Gospel Message.* St. Louis, Mo., n.d.

WOOD, W. *Cultures and Personalities: Aspects of the Holiness Religion.* Le Hague, 1965.

SPEAKING WITH TONGUES

BRUMBACK, C. *What Meaneth This?* Springfield, Mo., 1947.

CUTTEN, G. *Speaking with Tongues: Historically and Psychologically Considered.* New Haven, Conn., 1927.

ERVIN, H. *These Men Are Not Drunken As Ye Suppose.* Plainfield, N.J., 1968.

GROMACKI, R. *The Modern Tongues Movement.* Philadelphia, 1967.

HOEKEMA, A. *What About Tongues Speaking?* Grand Rapids, Mich., 1966.

HORTON, H. *The Gifts of the Spirit.* London, 1962.

LOMBARD, E. *De la glossolalie chez les premiers chrétiens et des phénomènes similaires.* Lausanne, 1910.

ROBERTS, O. *The Baptism of the Holy Spirit and the Value of Speaking with Tongues.* Tulsa, Okla., 1960.

SHERRILL, J. *They Speak with Other Tongues.* Westwood, N.J., 1964.

STAGG, F., Hinson, E., and Oates, W. *Glossolalia: Tongue Speaking in Biblical, Historical and Psychological Perspective.* Nashville, Tenn., 1967.

DIVINE HEALING

CLEBSCH, W., and JAEKLE, C. *Pastoral Care in Historical Perspective.* New York, 1967.

CRESPI, G. *La guérison par la foi.* Paris, 1952.

EDWARDS, H. *The Power of Spiritual Healing.* London, 1963.

GEE, D. *Spiritual Gifts in the Work of the Ministry Today.* Springfield, Mo., 1963.

GERSTNER, J. *The Theology of the Major Sects.* Grand Rapids, Mich., 1960.

NELSON, R. *Modern Divine Healing.* New York, 1950.

ROBERTS, O. *If You Need Healing, Do These Things.* Tulsa, Okla., 1965.

SCHERZER, C. *The Healing Church.* Philadelphia, 1950.

SIMPSON, A. *The Gospel of Healing.* Harrisburg, Pa., 1925.

SQUIRE, F. *Divine Healing Today.* London, 1904.

PENTECOSTAL MISSIONS

BERG, D. *Enviado per Deus.* São Paolo, Brazil, 1958.

CONDE, E. *História das Assambleias de Deus do Brasil.* Rio de Janeiro, 1960.

DAMBORIENA, P. *El protestantismo en la América Latina.* 2 vols. Madrid, 1963.

GLOVER, R., and KANE, J. *The Progress of World-Wide Missions.* New York, 1960.

GODDARD, B., ed. *The Encyclopedia of Modern Christian Missions.* London, 1967.

Hollenweger, W. J. *Handbuch der to Pfingstbewegung.* 10 vols. Geneva, 1965–67.

HOOVER, W. *Historia del Avivamiento Pentecostal en Chile.* Valparaiso, 1948.

LATOURETTE, K. *Christianity in a Revolutionary Age.* New York, 1962.

PERKIN, N., and GARLOCK, J. *Our World Witness: A Survey of Assemblies of God Foreign Missions.* Springfield, Mo., 1963.

REED, W. C. *New Patterns of Church Growth in Brazil.* Grand Rapids, Mich., 1965.

SUNDKLER, B. *Bantu Prophets in South Africa.* London, 1961.

TAYLOR, C., and COGGINS, W. *Protestant Missions in Latin America.* Washington, D.C., 1961.

INDEX